Henry Abbott

The American watchmaker and jeweler

An encyclopedia for the horologist, jeweler, gold and silversmith

Henry Abbott

The American watchmaker and jeweler
An encyclopedia for the horologist, jeweler, gold and silversmith

ISBN/EAN: 9783337135843

Printed in Europe, USA, Canada, Australia, Japan

Cover: Foto ©Lupo / pixelio.de

More available books at **www.hansebooks.com**

THE
AMERICAN WATCHMAKER

AND JEWELER

AN ENCYCLOPEDIA

FOR THE HOROLOGIST, JEWELER, GOLD AND SILVERSMITH

CONTAINING HUNDREDS OF PRIVATE
RECEIPTS AND FORMULAS COMPILED FROM THE BEST
AND MOST RELIABLE SOURCES. COMPLETE DIRECTIONS FOR USING
ALL THE LATEST TOOLS, ATTACHMENTS AND DEVICES
FOR WATCHMAKERS AND JEWELERS

—

BY HENRY G. ABBOTT

ILLUSTRATED WITH 200 E

—

CHICAGO:
GEO. K. HAZLITT & CO., PUBLISHERS
1891.

PREFACE.

FOR some years there has been a demand among the watchmaking and jewelry fraternity of this country, for a book that would furnish them some information in regard to tools of American manufacture, drawings and descriptions of the various escapments, definitions of various words and phrases used in the trade, etc. There are upon the market several very valuable works, compiled by English, French and German authors, but these works are silent in regard to tools and methods distinctively American. Most of these works devote considerable space to the use of the bow lathe, the turns and other devices long ago relegated to the shades of obscurity by the American watchmaker.

The ambitious workman is always in search of knowledge, in search of new ideas, new tools and new methods. Patient study, constant practice and ambition are requisite to become a proficient in any art. The demand for skilled workmen is constantly increasing, and a person wishing to thoroughly master any art, must be to a certain extent capable of self instruction. To be a proficient in any art a man must not be deft of touch alone but the head must also play its part. In America the watchmaker is somewhat differently situated from his European brothers. In the country towns he is often called upon not only to clean and repair watches and clocks, but is often asked to put in order or repair music boxes, fishing reels, musical instruments, sewing machines, electric motors, statuettes, pipes and a variety of other articles too numerous to mention. It would be next to impossible for the ordinary workman to remember all the various instructions, hints, pointers, formulas and recipes which he has read or heard about, and the author believes such persons will welcome this little volume and that it will prove valuable for reference in cases of emergency.

THE AMERICAN
WATCHMAKER AND JEWELER

AN ENCYCLOPEDIA FOR THE
HOROLOGIST, JEWELER, GOLD AND SILVERSMITH

ACCELERATION. This term in horology is applied to the steady gaining in the rate of a time-keeper, particularly to be observed in new movements. It is positively known to occur in marine chronometers, watches as a rule not being subjected to tests sufficiently accurate to detect it in them. There is but little doubt that the hairspring is the cause of acceleration. Old movements after being re-sprung some times accelerate, particularly if the overcoil is manipulated too much when timing. Britten declares that there is little doubt that the tendency of springs is to increase slightly in strength for some time after they are subjected to continuous action just as bells are found to alter a little in tone after use. Sometimes the very best chronometers, after going for a year or two, will accelerate by about three to four seconds per day. M. Jacob attributes this acceleration to the fact that chronometers are exposed to heat oftener and for longer periods than to cold, and since the balance is thus more frequently contracted it follows that after a time the segments will not return exactly to their initial positions. There will therefore be necessarily a slight acceleration of the rate.

Dent believed that it was due to the combination of oxygen of the air with the steel hairspring, so that after a time its rigidity is increased.

M. Villarceau attributed it to the influence of the escapement and that it arises from the fact that the impact communicating the impulse occurs before the balance has arrived at its neutral position.

M. H. Robert attributes it to the fact that the resistance opposed by oil at the pivots of the escape wheel differs from that at the pivots of the balance.

Flat springs do not accelerate as much as those having overcoils. Palladium springs accelerate very much less than hardened steel springs.

ACIDS AND SALTS. Acids and salts of various kinds are employed by the watchmaker and jeweler, but he should never keep them in proximity to his tools or work or he may have cause to regret it some day. It is advisable to keep them in glass-stoppered bottles.

Alum is sometimes used for removing the stains left by soldering in lieu of acids, and is also used in removing broken screws from brass plates by immersing the plates in a strong solution of alum and water, the best results being obtained from a boiling solution, which rapidly converts the steel into rust, while it does not attack the brass plate.

Aqua Fortis or Nitric Acid. This acid either in a pure or diluted form is a powerful corrosive and will dissolve silver, German silver, nickel, mercury, zinc, copper, brass, lead, steel, or iron. Tin when treated with this acid is reduced to a white powder called metastannic acid, and alloys containing tin when treated with this acid deposit the tin as mentioned above while the other ingredients pass into solution.

Aqua Regia, a mixture of about two parts by weight hydrochloric and one part nitric acid, will dissolve gold, platinum, brass, tin, copper, iron, steel, zinc, nickel and German silver. Neither of the two acids which combined form aqua regia will attack gold or platinum.

Borax is used as a flux in soldering gold, silver, platinum and other metals. It is ordinarily used in the form of a paste which is obtained by rubbing the borax on a slate or stone slab.

Hydrochloric Acid will dissolve slowly German silver, nickel, brass, copper, iron, steel, zinc and tin.

Hydrofluoric Acid will dissolve nearly all metals except silver, platinum and lead. It is a dangerous acid to handle unless you are thoroughly acquainted with its nature. It is used for etching on copper, enamel and glass.

Sal-Ammoniac or Chloride of Ammonium is used as a flux in soldering tin and other metals in the form of a paste obtained by combining with sweet oil. It is also used in battery solutions in electro-plating.

FIG. 1.

ACID BOTTLE. A neat form of acid bottle is shown in Fig. 1. The acid is kept in a glass bottle having a twisted glass dropper attached to the cork, and the bottle is kept in a screw-top wooden case, doing away with all chances of breakage and lessening to a minimum the chances of destruction of work, clothes and tools.

ADENDUM CIRCLE. The distance or space between the pitch line of a gear and the circle touching the ends of the teeth.

ADHESION. Adhesion is the mutual attraction which two bodies have for one another, as attraction between the liquid and the substance of the vessel containing it. See also *Oil* and *Capillarity*. Saunier says that the working parts in contact with each other should separate by sliding action and not by a sudden drawing assunder in a direction perpendicular to their touching surfaces, as such an action would involve the inconvenience of variable resistances, depending on the greater or less adhesion or cohesion of these surfaces. The amount of adhesion between clean surfaces is difficult to determine and it is impossible to give its exact proportion. In the case of oiled surfaces the resistance due to adhesion is proportional to the extent of the surfaces in contact.

ADJUSTING ROD. A device for testing the pull of the mainspring.

ADJUSTMENT. The manipulation of the balance, its spring and staff, for the purpose of improving the time-keeping qualities of a watch. Three adjustments are usually employed for this purpose, viz.: positions, isochronism and compensation.

Adjustment to Positions. The manipulation of the hairspring and balance so that the movement keeps time in the different positions. In ordinary watches two positions are taken, viz.: pendant up or vertical and dial up or horizontal. In the finer grade of work adjustments are made in the quarters, that is, with 3 up and 9 up. This adjustment is a delicate and often a difficult operation and it is only by constant study and application that the watchmaker can hope for success.* The object of timing or adjusting to positions is to ascertain how far a change of position modifies the compensation and isochronism and to verify the poising of the balance. Saunier says the balance cannot possibly be accurately poised in all positions if the pivots and pivot holes are not perfectly round, and the poising will be modified with a change of temperature if the two arms do not act identically; as will be the case when the metals are not homogeneous, when one or both arms have been strained owing to want of skill on the part of the workman, or careless work, etc. After accurately timing in a vertical position with XII. up, make it go for twelve hours with VI. up and the same number of hours with III. and IX. up. Observe with care both the rates and the amplitude of the arcs and note them down. Assuming the pivots and pivot holes to be perfectly round and in good condition

---

*Several excellent essays on this subject are in print, among which may be mentioned Modern Horology in Theory and Practice and the Watchmaker's Hand-Book by Claudius Saunier, the Watch and Clockmaker's Hand-Book by F. J. Britten, and Adjustments to Positions, Isochronism and Compensation, published by G. K. Hazlitt & Co., Chicago. Isochronal adjustments are thoroughly reviewed in an excellent little work by Moritz Immisch entitled Prize Essay on the Balance Spring.

and that the poising of the balance has been previously tested with care by the ordinary means, if the variations in the four positions are slight the poising may be regarded as satisfactory. As a general, but not invariable rule, a loss in one position on the rate observed in the inverse position may be taken to indicate that the weight of the upper part of the balance is excessive when it does not vibrate through an arc of 360° or the lower part if the arcs of motion exceed this amount. Independently of the balance this loss may be occasioned by excessive friction of the pivots due to a too great pressure owing to the calliper being faulty, or to a distortion of the hair-spring causing its center of gravity to lie out of the axis of the balance. If these influences become at all considerable their correction will be beyond the power of the isochronal hair-spring, and indeed it will be impossible to counteract them. Changes in the rate on changing from the vertical to the horizontal position may also arise from the following causes: 1. The action of the escape wheel, which is different according as it tends to raise the balance staff or to force it laterally. 2. A hairspring that starts to one side and so displaces its center of gravity, a balance that is not well poised, pivots or pivot holes that are not perfectly round, faults which although of but little importance in the vertical position of the balance staff become serious when it is horizontal. 3. The more marked portion of the friction of the pivots may take place against substances of different degrees of hardness in the two cases, the end stones being frequently harder than the jewels. Saunier further says that satisfactory results will be obtained in most cases by employing the following methods, either separately or two or more together, according to the results of experiments or the rates, the experience and the judgment of the workman:

1. Flatten slightly the ends of the balance pivots so as to increase their radii of friction; when the watch is lying flat the friction will thus become greater.

2. Let the thickness of the jewel holes be no more than is absolutely necessary. It is sometimes thought sufficient to chamfer the jewel hole so as to reduce the surface on which

friction occurs; but this does not quite meet the case since an appreciable column of oil is maintained against the pivot.

3. Reduce the diameters of the pivots, of course changing the jewel holes. The resistance due to friction, when the watch is vertical, increases rapidly with any increase in the diameters of pivots.

4. Let the hair-spring be accurately centered, or it must usually be so placed that the lateral pull tends to lift the balance when the watch is hanging vertical. In this and the next succeeding case it would sometimes be advantageous to be able to change the point at which it is fixed, but this is seldom possible.

5. Replace the hair-spring by one that is longer or shorter but of the same strength; this is with a view to increase or diminish the lateral pressure in accordance with the explanation given in the last paragraph.

6. Set the escapement so that the strongest impulse corresponds wiih the greatest resistance of the balance.

7. Replace the balance. A balance that is much too heavy renders the timing for positions impossible.

8. Lastly, when these methods are inapplicable or insufficient there only remains the very common practice of throwing the balance out of poise.

Adjustment to Isochronism. The manipulation of the hair-spring so that the long and short arcs of the balance are performed in the same time. The theory of isochronism advanced by Dr. Robert Hooke and more commonly known as Hooke's law, "as the tension so is the force," is an axiom in mechanics with which everybody is, or should be familiar. This law has like nearly all others its exceptions, and it is only partially true as applied to hair-springs of watches; "otherwise," says Glasgow, "every spring would be isochronous." Pierre Le Roy says that there is in every spring of a sufficient extent a certain length where all the vibrations long or short, great or small, are isochronous, and that this length being secured, if you shorten the spring the great vibrations will be quicker than the small ones; if, on the contrary, it is lengthened the small arcs will be performed in less time than the great ones. Glasgow says that a hair-spring of whatever form to be isochronous must satisfy the following conditions: Its center of gravity must always be on the axis of the balance, and it must expand and contract in the vibrations concentrically with that axis. When these conditions are secured in a properly made spring it will possess the quality of isochronism, that is, its force will increase in proportion to the tension, and it will not exert any lateral pressure on the pivots.

Britten says, it should be remembered that if the vibrations of a balance are to be isochronous the impulse must be delivered in the middle of its vibration, and that therefore no spring will be satisfacrory if the escapement is defective in this particular.

The recognized authorities conflict considerably in their various theories in regard to adjustment to isochronism and particularly in regard to the length of spring. Immisch says that mere length has nothing to do with isochronism. Glasgow contends that length has everything to do with it and that a spring too short, whatever its form, would make the short arcs of the balance vibration be performed in a less time than the long arcs, and a spring too long would have just the contrary effect. Charles Frodsham advanced the theory that every length of spring has its isochronous point. Britten declares that the length is all important; that a good length of spring for one variety of escapement is entirely unfitted for another variety. Saunier says that the discussion of the question whether short springs are preferable to long ones is a mere waste of time and can result in no good. In horology everything must be relative. Whatever be the escapement under consideration, it requires neither a long nor a short hairspring, but one that is suited to its nature and mode of action, that is to say, the length must bear a definite relation to the extent of the arcs of vibration, etc.

Owing to this conflict of opinion it is advisable that the student read the various arguments set forth in the works referred to above and form his own conclusions.

ADJUSTMENT HEATER. The Simpson heater, shown in Fig. 2, will be found invaluable when adjusting movements to temperature. The variation of temperature in this heater is one and one-half dedrees in twenty our hours. It is designed to be heated by gas, the cost of heating being but about three cents in twenty-four hours. A small lamp can be used if the watchmaker has no gas at command.

FIG. 2.

ALCOHOL OR BENZINE CUP. The watchmaker should keep the alcohol and benzine on his bench in a glass cup having a tight-fitting cover to prevent evaporation and contamination with dust. It also adds to the appearance of his bench and is a great improvement over an old saucer and bottle. The cup shown in Fig. 3 has a ground glass cover or stopper that fits tightly into the neck of the cup.

ALCOHOL LAMP. The Clark patent simplicity lamp shown in Fig. 4, is a favorite one with American watchmakers. It has nine facets on the

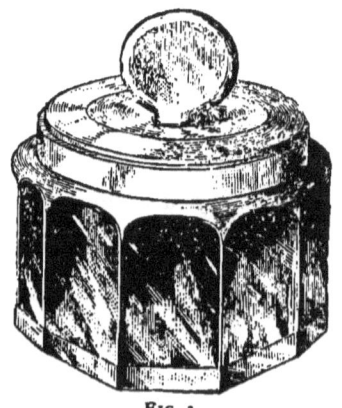

FIG. 3.

font that it may readily be adjusted to any required position. The wicks of alcohol lamps should not be too tight and the interior and exterior of the font should be kept free from dirt. The Clark lamp should not be filled more than one-third full. The wick should be removed when it gets so short that it fails to reach well down into the alcohol.

FIG. 4.

The Bush Self-Generating Gas Blow-Pipe Lamp, shown in Fig. 5, is divided into two compartments, one for alcohol and the other for benzine. Fill with alcohol at D and at E fill nearly full with benzine. Light the small burner at D, bring one of the tubes, A, B or C, to bear on the burner and above it as in cut; blow in rubber tube F and the gas formed by the action of blowing will be ignited. Empty out old benzine occasionally. Where a flame is desired still larger than that afforded by benzine, use gasoline. This lamp requires no more care than an ordinary lamp.

FIG. 5.

The great advantage of this lamp is that it leaves both hands free to manipulate the work, and that the size of the flame can be instantly regulated to suit the exigences of the case.

ALLOY. A compound of two or more metals. It is usual to melt the less fusible metal first and add the more fusible.

Alloys for Compensation Balances. Breguet used for his compensation balances the following alloy: Silver, two parts, by weight; copper, two parts; zinc, one part. First melt the silver and throw in the zinc, reduced to small pieces, stirring the metals and leaving it on the fire for as short a time as possible to prevent the volatilization of the latter metal; then pour it out and let it get cold. Melt the copper and add the cold alloy, stirring the three together until intimately mixed. Pour out, cut into pieces, and smelt anew to obtain a perfect incorporation. Be careful, however, to leave the alloy as short a time as possible over the fire, because the zinc dissipates easily. This alloy is hard, elastic, very ductile, and quickly smelts in the furnace. It does not stand much hammering.

Alloy for Composition Files. These files, which are frequently used by watchmakers and other metal workers, for grinding and polishing, and the color of which resembles silver, are composed of 8 parts copper, 2 parts tin, 1 part zinc, 1 part lead. They are cast in forms and treated upon the grindstone; the metal is very hard, and therefore worked with difficulty with the file.

Aluminium Alloys. Aluminium is alloyed with many metals, but the most important are those with copper. Lange & Sons have obtained a patent in the United States for an alloy consisting of ninety-five parts of aluminium and five of copper, which is malleable and is used for clock springs. An alloy of ten parts of aluminium and ninety of copper is hard but nevertheless ductile. It takes a high polish and somewhat resembles gold.

Aluminium Bronze. This alloy contains from 6 to 10 per cent. of aluminium, and is prepared by fusing chemically-pure copper with aluminium. The standard bronze in use consists of ninety parts of copper to ten of aluminium. It gives sharp castings, is easier to work than steel, can be engraved, rolled into sheets or drawn into wire and when exposed to the air suffers less change than cast iron, steel, silver or brass. It can be soldered only with an aluminium alloy.

Aluminium Silver. Aluminium and silver are easily alloyed and these alloys are more easily worked than silver although harder. An alloy of ninety-seven parts aluminium and three of silver is not affected by ammonium hydrosulphide and has a beautiful color. An alloy of ninety-five parts of aluminium and five of silver is white, elastic and hard. It is used for making blades of desert and fruit knives.

Aluminium Gold. One part of aluminium to 99 of gold gives a metal the color of green gold, very hard but not ductile. An alloy of 5 parts of aluminium to 95 parts of gold gives an alloy that is nearly as brittle as glass. An alloy of 10 parts of aluminium to 90 parts of gold is white, crystalline and brittle. An imitation of gold, used as a substitute for the precious metal in cheap jewelry, is made by fusing together 5 to 7½ parts of aluminium, 90 to 100 parts of copper and 2½ of gold. The color of this alloy resembles gold so closely as to almost defy detection.

Aluminium Zinc. Alloys of aluminium and zinc are very hard and take a beautiful polish. An alloy of 97 parts of aluminium and 3 of zinc gives a result that is as white as the pure metal, harder than aluminium and very ductile.

Artificial Gold. A metallic alloy, at present very extensively used in France as a substitute for gold, is composed of: Pure copper, 100 parts; zinc, or preferably tin, 17 parts; magnesia, 6 parts; sal-ammoniac, from 3 to 6 parts; quicklime, ⅛ part; tartar of commerce, 9 parts, are mixed as follows: The copper is first melted, and the magnesia, sal ammoniac, lime and tartar are then added separately and by degrees, in the form of powder; the whole is now briskly stirred for about one-half hour, so as to mix thoroughly, and then the zinc is added in small grains by throwing it on the surface and stirring until it is entirely fused; the crucible is then covered and fusion maintained for about 35 minutes. The surface is then skimmed and the alloy ready for coating. It has a fine grain, is malleable, and take a splendid polish. It does not corrode readily, and is an excellent substitute for gold for many purposes. When tarnished, its brilliancy can be restored by a little acidulated water. If tin be employed instead of zinc, the alloy will be more brilliant.

Bell Metal. An alloy of copper and tin, in proportions varying from 66 to 80 per cent. of copper and the balance tin.

Brass. An alloy consisting of about 65 parts of copper to 35 parts of zinc. This proportion is varied according to the uses to which the alloy is to be put. See *Bronzing*, *Plating* and *Coloring Metals*.

Britannia. This alloy as prepared by Koller consists of 85.72 parts of tin, 10.34 of antimony, 0.78 of copper and 2.91 of zinc.

Chrysorine. This alloy is sometimes used for watch cases and parts of the movement. In color it closely resembles 18 to 20 carat gold. It does not tarnish when exposed to the air and has a beautiful luster. It consists of 100 parts of copper and 50 of zinc.

Fictitious Silver. No. 1: Silver, 1 oz.; nickel, 1 oz. 11 dwts.; copper, 2 oz. 9 dwts.; or No. 2, silver 3 oz.; nickel, 1 oz. 11 dwts.; copper, 2 oz. 9 dwts.; spelter 10 dwts.

Malleable Brass. A malleable brass is obtained by alloying 33 parts of copper and 25 parts zinc; the copper is first thrown into the pot, which is covered slightly and fused. As soon as the copper is smelted, the zinc, to be free from sulphur, is added, and cast into ingots.

Composition of some Valuable Alloys.

	Cadmium.	Manganese.	Black Cobaltic Oxide.	Nickel.	Platinum.	Iron.	Antimony.	Copper.	Lead.	Zinc.	Tin.	Bismuth.	Silver.	Gold.	Aluminium.	Palladium.
Alloy for Tea Pots							9.53	0.88		9.94	88.55					
Alloy for Knives and Forks											10					
Alloy for Opera Glasses											20					
Alloy Resembling Silver		25		100	1					20			20 to 25			
Alloy Resembling Silver		20		100	20											
Alloy for Gongs and Bells				6.5		5		55			25		5			
Alloy, Non-Magnetic								57								45 to 75
Bell Metal, American								100			11					
Bell Metal, Japanese						0.55		15 to 30	2	1	4.36					
Bronze, Japanese								39	9.19	1.86	4					
Bronze, Manganese								10	2	20	3					
Bronze for Medals								82.72	1.37	18	1.70					
Bronze for Ornaments								54.50		5.33	24.3					
Bronze, Paris						0.74		50		2.7	25					
Clock Bells, German								82			26.56					
Clock Bells, Swiss						0.24		99.60		36.88	1.35					
Clock Bells, French								73		25			1.44			
Clock Wheels, Black Forest								74.5								
For Spoons								72		13.52	0.48				7.5	
Nurnberg Gold								60.66			1			2.5		
Oroide		25.50						50								
Prince's Metal								90		30						
Pinchbeck								68.21								
Soft Solder								6			18	7				
White Metal	1		20	140				90	6	72						

Gold Alloys used by Jewelers.

Color.	Gold.	Silver.	Copper.	Cadmium.	Steel.
Blue	250				250
Blue	500				250
Gray	800				200
Gray	857	86			57
Gray	725	275			
Green	750	125		125	
Green	750	166		84	
Green	746	114	97	43	
Red	666	67	268		
Red	750	104	146		
Red, Pale	600	200	200		
Red, Very	583	42	375		
Yellow	583	250	167		
Yellow	666	194	139		
Yellow	750	146	104		
Yellow, Dark	583	125	292		
Yellow, Pale	666	333			

Resembling Silver.—The following alloys have a close resemblance to silver: Minargent is composed of 100 parts copper; 70 nickel; 1 aluminium and 5 of tungstate of iron. Trabak metal is composed of tin 87.5, nickel 5.5, antimony 5 and bismuth 2. Warne metal is composed of tin 10, bismuth 7, nickel 7 and cobalt 3.

ALUMINIUM. Aluminum is an extremely light metal, rapidly coming into favor in America for all purposes of manufacture. Its weight is only about one-quarter that of silver. Its density is only 25.6. It withstands a very great heat and cools less rapidly than all other metals. It is particularly applicable where lightness combined with strength is desirable, and being extremely ductile, is easily worked. See *Alloys.*

AMALGAM. A compound of mercury with another metal; as an amalgam of tin.

ANCHOR ESCAPEMENT. The recoil escapements used in most house clocks. A variety of the lever escapement made with a very wide impulse pin, is also known as an anchor escapement. Authorities differ as to the inventor of the anchor escapement. Britten gives the credit of the invention to Dr. Hooke, whom he claims invented it in 1675, while Saunier says that the first anchor escapement appears to have been invented in 1680, by Clement, a London clockmaker.

Glasgow says: This escapement was the first step in the direction of securing isochronism in the vibrations of the pendulum, as it involved a longer pendulum, shorter arcs, a heavier pendulum bob and less motive power. Consequently this combination resulted in the pendulum being less controlled by the escapement, and therefore less influenced by variations in the impulse, although the escapement cannot be considered detached in the sense that a dead-beat one is.

In Clement's escapement, the entrance pallet was convex and the exit pallet concave, and they were afterwards made flat, but in both cases they were found to cut away very fast, owing to the friction when the recoil takes place; to prevent this, they were subsequently made both convex, as shown in the Fig. 6 , which lessens the angle, and consequently the friction at the recoils.

There are still people, says Britten, who believe the recoil to be a better escapement than the dead beat—mainly because the former requires a greater variation of the driving power to affect the extent of the vibration of the pendulum than the latter does. But the matter is beyond argument; the recoil can be cheaply made, and is a useful escapement, but is unquestionably inferior to the dead beat for time-keeping.

There is no rest or locking for the pallets, but directly the pendulum in its vibration allows a tooth, after giving impulse, to escape from the impulse face of one pallet, the course of the wheel is checked by the impulse face of the other pallet receiving a tooth. The effect of this may be seen on looking at the drawing (Fig. 6), where the pendulum, traveling to the right, has allowed a tooth to fall on the left-hand pallet. The pendulum, however, still continues its swing to the right, and in consequence the pallet pushes the wheel back, thus causing the recoil which gives the name to the escapement. It is only after the pendulum comes to rest and begins its excursion the other way that it gets any assistance from the wheel, and the difference between the forward motion of the wheel and its recoil forms the impulse.

ANCHOR ESCAPEMENT. 24

SETTING OUT THE ESCAPEMENT.

Draw a circle representing the escape wheel, which we assume to have thirty teeth, of which the anchor embraces eight. Mark off the position of four teeth on each side of the centre one, and draw radial lines which will represent the backs of the teeth.

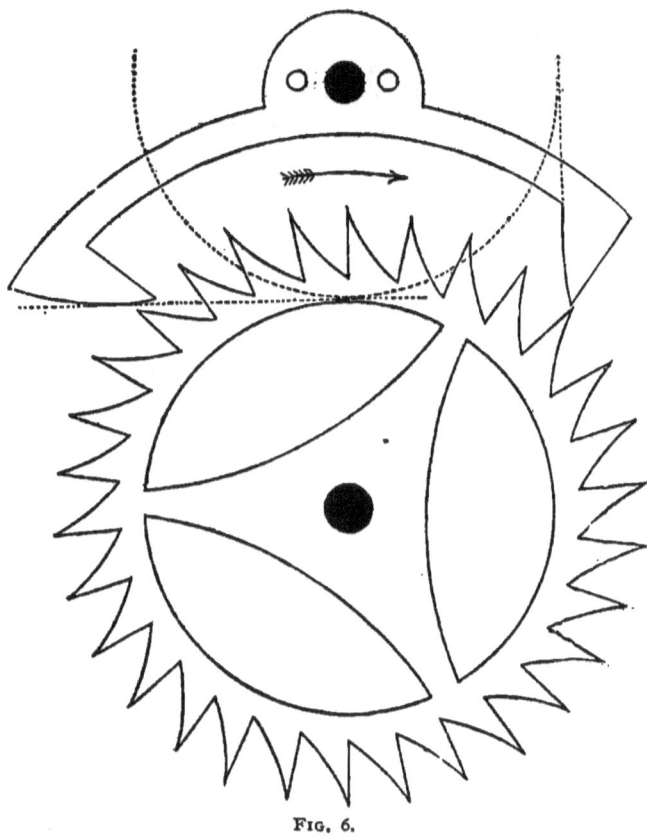

FIG. 6.

NOTE.—Space between one tooth and the next $=\frac{360}{30}=12°$; and 8 spaces $= 96°$. Then $\frac{96}{2}=48°$ to be set off on each side of the centre.

The distance of the pallet staff centre from the centre of escape wheel $=$ radius of wheel $\times$ 1.4. From the pallet staff

ANCHOR ESCAPEMENT.

center describe a circle whose radius = seven-tenths of the radius of escape wheel, that is, half the distance between the escape wheel and pallet staff centers. Tangents to this circle just touching the tips of the teeth already marked, as shown by dotted lines in the drawing would then form the faces of

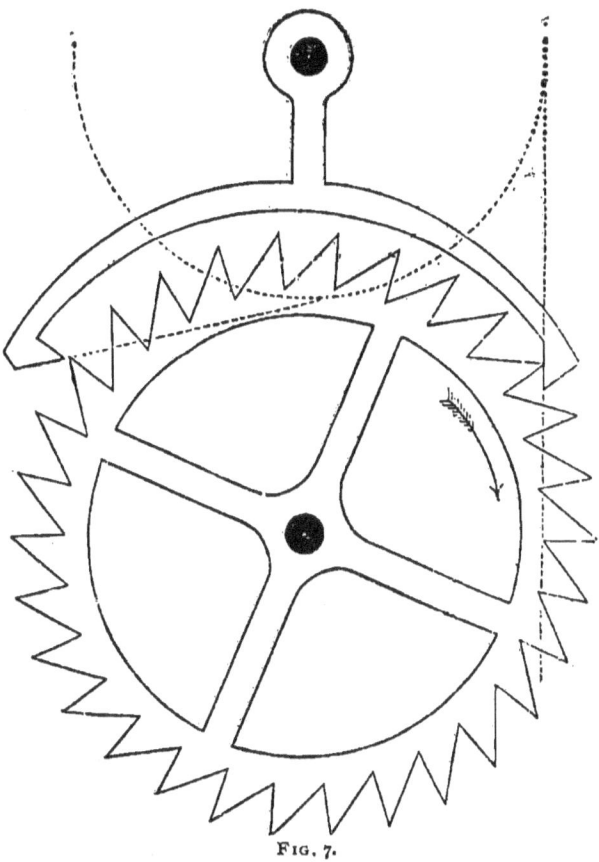

FIG. 7.

the pallets if they were left flat. When a tooth has dropped off the right-hand pallet, which is the position of the escapement in the drawing, the amount of impulse is shown by the intersection of the other pallet in the wheel. The impulse, measured from the pallet staff center, is usually from 3 to 4°.

The pallet faces are generally curved full in the middle, as shown in Fig. 6. The object of curving the pallets is to lessen the "pitting" which the wheel teeth make on the pallets. There will, however, be very little "pitting" if the wheels are made small and light, and there is not excessive drop to the escapement.

The advantage of making the backs of the escape wheel teeth radial and the foresides curved, as shown in Fig. 6, is that if the pendulum gets excessive vibration the pallets butt against the roots of the teeth and the points are uninjured.

There is another form of the recoil escapement often used in long-cased clocks, in which the anchor embraces ten teeth of the escape wheel, and the foresides of the teeth are radial. It is shown in Fig. 7. In other respects the construction is substantially the same as the one just described.

ANGULAR VELOCITY. The angle through which an arm turning on its axis is displaced in a unit of time. It is entirely independent of the length of this arm The approximate ratio of the angular velocities of the balances with the cylinder and (pocket) chronometer escapements in the same unit of time (one-fifth second when there are 18,000 vibrations per hour), is about 270°: 360°. The velocity properly so called is the space transversed in a unit of time by the point under consideration (which in this case is taken on the circumference of gyration). For a given angular movement we obtain the approximate ratio of the velocities by multiplying each radius by the number of vibrations in a unit of time.— *Saunier*.

ANNEALING. The process of heating metals and then manipulating them in order to increase their ductility. Gold, silver, copper and brass are annealed by beating them to redness and then plunging them in water, while steel is annealed by heating and then allowing it to cool slowly.

ANODE. The positive pole of an electric battery; opposed to cathode.

ARBOR. An axle or spindle on which a wheel turns.

ARC. Any given part of the circumference of a circle.

ARCOGRAPH. An instrument sometimes used by watchmakers for drawing a circular arc without the use of a central point.

ASSAY. To subject an ore, alloy or metallic compound to chemical examination in order to determine the amount of a particular metal contained in it.

AUXILIARY. See *Balance*.

BALANCE. The wheel in a watch, clock or chronometer which is kept in vibration by means of the escapement and which regulates the motion of the train. The size and weight of a balance are important factors in the time-keeping qualities of a watch although the dimensions of a balance are not criteria of the time in which the balance will vibrate. The balance is to a pocket time-piece what the pendulum is to the clock; although there are two essential points of difference. The time of vibration of a pendulum is unaffected by its mass, because every increase in that direction carries with it a proportional influence of gravity; but if we add to the mass of the balance we add nothing to the strength of the hairspring, but add to its load and therefore the vibrations become slower. Again, a pendulum of a given length, as long as it is kept at the same distance from the earth's center, will vibrate in the same time because the gravity is always the same; but the irregularity in the force of the hairspring produces a like result in the vibration of the balance. Britten says there are three factors upon which the time of the vibration of the balance depends:

1. The weight, or rather the mass, of the balance.*
2. The distance of its center of gyration from the center of motion, or to speak roughly, the diameter of the balance. From these two factors the moment of inertia may be deducted.

---

*The mass of a body is the amount of matter contained in that body, and is the same irrespective of the distance of the body from the center of the earth. But its weight, which is mass × gravity, varies in different latitudes.

3. The strength of the hair-spring, or more strictly its power to resist change of form.

Balances are of two kinds, known as plain or uncut, and cut or compensation. The plain balance is only used in this country on the very cheapest variety of movements. The compensation balance is used on the better grade of watches. The plain balance is usually made of brass or steel while the compensation balance is made of steel and brass combined. Some English makers use gold for plain balances, it being denser than steel and not liable to rust or become magnetized. The process of compensation balance making as carried on in our American factories is as follows: A steel disc, one-eighth of an inch thick and five-eighths of an inch in diameter is first punched from a sheet of metal. It is then centered and drilled partially through, the indention serving as a guide in the operations to follow. A capsule of pure copper three-fourths of an inch in diameter is then made and in the center of this capsule the steel disc is lightly secured. A ring of brass one-sixteenth of an inch in thickness is then made and placed between the copper capsule and the blank, and the whole is fused together. It is then faced upon both sides. It is then placed in a lathe and cut away in the center until a a ring is formed of steel, which is lined or framed with brass. It then goes into the press, where two crescents are cut from it, leaving only the inner lining of the ring and the cross-bar of steel. The burr is then removed and the balance is ready to be drilled and tapped for the balance screws. This method of making balances is known as the "capsule method."

The Expansion and Contraction of Balances. The American Waltham Watch Co. use a simple little contrivance shown at Fig. 8 for indicating the expansion and contraction of balances. It is composed of a steel disc, on one side of which a scale is etched and opposite the scale a hole is drilled and tapped to receive the screw that holds the balance. One of the screws of the balance to be tested is removed and the indicating needle is screwed in its place. The steel disc is held by means of a pair of sliding tongs over an alcohol lamp, or can be heated in any other way, and the expansion will be indicated by the movement of the needle on the scale. Fig. 9 illustrates the expansion and contraction of balances. With an increase of temperature the rim is bent inward, thus reducing the size of the balance. This is owing to the fact that brass expands more than steel, and in endeavoring to

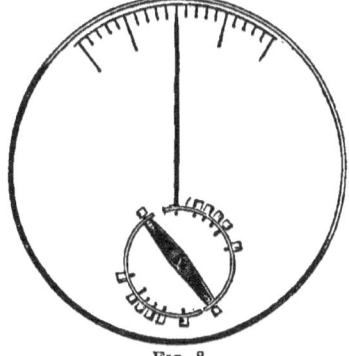

FIG. 8.

expand it bends the rim inward. The action is, of course, reversed by lowering the temperature below normal. Some adjusters spin a balance close to the flame of a lamp before using, in order to subject it to a higher temperature than it is likely to meet in use. The balance is then placed upon a cold iron plate and afterward tested for poise. The balance is then trued, if found necessary, and the operation is repeated until it is found to be in poise after heating. Britten says that it has been demonstrated that the loss in heat from the weakening of the hair spring is uniformly in proportion to the increase of temperature. The compensation balance, however, fails to meet the temperature error exactly, the rims expand a little too much with decrease of temperature, and with increase of temperature the contraction of the rims is

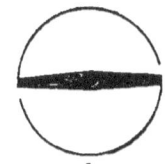  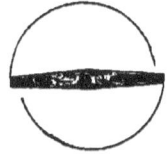

FIG. 9.

ginal Position of Rim.   Position Under Extreme Cold.   Position Under Extreme Heat.

insufficient, consequently a watch or chronometer can be correctly adjusted for temperature at two points only. Watches are usually adjusted at about 50° and 85°. In this range there would be what is called a middle temperature error of about two seconds in twenty-four hours with a steel hair-spring.

The amount of the middle temperature error cannot be absolutely predicated, for in low temperatures, when the balance is larger in diameter, the arc of vibration is less than in high

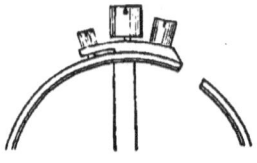

FIG. 10.

temperatures when the balance is smaller, and consequently its time of vibration is affected by the isochronism or otherwise of the hair spring. Advantage is sometimes taken of this circumstance to lessen the middle temperature error by leaving the piece fast in the short arcs. To avoid middle temperature error in marine chronometers, various forms of compensation balances have been devised, and numberless additions or auxiliaries have been attached to the ordinary form of balance for the same purpose. Poole's auxiliary, shown in Fig. 10, and Molyneaux's, shown in Fig. 11, may be taken to represent the two principles on which most auxiliaries are constructed. Poole's consists of a piece of brass attached to the fixed ends of the rim and carrying a regulating screw, the point of which checks the outward movement of the rim in low temperatures. Molyneaux's is attached to

FIG. 11.

each end of the arm by a spring, the free ends of the rim acting on it in high temperatures only. Fig. 11 illustrates this auxiliary when the temperature has been raised, its free ends, to which the adjusting screws are attached, having approached nearer the center of the balance, carrying with them the free ends of the auxiliary, so that the small projection no longer comes in contact with the short end of the balance rim, as it would in a temperature of 55°. This auxiliary is made of steel.

Sizes and Weights of Balances. The size and weight of the balance are two very important elements in the timing of a watch and especially in adjusting to positions. The rules governing the sizes and weights of balances, says Mr. Chas. Reiss, are of a complex nature, and though positive are difficult of application on account of the impracticability of determining the value of the elements on which we have to base our calculations. These elements are the main-spring or motive power, the hairspring representing the force of gravity on the pendulum, momentum and friction. The relation of the motive power or the main-spring to the subject under discussion lies first in the necessary proportion between it and the amount of tension of the spring to be overcome, according to the extent and number of vibrations aimed at; and, second, to that of friction affecting the motion of the balance and incidental to it. In an 18,000 train the main-spring has to overcome resistance of the hairspring for 432,000 vibrations daily. The hairspring having its force established by the relative force of the motive power circumscribes the proportions of the mass called balance and is so co-agent for overcoming friction.

Momentum overcomes some of the elastic force of the spring and friction. It is the force of a body in motion and is equal to the weight of the body multiplied by its velocity. Velocity in a balance is represented by its circumference, a *given point* in which travels a *given distance* in a *given time*. Weight is that contained in its rim. A balance is said to have more or less momentum in proportion, as it retains force imparted to it by impulsion. If a watch has a balance with which it has been brought to time, and this is changed to one-half the size, it requires to be four times as heavy, because its weight is then only half the distance from the center, and any given point in its circumference has only half the distance to travel. On the other hand, a balance twice the size, would have one-fourth the weight. In the first case the balance would have twice as much momentum as the original one, because if we multiply the weight by the velocity we have a product twice as great. In the latter case a like operation would give a product half as great as in the original balance.

It follows that the smaller and heavier a balance the more momentum, and vice versa the less momentum it has, always on condition that the hair-spring controls both equally. Friction, affecting the vibration of the balance, is that of the pivots on which it moves and that of the escapement. It is in proportion to the force with which two surfaces are pressed together and their area. In a balance, weight is synonymous with pressure, area is represented by the size of its pivots and the thickness of the pivot holes. The first, pivot friction, is continuous and incidental and is overcome by combined forces, the motive power, the elasticity of the hair-spring, and the momentum of the balance. The latter, or escapement friction, is intermitting and is overcome by contending forces, the hair-spring and the momentum of the balance on one side and the motive power on the other.

Having it in our power, as shown above, to obtain the desired momentum of the balance by differing relative pressure and diameter, we can regulate pivot friction within certain limits and distribute the labor of overcoming it, among the co-operative forces, in such a manner that the proportions of such distributions shall not be disturbed during their (forces) increase or decrease. Incidental pivot friction is that caused by the contact of the balance with the escapement. Escapement friction is that caused by the unlocking on the impulse. The first causes retardation, the latter acceleration in the motion of the balance, regardless of isochronism. It is easy to comprehend that a heavy balance would, by its greater momentum, unlock the escapement with less retardation than a light one; but, on the other hand, the acceleration by the impulse would be less also; and with a varying motive power a disturbing element would be introduced by a change in the relative proportions of these forces, the momentum of the balance decreasing or increasing faster than the motive power, constituting as it does relatively a more variable force. In argument the reverse of this might be advanced in regard to a balance which is too light. Without, however, entering further into the subject it is plain how the rate of a watch under such conditions might be affected after being apparently adjusted in stationary positions by being used on a locomotive or under conditions where external disturbances should lessen the extent of vibration, and making the contact between the balance and the escapement of less duration.

The almost universal abandonment of watches with uniform motive power and the introduction of stem-winders with going barrels, invest the subject with special interest; and as stated in the beginning, applying rules for defining these desirable proportions being impracticable, the only solution of the problem which remains to us is the study by observation of certain symptoms which do exist, to determine that which by other means cannot be done. During the progress of horology similar difficulties had to be met in every kind of watch which happened to be in use. The old Verge watch had its balance proportioned thus; that it could lie inside in the mainspring barrel, and the watch, when set going without a balance spring, would indicate by the hand on the dial a progress of twenty-seven and one-half minutes during one hour running. It was said that under these circumstances it would be least affected by inequalities of the motive power, and the verge would not be cut by the escape wheel. The balance in the Cylinder watch was to be sized according to the proportion of the train, each successive wheel to be one-half smaller than the preceding one and the balance to be twice the size of the escape wheel, the weight to be determined by the equal running of the watch during all the changes of an unequal motive power. The cutting of the steel pallets in Duplex watches or chronometers is caused more by too heavy balances than by any other defect in their parts. It might be well to note the following, which is very important and too often neglected, and that is the arrangement of the mainspring in the barrel so as to avoid coil friction, and the smallest advantage of the old Fusee watch was not the facility of obtaining five turns of the fusee to three or three and one-half of the main-spring, but being enabled thereby to arrange the latter around a small arbor in such a manner that the coils never touched, insuring a smooth motive power and lessening the chances of breakage beyond estimation.

Poising the Balance.—In merely poising a balance for a cheap movement there is no great diffiulty, that is, putting it in equipoise sufficient for the reasonable good performance

BALANCE. 34

of the movement, but to well and thoroughly poise for a high grade of movement embraces means and methods not necessary in the first mentioned. In a cheap balance a high degree of accuracy is not expected, and so the manipulations are in the poising simple, provided all the parts are in condition to admit of poising. The following will be about all the conditions and means used generally: In the outset the balance should be in poise without its staff, and this is approximated before the staff is in by putting into the staff socket in the arm a piece of true wire, sufficiently tight to allow of the balance being held on to it with friction, so that the balance can be trued in the flat by the fingers or with tweezers and remain while poising on the parallel bars.

Fig. 12 illustrates a form of tweezers made especially for balance truing. To here explain the parallel bars and give a few points regarding the essential features will be well, and help to make clear some points that follow in the poising instructions.

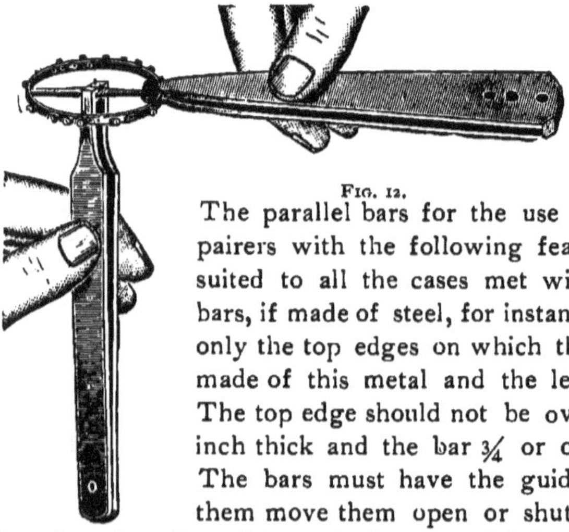

FIG. 12.

The parallel bars for the use of watch repairers with the following features will be suited to all the cases met with: The two bars, if made of steel, for instance, must have only the top edges on which the pivots rest made of this metal and the less the better. The top edge should not be over $\frac{1}{160}$ of an inch thick and the bar $\frac{3}{4}$ or one inch long. The bars must have the guides that carry them move them open or shut for different lengths of staffs, and keep the bars parallel during the movements. The bars after they are in their places and securely fastened to the stand carrying them, must be ground true, straight and parallel, on a flat piece of glass (plate glass is the best), charged with emery of about 140, with oil sufficient to make a paste. The glass can be held and used as a file or the bars can be held down on the glass and moved about with a circular stroke, but if the stand is large and heavy this operation will not be readily performed with good results. The main reason for using the glass referred to, is that it is a ready way of getting a grinding bed comparatively true without labor or preparation. A flat metal surface, marble or stoneware, would answer well, but would not be as readily had. After the emery has ground the surfaces true, clean off all the emery and use fine oil stone powder or pumice stone; clean, and follow the pumice stone with any polishing powder, or follow the pumice stone with a large and true burnishing file, keeping the surface wet slightly. In making the parallel edges, the object is to give them a perfectly straight surface on the edge and highly polished. These parallels are probably best made of bell metal, as there is then no danger of their being affected or accumulating magnetism. In the construction of a poising tool, to avoid the use of iron or steel in its make up, will be found the most satisfactory, as then magnetism will not be a disturbing element that it might otherwise be. The whole tool should be heavy and low and stand on the bench firmly, and if a fine one have two level vials set in its base to level up the parallels with, before using. With a level bench and a tool made so that the feet are parallel to the top edge of the parallels, there will be little trouble in the balance rolling by gravity while poising. There are a great variety of poising tools and any that have the parallel bars true and straight and parallel to one another, readily adjusted for distance, and have a firm and heavy stand, will be easily and satisfactorily handled.

Holes for the staff pivots are not good for poising, although jeweled, as the pivots must turn in them with a slipping action, whereas they roll without slip or friction on the parallels. The extreme top edge of the parallels, if of hard substance, can be made as thin as the $\frac{1}{500}$ of an inch and be all the better, as will be explained. The plain straight portion of a conical pivot of a fine staff is frequently not over the $\frac{1}{100}$ of an inch long, and this is the part of the pivot that is to be exactly concentric with the center of gravity of the balance after poising

BALANCE. 36

is accomplished and is that part of the pivot that rests on the jewel. Now, from this it will be seen that the thickness of the parallels cannot be great, not over the $\frac{1}{100}$ of an inch, as the conical part of the pivot must not touch the parallel, and the end of the pivot should be outside of the parallel. Fig. 13 will show the situation and give the best idea. After the balance has been trued on the wire, then test on the straight edge, and if the balance rolls freely and gravitates, then lighten it on the down or heavy side. Or in the event that the balance is rather light it may be advisable to weight it on the top or light side.

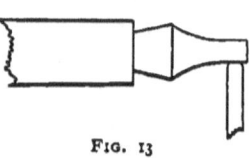

FIG. 13

It will take a little practice to poise in this first operation, and there are several points to look at. First, if the balance is a heavy one, then in poising take away weight; second, if a plain (not comp.) remove little bits from the under side of the rim with a graver or drill; if very light, add weight by small pins being added by drilling in the rim and driving in several pins and then filing away till poised. The pins must be put into the rim at such points as are indicated by the circumstances. Soft solder, if used on the under side of a plain balance, is very easily handled, but the risk from the soldering fluid is great and requires great care in cleaning, but when all is well done, it serves a good purpose. As the wire on which the balance is hung is large in diameter, the poising will not be very delicate, but can be made good enough for the end served. In poising a compensating balance, the balance must be hung on a wire with each end pointed, turned to points, so that the wire can be held in the calipers and the balance made true in the round.* Set the gauge of the calipers so that the rim at the end of one arm shall exactly conclude with it, and then turn the balance slowly under the gauge and see if the rim turns truly under it. If not true, bend in or out with the fingers and try by gauge till the balance will turn true in the round, then put onto the parallels and poise as in case of the plain balance, but alter the weight with the screws. The

---

*See *Gauges*.

screws that are at the bottom can be put into a split chuck and a little turned away from the under side of the head, or a washer * can be put under the head of the top screw, and this method pursued till a reasonably fine poising is obtained. In these operations all the points relating should be well considered, and not make moves without method and good reasons. Care is required all through poising in all its branches.

These washers are very convenient to use in cases where a balance requires a little more weight, and where it is not advisable to change the hairspring or regulator when regulating to time, and in such cases must be put under the heads of the screws at the ends of the arms. All things being equal, in poising a weighted balance, it is better to add a little weight than take away any, by turning the heads of screws as described, as then the balance is not in any way injured, and if it was all correct when found, although indications led to other conclusions, by removing a washer or two the balance would be left as original and much trouble saved in trying to remedy a mistake. Never make any changes in a fine compensated balance as in all probability it was correct when made and some injudicious handling to blame for any defect. After a balance has been trued in the calipers as described, so that the rim is truly concentric with the hole in the arm, it should if it has not been injured, be virtually in poise, but if it is not, add washers to the screws on the light side and by them try to poise it rather than by lessening the weight. Many times, taking a screw from the heavy side and putting it in place of one on the light and the light in place of the heavy, will tend to an equilibrium, and so far as it does is so much gain. In removing the screws in a compensating balance, care must be used when they are replaced to see that they are left just tight enough to stay in place and at the same time not bind the head hard down on the rim. Screws badly handled in this respect may derange the compensation, also the poising. All the screws of a balance, except those at the ends of the arms and occasionally a pair at the quarters, should be down heads, close to the rim. The others can be turned in and out at pleasure to

---

*See *Balance Screw Washer*.

poise or for timing, as required. With a balance with a screw at each end of the arm, it is best not to move them in or out in poising, but proceed as described and leave these screws to be moved in timing afterward, if required, as it helps make that operation easy. When a balance has four screws they may be moved to do all the poising and afterward any pair opposite, or the whole, may be moved in timing and not disturb the poising. A compensating balance with four screws as described is much the easiest balance to handle, for by these screws the finer adjustments in poising and timing can be easily performed with greater certainty than by the old methods as described.

The balance staff is a very important element in poising and its pivots should be perfect, that is, perfect cylinders, and all that part that touches the hole jewel be of equal diameter. By referring to cut of staff it will be seen that the end after leaving the cone is straight, of equal diameter throughout its whole length, and this is the shape of all staff pivots at that point riding in the jewel holes, no matter what curve or shape may be given to the balance of the pivot. When there is a different diameter in the top and bottom pivots they are each true cylinders and their cylindrical diameters are parallel to each other and to the axis of the staff. When pivots are bent or out of parallel with the axis of the staff they are then not in condition to make poising possible, as a bent pivot will make a balance gravitate and act as though out of poise in itself, and with a bent pivot, poising can only be approximately attained. Perfectly cylindrical and parallel pivots to a staff are, in poising, a very essential feature, and without which poising cannot be attained.

When a balance has been poised as indicated and a staff made and fitted with perfectly cylindrical and parallel pivots, proceed as follows, and there will be little to do to complete the operation: First put the balance on the staff with a hollow punch and only press it on sufficiently to hold for preliminary tests; then place on the parallels of the poiser and examine; should the balance appear in poise, it must not be taken for granted that it is so, but try a very slight jar given the poising tool, like rubbing over the bottom of the frame an old file, which will impart to it a very slight vibration, and if the balance is actually out, it will roll and then remain with the heavy side down. If a jar, such as a series of taps with a hammer, be given, the balance will rotate and stop for an instant and then rotate again, and finally jar off the bars and the operation will not prove anything. The jar is such that the balance raises up bodily, when made with the file, and then falls down exactly on the same place on the parallels, rather the pivots come to rest always at the same point and it will be seen by this means that if any point of the rim is in reality heavier from gravity, that it will by the momentum imparted, fall, overcoming the pivot friction and finally seek a point in a direct line under the staff.

Repeated movements of a balance while on the parallels are necessary, together with great cleanliness of pivots and parallels, to thoroughly ascertain the true poised condition of the balance. When it is ascertained that a balance is out of poise or has a heavy side, punch out the staff and put the balance again on it only turned just one-half way around, and repeat as above. In this way a staff can be put into a balance to the best advantage and such little items all tend to save time and make easy the whole handling. When the best position is found for the staff, stake it, and true in the flat, and test again on the bars, and if necessary make further changes as above to affect a poise. When a balance is in poise and a staff perfectly true as has been described, and well staked on, it will in the most cases be found poised and nothing further to do. After putting on the roller it is advisable to test again for position, but it is generally unnecessary, as this will not disturb the poising only in exceptional cases. By staking on the roller too tight the staff may be bent and may destroy the poise.

Care is necessary in handling a balance for any purpose, not to bend the rim, soil or corrode the metal and finish, and in making slight alterations in the curve of the rim, not to bend it at the holes and so destroy its true circle and injure the strength of the metal and change its adjustment.

Any one, after poising a balance and testing the movement carefully in different positions, will in many cases be aware of quite a change of rate in the changes of position, and this, at the first thought, would seem to rather reflect on the accuracy of the posing; but it will be found to occur at times with the most carefully poised balance, and that the operation of poising by the parallels does not comprehend the whole, nor the very nicer requirements. In any case, the most careful mechanical posing must be attended to first, before any operations of a more delicate nature are attempted. In short, the parallels are to be used in the most delicate methods, but precede the others. When a movement is placed in its case and hung up, after poising on the parallels, its rate should be carefully noted for a given time, then it should be just reversed and set up with the pendant down, when it will be found, as a rule, that after a trial of same duration as the first, that the rate will not be the same. Now, when this occurs in a fine movement, it will be advisable to investigate all the parts which in any way relate to this action. Both hole jewels must be examined, for finish, thickness and truth of the bore; the roller jewel and the lever-fork examined; guard pin and its action with the table; the hairspring and all its relations and connections; the balance must be removed and then the lever, and the lever placed on the parallels by its staff pivots, as in the balance, and tested for poising. The lever should, when placed on the parallels, lay horizontal, like the beam of pan scales, and not swing or hang either end down; the weight should be removed from the heavy end, in such an event, until the lever will lie as indicated. Levers can be, and are made, that will stand in any position, like a poised balance, but it will, in most cases, be difficult to poise a lever for any position other than horizontal. Next, the escape wheel must be poised so that it will perform as a poised balance, when on the parallels; lever and escape jewels examined, as in those of the balance staff.

After all has been so far attended to, and the parts in place again, the balance must stand, when the mainspring is entirely run down, with its arms either perpendicular or horizontal;

with a movement, whose balance is near the center, the arms can stand pointing to 6 and 12, or 3 and 9, as the most convenient. In requiring balance arms to stand in some fixed relation to prominent points of the movement, the manipulations are greatly facilitated, though any position the arms may chance to have will not interfere with the result, but a more expert hand will be required to get along with ease and certainty.

When all the foregoing operations are attended to, hang up the watch and take its rate for 12 hours, with main spring fully wound up; then reverse its position, with mainspring wound up, and test for another 12 hours. On examination, if there should be any considerable variation in the rates in the two positions, say 10 to 15 seconds, then proceed by changing the screws as follows: In a case where the watch loses, when hanging, it indicates that a screw of the balance nearest to 12 or 6, when the movement is entirely run down, must be moved a very little in or out. In this case, it is fair to suppose that the balance is too heavy on the side nearest 6—that this side gravitates, and to an extent acts like a pendulum. Assuming this to be the case, turn the lower screw in and the upper one out, where there are four timing screws, and where not, washers may be added to the top screw, and the two trials repeated. After trial, if the result is improved, then the lower screw may be made a little lighter, but not at the first trial. In the first trials the balance should not be altered in weight, as indications in these manipulations are changed or modified by conditions not yet mentioned.

We will assume that the balance has four screws, and when one is turned in and the other out, as indicated, and the end attained, then the watch is to be placed with 3 or 9 up, and two trials made, as in the first, and the same method used, if indications are similar.

When the handling of the balance has been correctly done, the poising will be found to equalize the rates of the different positions, and the total performance improved. There is, of course, many chances for mismoves, but with caution they will do no harm, for if the balance is not changed other than a change in distribution of its weights, the act of restoring will be merely setting all the screws back to the position they were when poised by the parallels, and then proceed again on a new method, reversing the first, and then gradually it will be made clear to the most inexperienced, remembering that what held good in one case may not in another, and that various cases are only compassed by trial, and that the indications in the one may be just reversed in the other.

Instead of changing the lower screw as previously suggested, another trial is to be made with 12 down, and the rate taken for the same period as for 6 down, and the two compared. Now if the watch maintains its former record it is pretty good evidence that the two rates will be its rates for these two positions, and then the alterations may be made. Now, while hanging in this case the watch lost, 6 down, and relatively gained with 12 up, and a very natural conclusion would be that if losing with 6 down that the lower side of the balance would be the heaviest, but such is not the case, but the indications are that the upper side is the heaviest, and that the screw there should be turned in, and that the lower one may or may not be changed. Change the top screw first, in this case, and then make another trial and compare with the first. In all average cases, after changing the screw, the two rates would be found to be closer than in the first trial, and this will give a pretty good index of how to proceed. The philosophy of the action is the same as that of the action of the musical measuring instrument used to beat music measures, called a metronome. It has a short pendulum with the rod prolonged above the shaft that it swings on, and on the upper end of this rod is a small weight that slides up and down and so regulates the beats. The position of this weight being above the center of motion has a very great control of the vibrations and controls them for a wide range. For instance, the whole pendulum of one of these instruments is not over 2 or 2½ inches long, but with the little counter weight it can be made to beat seconds and slower measures, which could not be accomplished with anything short of a 39 inch pendulum and over. Then move the screw as already indicated, keeping in mind the compared pendulum action and its philosophy.

Gravitating on the principle of the simple pendulum is not the whole problem in moving the screws of the balance, but they embrace the philosophy of the instrument described, and this must be kept in mind in the handling. In experiments it will be found that a screw moved at the top of a balance, will make twice as much changing in the rate as the same movement of a screw at the bottom. Hanging up a watch and turning out the lower screw one-half a turn, and the rate will be, for instance, ten seconds slow in six hours. Now put up just reversed, and for the next six hours the watch will be found twenty seconds slow or more. Now, if we proceed in this case on the simple pendulum philosophy, we should make a mistake in moving the screws.

In practice it is not necessary to make only tests for 3 and 9, assuming we have an open face watch. First, regulate on full spring for 6 or 8 hours hanging, and when well regulated place the watch 3 up and then 9 for the same period on full spring, and if any material change in rate in the two last, then move the screw as already indicated, keeping in mind the compound action and its philosophy.

The handling of the screws in poising on the parallels and in the running watch are for some indications just reversed, and this is due to the action of lever and hairspring on the balance, with gravity in one case and to gravity alone in the other. In experimenting with the running watch always wind fully up for each trial, and periods of six to eight hours will be found the most convenient. The upper coils of a mainspring are much the most equal in power, and consequently give best results; that is, the fourth, fifth and sixth turns of a spring are much nearer each other in strength than are the second, third and fourth. If a balance is perfectly poised mechanically, and the whole train in perfect mechanical poise and condition, then the running watch should not give any very considerable difference in rate in four positions, but as this is not the case generally there will be a change of rate in the positions and the balance can be then manipulated to correct the error, although it in itself may not be at fault. The reason for not testing a watch for the whole range of four positions, is that in the pocket, a watch is not supposed to get into a position with the stem down, three and nine are apt to be up and down, and so with twelve are the three positions used. The isochronal condition of the hairspring is apt to make trouble in these experiments, and this is another reason for using full spring invariably. The motion and its extent of the balance is another element in the matter, and any movement when in perfect poise for a balance motion of $\frac{3}{4}$ of a revolution, each side of the center or dead point ($1\frac{1}{2}$ revolution) would not be found in as accurate poise for $\frac{3}{4}$ of a revolution. A balance making one and a half revolutions, to a certain extent, is self-correcting, as will be seen, and is to be preferred to any other movement, for if any point of the rim is out of poise then the fault is brought just opposite in each excursion, and so does not relatively gravitate. Owing to the fusee, an English lever with a balance making one and one-half revolutions, is the highest form of movement for accurate adjustments of any kind, and so is the easiest to realize perfect poising. The American watch is so uniformly well and evenly made by machinery that poising is in it quite easy, and much more so than in foreign makes. A Waltham movement that I tested, just as it left the factory, only changed its rate about three seconds for the four positions. This could not be realized in any medium grade of foreign watch, and I presume this is not a single case, but probably rather a type. The American movement is made mechanically so near perfection that the watch maker will find poising a balance comparatively easy, and that what he finds to hold good in one case will be pretty sure to in another, due to this mechanical perfection.   J. L. F.

BALANCE ARC. That part of the vibration of a balance in which it is connected with the train, used only in refence to detached escapements.

BALANCE BRIDGE OR COCK. The standard that holds the top pivot of the balance in an upright position. In some of the old English and French full plate watches the balance cock was spread out to cover the entire balance, as shown in Fig. 14, and was sometimes artistically wrought and set with precious stones.

FIG. 14.

BALANCE PROTECTOR. No matter how careful a person may be, accidents will happen, and the least accident to a compensation balance gives the workman considerable trouble. The Arrick patent balance protector, Fig. 15, is intended for guarding balances from contact with turning tools, polishers and the hand rest, while work is being done upon the pivots. The staff is passed through the hole in the protector and held in a wire chuck, and the protector is secured to the arms of the balance by two screws. The Bullock protector, shown in Fig. 16, is designed to protect the balance and other wheels from heat while drawing the temper from staff or pinion for the purpose of pivoting.

FIG. 15.

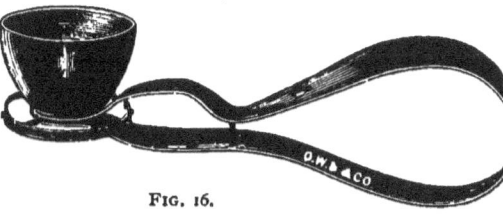

FIG. 16.

BALANCE SCREW WASHERS. All watch adjusters and expert repairers time their watches by the balance screws, without unpinning the hair spring, and have their regulator in the center. After the curve of the hair spring is once correct it should never be let out or taken up. The portion of the spring where it is pinned is naturally stiffer and often abruptly bent to make the first coil conform to the stud and regulator. In unpinning the spring this curve is necessarily altered and the spring thrown out of the center, the heat and cold adjustment is altered and the isochronal adjustment often entirely destroyed.

Where a watch has timing or quarter screws and they move in or out friction tight, you can very soon bring your watch to time without molesting the spring and have the regulator in the center, and also poise by these screws. Very often some of these timing screws are so tight that there is danger of twisting them off. You will also find that two-thirds of the watches of the best makes do not have timing screws. In this case time by a pair of screws opposite the balance arms. If it runs too slow lighten an opposite pair of screws (just mentioned) in a split chuck or file in the slot with slotting file. If it runs too fast put a pair of washers under the screws near the balance arms, or four at right angles or more under other screws. Whatever may be required in poising put the required amount on the light side of the balance rim. Do not tamper with an adjusted hair-spring or any other. If you are anxious to do your work quickly and accurately compare your seconds hand with that of the regulator. See *Poising the Balance.*

BALANCE SPRING. See *Hair Spring.*

BALANCE STAFF. The axis or staff to which the balance is attached. In some makes of watches the balance staff and colet are one piece, while in others the colet is made of brass and is fitted tightly to the staff.

Making a New Staff.—It is a very common thing for American workmen, especially those who reside in the large cities, to depend upon the stock of the material dealer for their staffs. The country watchmaker must, however, rely upon his mechanical ability, and even in the large cities the workman will have to make his own staffs when repairing many foreign watches. The following instructions relate more particularly to staffs for American watches, though they may be applied to foreign watches as well. Before proceeding further I would call the attention of the trade to a most valuable series of essays on the balance staff published in the columns of *The American Jeweler*, and would advise those interested to read them carefully.*

The material used should be of the best, say Stubb's steel wire, a little larger in diameter than the largest part of the staff and a trifle longer that the old one. A wire that fits the No. 45 hole in the pinion guage will be about right in the majority of cases. Put this in the split chuck of your lathe, if you use an American lathe, and rough it out to the form shown at *B* in Fig. 17. If you use a Swiss or wax-chuck lathe, the form of chuck shown at *A*, Fig. 17, will be found very useful.† It is made from a piece of brass rod, threaded to fit the lathe spindle and bored out to receive the work, which is held by set screws, three or four at each end of the chuck. By the aid of these screws the work may be held very firmly and yet can easily be brought to center.

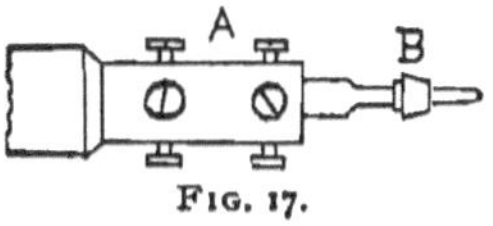

FIG. 17.

After bringing the work to the general form of the staff, in the rough, remove from the lathe, smear with soap and harden by heating to a cherry red and plunging endwise into oil. Re-chuck in the lathe, and while revolving, whiten by applying a No. 000 emery buff so that you may observe the color while drawing the temper. Now place the roughed-out blank in the bluing pan, and draw to a deep blue in color.

The heights may be taken from the old staff providing it was not faulty and is at hand, but all things considered it is better to make your measurements and construct the new staff independent of the old one. A simple tool, and one which any wachmaker can make, is shown in Fig. 18. It will be found very convenient in taking the measurements or heights of a staff.‡ It consists of a hollow sleeve *A*, terminating in a foot *B*.

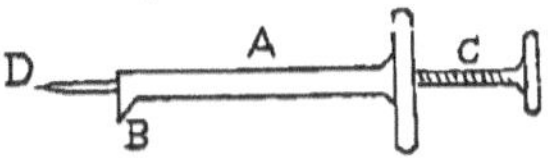

FIG. 18.

---

*Making and Replacing the Balance Staff, a series of seventeen essays published in *The American Jeweler* for December, 1888, and January to September, 1889, inclusive. The illustrations are from these essays.

† From the essay by "Pasadena," *American Jeweler* March, 1889.

‡ Other measuring instruments for this purpose will be found under *Guages*.

BALANCE STAFF. 48

Through this is screwed the rod C, terminating in a pivot D, which is small enough to enter the smallest jewel. To ascertain the right height for the roller, place it upon the foot B, indicated in Fig. 19, and set the pivot of the tool in the foot jewel, and adjust the screw until the roller is in the proper relation to the lever fork as shown in the illustration. In Fig. 19 the potence and plate of the watch are shown in section at A. The roller is indicated at c and the lever fork at d. After the adjusting of the roller is completed, remove the tool and apply it to the rough staff as indicated in Fig. 20, at A, and the point at which the seat for the roller should be cut will be shown. In order to ascertain the height of the balance, apply the gauge as before and bring the point e, so as to give sufficient clearance below the plate as indicated by the dotted lines at B, Fig. 19. Then apply the gauge to the work as indicated at B, Fig. 20, and turn the balance seat at the point indicated. The diameter of the seat for the roller, balance and hairspring collet, can be taken from the old staff, or guage the holes with a taper arbor or a round broach, and then take the size from the broach with calipers.

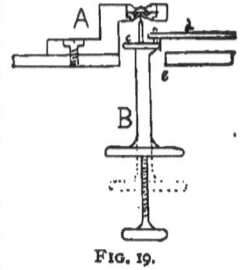

FIG. 19.

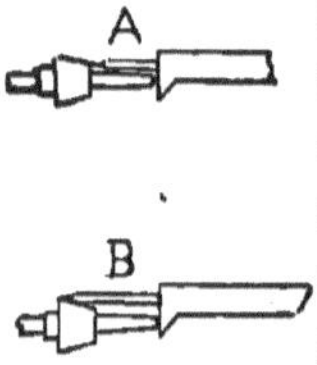

FIG. 20.

The diameter of the lower pivot should be taken from the jewel, and the ordinary pivot gauge when used in connection with a round pivot broach is all that is necessary even for the finest work. At A, in Fig. 21, is shown the gauge, each division of which corresponds to about $\frac{1}{3500}$ of an inch. Slip the jewel on the broach as far as it will go without forcing, as shown at B, Fig. 21, and then take the size of the broach, close up to the jewel, by means of the slit in the guage. This will not give you the exact size of the jewel hole, but will be just enough smaller to allow of the proper freedom of the pivot.

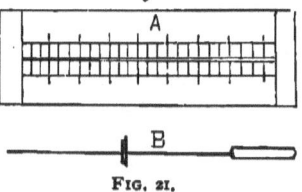

FIG. 21.

BALANCE STAFF.

The best shape for the pivots is shown in Fig. 22, known as conical pivots; the straight portion of the pivot which enters the jewel hole being truly cylindrical and about $\frac{1}{100}$ of an inch long.

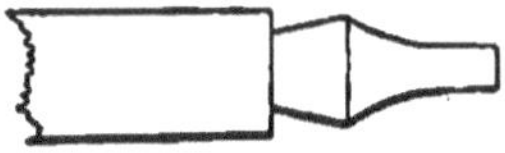

FIG. 22.

Many very good workmen employ but one graven for performing the entire work, but it is better to have at least three, similar in shape to those shown in Fig. 23; A for turning the staff down in the rough, B for undercutting, and C for turning the conical shoulders of the pivots. A graver like that shown at D will be found excellent for beginners and others who find it difficult to turn the shoulder square and at right angles to the staff E, without leaving a groove in one or the other. The all important thing is to keep the gravers sharp. Upon the least sign of their not cutting, stop the work and sharpen them.

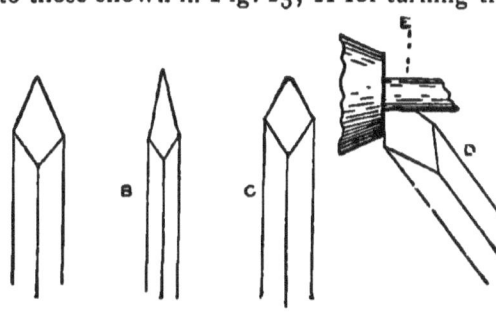

FIG. 23.

Next in importance is the position in which the graver is applied to the work. It must, under all circumstances, *cut* and not *scrape*. If held as shown at A, Fig. 24, it will cut a clean shaving, while if applied as at B, it will only scrape. If held as shown at C, the force of the cut will be in the direction of the hand, as indicated by the arrow. If the point should catch from any cause, the hand would yield and no harm would be done, while if held as at D, the force of the cut would be downward upon the rest, as indicated by the arrow, and the rest being unyielding catching would be dangerous.

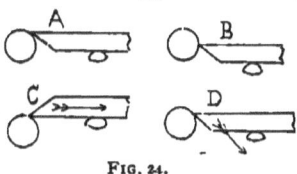

FIG. 24.

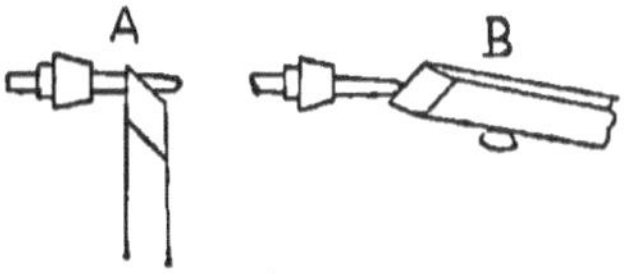

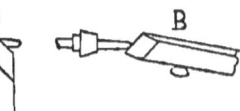

FIG. 25.

The roughing out should be done with the point of the graver held as at C, Fig. 24, and then finished with the edge held diagonally as at A, Fig. 25. It is difficult to show the exact position in the cuts, but the idea is to have the shavings come away in a spiral, may be as fine as a hair, but in perfect coils.

To turn the pivot, hold the graver nearly in line with the axis of the lathe, as shown at B, Fig. 25, and catching a chip at the extreme end with the back edge of the graver, push forward and at the same time rolling the graver towards you, which will give the pivot the conical form. Very small pivots can be turned in this way with perfect safety, and very smoothly. Of course, this method of turning will not give sharp corners; such places as the seat of the roller, balance, etc., must be carefully done with the point of the graver.

The pivot and seat of the roller should be left slightly larger than required, to allow for the grinding and polishing, the amount of which will depend upon how smoothly the turning is done. The grinding is done with a slip of bell-metal or soft iron or steel of the shape shown at E, Fig. 26. F is a bell-metal polisher, and G, is for the same purpose, but made of box-wood. E should be used with oilstone powder and oil, and F and G with crocus and diamantine for polishing.

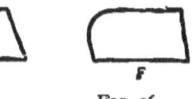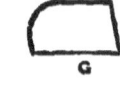

FIG. 26.

When the staff is finished from the lower pivot to the seat of the balance, the upper part should be roughed out nearly to size, then cut off, reversed in the lathe and the top part finished. It is better to do this in a wax chuck even if you use a split chuck, for the lower part of the staff is tapered and it is ten chances to one that you could select a split chuck that would hold it true and firm. In using a wax chuck the important point is to get a perfect center. It should be turned out with the graver at an angle of about 60°, care being taken not to leave a little "tit" in the center. Before setting the staff in the wax it is necessary to get its full length as follows: Screw the balance cock in place with both cap jewels removed, and if the cock has been bent up or down, or punched to raise or lower it, see that it is straightened and put right; then with a degree gauge or calipers take the distance between the outer surfaces of the hole jewels, and shorten the staff with a file to that length.

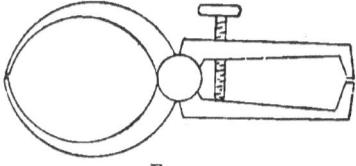

FIG. 27.

A very handy tool can be made by adding a stop-screw to the common double calipers as shown in Fig. 27. The improvement is that they can be opened to remove from the work and closed again exactly the same.

When fixing the staff in the chuck, care should be taken not to burn the wax. Use a small lamp and heat the chuck until the wax will just become fluid. The staff should be set in the wax about to the seat of the balance, the finished pivot resting in the center of the chuck, and the outer end trued up by the finger and the point of a peg while the wax is still soft.

Fig. 28 shows it with the staff finished, but, of course, it is not, when put in the wax. The dotted lines show about the right quantity and shape of the wax, which must be true and round, or in cooling it will draw the work out of center.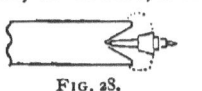

FIG. 28.

If necessary, when cool, the wax can be turned true with the graver, again heated and centered. The turning and finishing is to be done as previously described. The seat for the balance should be slightly undercut and fitted to drive on tightly without riveting. Take the size of the top pivot from its jewel the same as the lower. The ends of the pivots should be finished as flat as possible, and the corners slightly rounded. When done, remove from the wax and boil in alcohol to clean, and it is ready to receive the balance, which should first be poised as described on page 33.

BANKING PINS. The two pins that limit the motion of the lever in the lever escapement are known as banking pins. The pins used for limiting the motion of the balance in verge and horizontal escapements are also known as banking pins. The two pins in the balance arm which limit the motion of the balance spring in pocket chronometers are also known as banking pins.

BARREL. The circular brass or steel box that encloses the mainspring of a watch or clock.

Barrel Arbor. The barrel axis, around which the mainspring coils.

Barrel Contractor. Clackner's patent barrel contractor will be found very useful for restoring distorted mainspring barrels to shape, and consists of a die with a series of tapered holes, as shown in Fig. 29, and punches to correspond. The defective barrel is placed in a hole of the proper size and a few light taps from a hammer on the punch quickly brings the barrel to the desired form and of a size to fit the cover. This tool will also be found useful for contracting rings, etc.

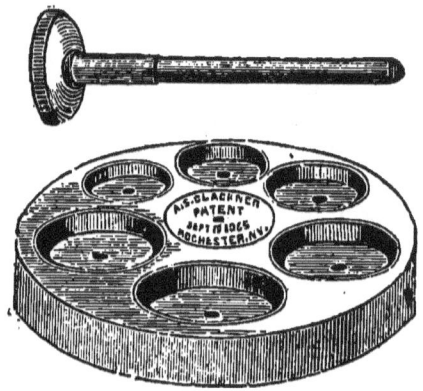

FIG. 29.

Barrel Hook. A hook in the barrel to which the mainspring is attached. The mainspring is sometimes attached by means of a hook on the spring which fits in a hole in the barrel.

Barrel Ratchet. A wheel which is placed on the barrel arbor and kept from turning backward, when the mainspring is wound, by a click or dog.

BEAT. The striking of the escape wheel upon the pallet or locking device.

Beat Block. A device for obviating the necessity of marking the balance to see that it is in beat.

FIG 30.

Before taking off the hair spring lay it on the block, turn the balance so the roller pin hits on the side the arrow points, then turn the table so that the line comes under the stud. In replacing the balance put the stud over the line and it will then beat the same as before. By using this tool you also avoid getting the balance out of true.

Beat Pins. Small screws or pins to adjust the position of the crutch in relation to the pendulum. The pins at the end of the gravity arms that give impulse to the pendulum in a gravity escapement.

BELL METAL. See *Alloys*.

BENCH. An excellent arrangement for a watchmaker's bench is shown in Fig. 32. This bench was designed by Mr. Laughlin and is complete in every detail. Benches can be purchased ready made from almost any tool and material house in the country but many prefer to make their own or to have them made in order to vary the details to suit their peculiarities. The bench shown in Fig. 31, is one of the latest designs on the market, the points

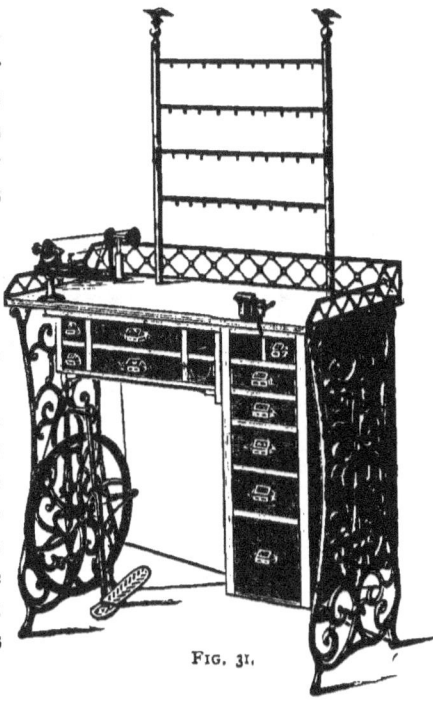

FIG. 31.

claimed for it being that it is raised sufficiently from the ground to allow sweeping under it, its small weight and its low price. The frame is made of iron and is similar to those used for sewing machines. The foot-wheel is fastened to the iron frame on the left, instead of being supported by uprights from the floor. It is neat in appearance, substantial, and quite

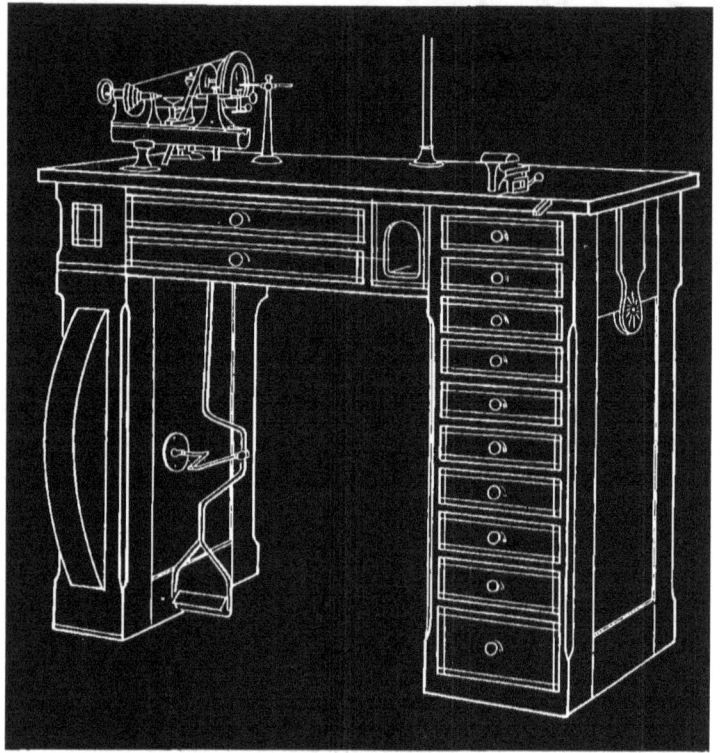

FIG. 32.

reasonable in price. From the sketch, (Fig. 32) any first-class cabinet maker should be able to make a good bench. This bench is made of black walnut, veneered with French walnut and birds' eye maple. The top is twenty-one inches wide by forty-one long, and is thirty-three inches high. The The drawers on the right hand side are ten inches wide. In the center are two drawers and the left hand side is entirely boxed in. The lathe wheel can be varied to suit the ideas of the watchmaker, a space of five inches being left for its reception. For the various styles see *Lathe Wheels*.

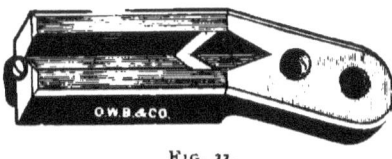

Fig. 33.

Well seasoned black walnut, cherry or red cedar are the best woods for a bench. The little pin attached to the right hand side of the bench is a pegwood cutter, an enlarged view of which is shown in Fig. 33.

BENZINE. A light oil of petroleum used for cleaning movements. For directions for use see *Watch Cleaning*.

BEVEL GEAR. A gear in which the two wheels working together stand at right angles to each other. See *Wheels*.

BEZEL. The grooved metal ring of a watch or clock that holds the crystal or glass in position.

BEZEL CHUCK. See *Chuck*.

BINDING WIRE. Fine malleable iron wire, used for binding articles while soldering, etc.

BITE. To adhere to; To hold fast; As a set screw *bites* a shaft. The eating of metal by means of acid.

BLOW-PIPE. A tapering metal tube, used to direct the flame from a lamp or gas jet upon an article for soldering, annealing and similiar purposes. See also *Alcohol Lamp*.

BLUESTONE. A soft blue stone, sometimes used for reducing brass and gold before polishing. It must not be confounded with blue vitriol, sometimes called blue stone.

BLUING. The changing of the color of steel by heat.

BLUING PAN. A pan used for bluing screws and other small articles. It is sometimes very desirable to match the color of screw heads in a watch. By making the following described simple little tool you can very readily color your screws straw, purple or blue as the case may require, to match the other screws in the watch. Select a very large mainspring barrel, drill a hole in the side of the barrel the size of an ordinary pendulum rod for an American clock, cut a thread in this hole and also on the piece of wire and screw it firmly into the mainspring barrel, cutting off about four or five inches long, to which attach a neat piece of wood to serve

FIG. 34.

as a handle. Now take out the head, and fill the barrel full of fine marble dust or brass or iron filings and replace the head in the barrel, after which drill any number and size of holes in the barrel you wish, to accommodate all sizes of watch screws, and the tool is ready for use. Bluing pans similar to the one shown in Fig. 34, can be purchased from material dealers and are similar to the one described. After fitting the screw to the proper place in the watch, harden and

FIG. 35.

temper in the usual manner. Polish out all scratches or other marks and selecting a hole in the tool to fit the screw loosely, press it down level with the face of the barrel and hold the tool over a small alcohol lamp flame until the color desired appears. Heat up slowly and the effect will be much better than if it is done rapidly. First blue the screws without any special regard as to uniformity of color. Should they prove to be imperfect, take a piece of clean pith and whiten the surface with rouge, without letting it be too dry. Pieces when thus prepared, if cleaned and blued with care will assume a very uniform tint.

Soft screws are sometimes very difficult to blue evenly, but this difficulty may be overcome by finishing them with a slightly soapy burnisher. Bluing shovels, like that shown in Fig. 35, can be purchased from material dealers. Another form is like that shown in Fig. 36, which is also known under the name of pickle-pan or boiling out pan. It is very useful for boiling out jewelry after soldering. For the latter purpose use sulphuric acid one part, and water fifteen to twenty parts. Pieces that are not flat will rarely assume an even

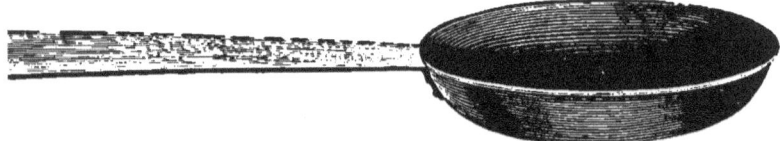

FIG. 36.

color when placed in a flat pan. To overcome this difficulty, sprinkle the bottom of the pan with fine brass filings or marble dust and press the article into it. The bluing pan or shovel should be thoroughly warmed before the articles are placed in it in order that any moisture present may be dispersed. The pan will also be found useful for tempering small steel articles by boiling them in oil.

BOILING-OUT PAN. See Fig. 36.

BOUCHON. A hard brass tubing sometimes inserted in watch and clock plates to form pivot holes, and known in America as bushing wire. See *Bushing*.

BOW. A device now obsolete which consisted of a strip of whalebone to both ends of which a cord or gut was attached and which was used to rotate a drill or mandril before the introduction of watchmakers lathes.

The ring of a watch case by which it is attached to the chain. See also *Pendant Bow*.

Bow Tightener. See *Pendant Bow Tightener*.

BRASS. See *Alloys*.

BREGUET SPRING. See *Hair Spring*.

BRIDGE. The standard secured to the plate, by means of screws, and in which a pivot works.

BROACH. A tapering piece of steel used for enlarging holes, made with from two to eight cutting edges. Some broaches are made without cutting edges and are called polishing broaches. They are used for burnishing pivot holes.

BRONZING. See *Electro-Plating*, *Bronzing* and *Staining*.

BUFF. A device for polishing or reducing metals.

Emery buffs are round or square sticks on which emery paper or cloth is glued. They are used to reduce the surfaces of

FIG. 37.

metal. Fig. 37 illustrates a ring buff used for polishing the inside of rings, preferably used on a polishing lathe.

BULLSEYE. A thick watch resembling a bulls eye in shape. A term usually applied to old fashioned English verge watches.

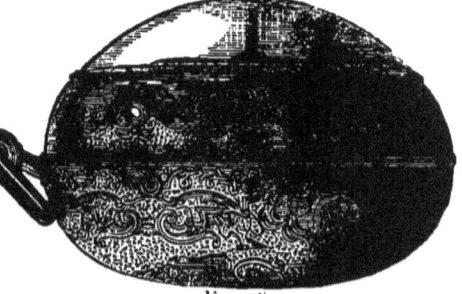

BURNISHER. A polished steel or agate tool used for glossing the surface of metals.

FIG. 38.

Fig. 39 is a jewel burnisher. The article to be burnished must be first freed from all scratches, for scratches would only be brought out more prominently by the use of the burnisher. The burnisher must be kept highly polished or you cannot expect to do good work with it. Saunier gives the following method of re-facing a burnisher: Prepare a dry smooth piece of wood, rather thick, and of a width equal to the length of the burnisher. On this board carefully glue a piece of emery paper of a fineness corresponding to the degree of cut required, stretching it as even as possible, and

FIG. 39.

turning the edges down towards the under side. Then lay the board on a firm smooth surface, resting a weight npon it, and allow it to dry. In using this lap, it is fixed or allowed to rest against the side of the bench; holding the burnisher with two hands at its extremities, the workman places himself at one end of the board, and draws the burnisher along it towards him, maintaining the surface quite flat and applying considerable pressure. On reaching the nearer end, raise it, and after again placing it on the furthest end, draw towards the body, and so on. By proceeeing in this manner all risk of rounding the angle will be avoided.

BUSH. A perforated piece of metal let into a plate to receive the wear of pivots. See *Bouchon*.

Bushing Pivot Holes. The bush may be either a turned or tapped one. A bush is selected as small as the pivot will admit. Open the hole in the plate or cock and finish with a a rat-tail file. Slightly taper the end of the bush with a fine file until it will fit the hole. With a knife score the bush just above the edge of the plate and press it firmly into the hole. Break off the bush at the point scored and drive it firmly into place by means of the bushing punch shown at Fig. 40 and you will find your bush is rivited firmly into the plate. Observe the endshake your pinion requires and make due allowance when finishing off your bushing. In bushing a plate, particularly where the bushing must be large, some watchmakers prefer to use a solid wire and drill the hole after fitting. If this method is followed be careful to see that you accurately center the work before drilling, and drill first with a shall drill, subsequently passing through a larger one, or open up the hole by means of a small broach. It is always

BUSHING PUNCH.

well to use bushing wire with a hole smaller than is ultimately required, and enlarging afterwards while the work is centered in the lathe. A tapped bushing is very firm, but unless the threads are well made is apt to be out of center. The closing hole punch shown at Fig. 40 often obviates the use of a bushing if skillfully used.

BUSHING OR CLOSING HOLE PUNCH. This tool is very simple in construction and will be found very useful in repairing both watches and clocks. Fig. 40,

FIG. 40.

Goeggels Bushing and Closing Hole Punch, consists of two counter-sunk steel punches, with a post in the lower punch. In using, fasten the lower punch in vise and place the work over it. They are made in various sizes for watches and clocks and are quite inexpensive.

BUSHING WIRE. Hard brass tubing for bushing the pivot holes of watches and clocks. This wire is kept by most material houses in the various sizes applicable to watch and clock work, and is put up in assorted sizes. See *Bouchon* and *Bush*.

BUTTING. The touching of the points of the teeth of two wheels acting with one another. It is caused by the wheels being planted incorrectly, or by pinions or wheels of improper size. See *Depthing Tool* and *Wheels and Pinions*.

CALIPERS. Compasses having two curved legs or fingers pivoted together and used either to measure the inside or outside diameter of bodies. Calipers are divided into two classes, known as inside and outside calipers. They are used by watchmakers for determining the diameter of staffs and pinions, for testing the truth of wheels, etc. Calipers are sometimes used in poising balances, the balance staff being centered between the points of the calipers. For this purpose a hole is drilled in the calipers and jewels are inserted.

Thompson's jeweled calipers, shown in Fig. 41, have garnet jewels inserted in the points of the arms at one end, and hardened steel bearings in the other. The Euclid Double Calipers are very useful tools, as they give on the lower limbs an inside measurement corresponding to the outside measurement of the upper limbs. See *Gauge*.

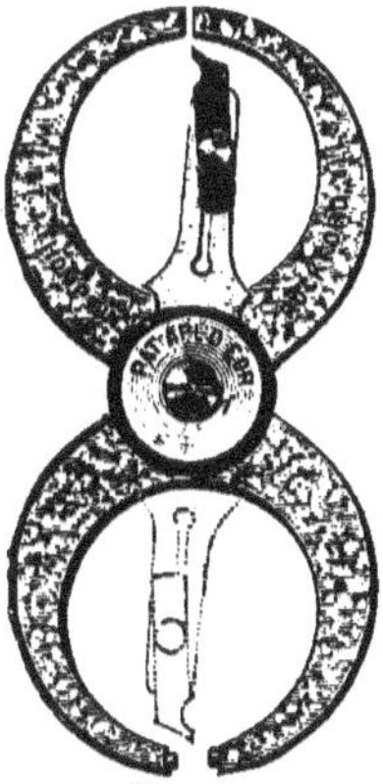

CAM. A movable piece of irregular contour, so shaped as to give a variable motion to another piece pressing against it by sliding or rolling contact.

FIG. 41.

CANNON PINION. The pinion to which the minute hand is attached; so called on account of the pipe attachment resembling a cannon.

CAP. The part of the case that covers the movement. A thin metal cover used in some English, Swiss and German watches to cover the movement and attached by studs and a sliding bar or spring.

CAPILLARY ATTRACTION AND REMPULSION. The cause which determines the ascent or descent of certain fluids when in contact with certain solid substances. See *Oil Sinks*.

CAPPED JEWEL. A jewel having an end stone.

CARDINAL POINTS. The four intersections of the horizon with the meridian and the prime vertical circle, or North and South, East and West. *Webster*.

CARRIER. A piece fastened to work in a lathe and connecting it with the face plate. A dog.

CASE-HARDENING. A process of carbonizing the surface of wrought iron, thus converting it into steel. See *Steel*.

CASE SPRINGS. The springs in a watch case that cause it to fly open and that keep it in position when closed.

Adjustable Case Springs. The Harstrom Adjustable Case Spring shown in Fig. 42 is easily fitted and is said to be a very excellent spring. The holder should be fitted securely in a vise and with a three cornered file cut down near the rear end on the back of the spring enough to rest a punch against; then with a tap of a hammer you can move it backwards. To move it forward, rest your punch against the end of the spring. Thus you can easily make it correspond with the screw hole in the case. Then, near to where it protrudes from the holder, bend the spring upward enough to make the front end level with the upper edge of holder, or move, if greater strength is required.

FIG. 42.

CASE SPRING VISE. The Boss case spring tool, shown in Fig. 43, is a very handy little tool. By turning the thumb screw you can bind the spring in the desired position and hold it there until the screw is inserted in its proper place. It will be found much handier than the ordinary plyer-shaped tools designed for the same purpose. Another form of case spring vise is Hall's, which is shown in Fig. 44.

FIG. 43.

FIG. 44.

CASE STAKE. A stake made with a large head, generally of steel, and used for taking out dents from battered watch cases. The stake shown in Fig. 45 is of the reversible pattern, and while using is held in the vise.

FIG. 45.

CELEBRATED WATCHMAKERS.

Abbey. To him or his assistant, Graham, is attributed the invention of the cylinder escapement.

Arnold, John. Born in Cornwall, England, in 1744 and died at Eltham, Eng., in 1799. He was the inventor of the helical form of balance spring and a chronometer escapement. The English Government awarded him £1,320 for the superiority of his chronometers in 1790, and his son, who followed up the successes of his father, was awarded £1,680 in 1805.

Berthoud, Ferdinand. Born in 1727 and died in 1807. An eminent Swiss watchmaker and author of many celebrated books on horology. He went to Paris at the age of 19 and remained there until his death.

Berthoud, Louis. A French chronometer maker and nephew of Ferdinand Berthoud. He died in 1813.

Breguet, Abraham Louis. Born in Switzerland in 1747 and died in Paris in 1823. An eminent watchmaker of French parentage and the inventor of the form of hairspring of that name. He was endowed with great ingenuity and a taste for complicated and remarkable mechanisms.

Callet, F. A thorough mechanic and skilled calculator. He was born at Versailles, France, in 1744, and died in 1798.

Dent, E. J. Born in 1790 and died in 1853. Builder of the great Westminster clock, London.

De Vick, Henry. A celebrated German watchmaker of the fourteenth century and the builder of the famous clock belonging to Charles V. of France. Also claimed by some writers to be the inventor of the Verge escapement.

Fetil, Pierre. A noted French watchmaker, born at Nantes in 1753, and died at Orleans May 18, 1814.

Graham, George. Born in Cumberland, England, in 1673 and died in 1751. He was buried in Westminster Abbey. He was the inventor of the mecurial pendulum, the dead beat escapement for clocks, and is credited with being the inventor of the cylinder escapement.

Grossmann, Moritz. A celebrated horologist, author and linguist. Though born and raised in Saxony, he was very conversant with the French, Italian and English languages, and contributed to many technical journals throughout the world. He was a member of the British Horological Institute, the Galileo Galilei, Milan, Italy, and the Polytechnic Society of Leipzig. It was while in the hall of the latter society, and just after delivering a lecture on horology, that he was stricken with apoplexy, which resulted in his death Ian. 23, 1885. He received his training as a watchmaker under the best masters of Saxony, Switzerland, France and England. He located in Glashutte, Saxony, in 1854, and began the manufacture of fine watches, tools and metric gauges, and later on large sized models of the various escapements. His first essay, " The Detached Lever Escapement," was written in 1864 and was awarded first prize by the British Horological Institute. In 1869 he took the first prize offered by the Chambre de Commerce, Geneva, on the subject of " The Construction of a Simple and Mechanically Perfect Watch." In 1878 he published a translation of Claudius Saunier's " Modern Horology."

Harrison, John. Born in 1693 and died in 1776. He is credited with being the inventor of the going fusee and the gridiron pendulum. He was celebrated for his chronometers.

Hooke, Robert. Born in 1635 and died in 1703. He was the inventor of the anchor escapement for clocks and the balance spring for watches.

Houriet, F. A noted Swiss watchmaker of the eighteenth century. He worked for nine years in Paris with such men as F. Berthoud, Romilly and Le Roy. He afterwards returned to Neuchatel, and much of the rapid progress made by the watchmakers of that canton was credited to his efforts.

Huyghens, Christian. Born in 1629 and died in 1695. He is credited with being the first person to apply the pendulum to clocks.

Janvier, Antide. He was celebrated for his skill in representing planetary movements by the aid of mechanism. He was a profound mathematician. He was born at Saint-Claude-du-Jura in 1751 and died in 1835.

Jodin, Jean. A clever French watchmaker of the eighteenth century. Author of a work on horology. He was the first to point out that success in the timing of horizontal watches depends on the correct proportioning of all their parts.

Jurgensen, Urban. Born in 1776 and died in 1830. He was a celebrated Danish watchmaker and the author of many valuable books on horology.

Kessels, M. A celebrated German clockmaker who worked for a long time with Breguet. He was the maker of a number of excellent astronomical clocks for Swiss, German and Russian observatories. He died in 1849.

Lepaute, J. A. One of the most celebrated of French horologists. He did much to improve his art, especially in regard to turret clocks. He was the author of a volume on horology, which in its time was a standard authority. He was born at Montmedi in 1709 and died in 1789.

Le Roy, Julien. A celebrated French horologist. He was the inventor of the horizontal mechanism for turret clocks. He introduced improvements in nearly all the branches of horology of his day. He died in 1759.

Le Roy, Pierre. A son of Julien Le Roy and unquestionably the greatest of all French horologists. He was born in 1717 and died in 1785. He was the inventor of the Duplex escapement.

Moinet, Louis. A clever watchmaker and writer of France. He was born at Bourges in 1768 and died in 1853.

Motel, H. A French chronometer maker, pupil and successor of Louis Berthoud. His chronometers were remarkable for their close rates and for their beautiful construction. He died in 1859.

Mudge, Thomas. Born in 1715 and died in 1794. He was the inventor of the lever escapement and was celebrated for his chronometers.

Perron, M. A celebrated French watchmaker and author. Born at Besancon in 1779.

Quare, Daniel. Born in 1632 and died in 1724. He was the first to apply the concentric minute hand to watches and clocks and was the inventor of the repeating watch.

Reid, Thomas. Born in 1750 and died in 1834. He was a celebrated Scotch horologist and the author of a treatise on watch and clock making.

Sully, Henry. Born in 1680 and died in 1728. A celebrated watchmaker and the author of a work on horology. He was an Englishman by birth, though he resided most of the time in France, where he died.

Robin, Robert. A celebrated French watch and clock maker. He built many large turret clocks for the public buildings of France. Born in 1742 and died in 1799.

Romilly, M. A clever Swiss horologist. He was held in high esteem in Paris, where he passed the greater portion of his life. He was born at Geneva in 1714 and died in 1796.

Roze, A. C. An eminent French watchmaker. Born in 1812 and died in 1862.

Tavan, Antoine. A celebrated French watchmaker who resided the better part of his life in Geneva. Born at Aost, France, in 1749 and died at Geneva in 1836.

Tompion, Thomas. Born in 1638 and died in 1713. He was buried in Westminster Abbey.

CEMENTS. Cement for use in the lathe can be purchased from material dealers generally at so small a cost that it will scarcely pay the watchmaker to bother in preparing it, but circumstances often arise where a cement is desirable for other purposes, such as attaching metal letters to show windows, etc., and the following receipts will be found very reliable.

Acid-Proof Cement. A cement that resists acid is made by melting one part India rubber with two parts linseed oil; add sufficient white bolus for consistency. Neither muriatic nor nitric acid attack it; it softens a little in heat, and its surface does not dry easily; which is produced by adding one-fifth part litharge.

Alabaster Cement. Melt alum and dip the fractured faces into it; then put them together as quickly as possible. Remove the exuding mass with a knife.

Alabaster Cement. 1. Finely powdered plaster of Paris made into a paste with water. 2. Melt rosin, or equal parts of yellow rosin and beeswax, then stir in half as much finely powdered plaster of Paris. The first is used to join and to fit together pieces of alabaster or marble, or to mend broken plaster figures. The second is to join alabaster, marble, and other similar substances that will bear heating.

Amber Cement. For cementing amber and meerschaum make a thick cream of finely powdered quicklime and white of egg, apply with a camels' hair brush, dry slowly and scrape off surplus after thoroughly dry.

Acid Proof Cement. Form a paste of powdered glass and a concentrated solution of silicate of soda.

Cement for Thin Metal Sheets. Cut isinglass into small pieces and dissolve in a little water at a moderate heat; add a small quantity of nitric acid, the quantity being determined by experiment; with too much acid the cement dries too slowly, while with too little it does not adhere well.

Cement for Glass and Brass. Melt together 1 part of wax and 5 parts of resin, and after melting stir in 1 part of burned ochre and ¼ part plaster of Paris. This is a good cement for attaching letters to windows. Apply warm to heated surfaces where possible.

Cement for Glass and Metals. The following cement is used extensively for fastening brass and enamel letters to show windows: Mix together boiled linseed oil 5 parts, copal varnish 15 parts, glue 5 parts, and oil of turpentine 5 parts; add to this solution 10 parts of slaked lime and thoroughly incorporate.

Cement for Paper and Metals. Dissolve dextrin in water, adding 20 parts of glycerine and 10 parts of glucose. Coat the paper with this mixture, and, after rubbing the metal with a piece of onion, attach the paper.

Cement for Knife and Fork Handles. Melt two parts of pitch and stir in one part of sand or brick dust; fill the cavity in the handle with the mixture, and push in the previously heated tang.

Engravers' Cement. Resin, one part; brick dust, one part; mix with heat.

Fireproof Cement. A very tenacious and fireproof cement for metals is said to be made by mixing pulverized asbestos with waterglass, to be had in any drug store; it is said to be steam tight, and resist any temperature.

Glass and Metal Cement. Brass letters, and other articles of a like nature, may be securely fastened on glass windows with the following: Litharge, two parts; white lead, one part; boiled linseed oil, 3 parts; gum copal, 1 part. Mix just before using; this forms a quickly drying and secure cement.

Gold and Silver Colored Cement. For filling hollow gold and silver articles. Consists of sixty parts shellac, ten parts Venetian turpentine, and three parts gold bronze or silver bronze, as the case may be. The shellac is melted first, the turpentine is then added, and finally, with constant stirring the gold or silver bronze.

Jewelers' Cement. Put in a bottle two ounces of isinglass and one ounce of the best gum Arabic, cover them with proof spirits, cork loosely and place the bottle in a vessel of water, and boil it until a thorough solution is effected; then strain for use.

Metal Cement. Take plaster of Paris, and mix it to proper thickness by using water containing about one-fourth of gum Arabic. This cement is excellent for metal exposed to contact with alcohol, and for cementing metal to glass.

Strong Cement. Mix some finely-powdered rice with cold water, so as to form a soft paste. Add boiling water, and finally boil the mixture in a pan for one or two minutes. A strong cement is thus obtained, of a white color, which can be used for many purposes.

Transparent Cement. A good transparent cement for fastening watch glasses, etc., in bezels or settings, is made by by dissolving seven parts of pure gum Arabic and three parts crystalized sugar in distilled water; the bottle containing the mixture should be placed in a utensil of hot water until the mixture assumes the consistency of syrup, and then left well corked for use.

Watchmakers' Cement or Wax. Eight ounces of gum shellac heated and thoroughly incorporated with one-half ounce of ultramarine makes the strongest and best wax for use on cement brasses and chucks.

CEMENT BRASSES. Attachments to a lathe to which work is fixed by means of cement. These brasses are made in various shapes and sizes by tool manufacturers, or the ingenious watchmaker can make them for himself during his leisure hours. The watchmaker should have a supply of these brasses, varying in diameter from one inch to the smallest size necessary. Should you have a watch that has a

CENTERS. 70

broken cock or foot jewel, and among your supply you are unable to find one that fits both the pivot and the recess in the cock or potence, you will find these brasses very useful. If

FIG. 46.

you find a jewel that fits the pivot nicely, and the brass setting is too large, select a cement brass that is just a trifle smaller than the recess in the potance, cement the jewel to the end of the brass, with the flat side of jewel to the brass, so that if the brass setting of the jewel is too thick it can be turned to exact thickness of the old setting at the same time that the diameter is turned. Bring to an exact center by the hole in the jewel, by means of a pegwood, and as soon as the cement is hard turn down with a sharp graver. With a full set of these brasses a watchmaker can utilize odds and ends, without waiting to send for new jewels. The above is only one of many uses to which these brasses may be brought.

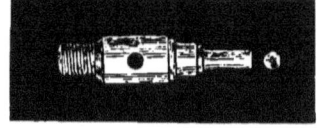
FIG. 47.

CENTERS. Pins used in conjunction with a lathe for holding work while revolving. They are usually made of steel. They are of two forms, known as male and female centers.

Female Centers. These very useful adjuncts to a lathe are easily made by any watchmaker. He should have at least six pairs, the largest being one-fourth of an inch in diameter, which will accomodate as large a piece as you will wish to handle on your watch lathe, viz.: winding arbors for clocks.

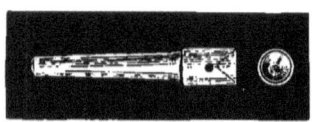
FIG. 48.

These female centers are made from steel tapers, the same as centers are made, but instead of turning the end to a sharp point they are countersunk. First place the taper in a chuck and turn off the outside and end true; drill a small hole in the center of the taper, while the lathe is running, and deep enough so the countersink will not reach the bottom of the hole, or one-eighth of an inch deeper than the countersink. Harden the end only and after tempering polish off the bluing. After you have made all the sizes you require, test all of them in your lathe to make sure they did not get out of true in tempering.

These female centers are very useful for holding or suspending any article in the lathe that is too large to be held in the split chucks. Pivots of clocks can be turned and polished very quickly and accurately in these centers.

Almost any kind of large work can be done on a medium sized watchmakers' lathe by fitting a face plate to the lathe, say one and three-fourths inches in diameter, with four slots, and fitted to a chuck with a taper hole to receive both male and female centers. The taper hole being standard, the centers are interchangeable, and with two styles of dogs almost any kind of large clock work can readily be handled.

These centers prove very useful for many odd jobs. As an example: It is a very common occurrence to hear an American clock beat irregularly, caused by the 'scape being out of round. Select a pair of female centers that will admit the ends of the pivots of the 'scape wheel snugly; place one center in the taper chuck and the other in the tail stock spindle, and suspend the 'scape pinion in these centers; fasten on a dog, run the lathe at a high speed and hold a fine, sharp file so it will touch the teeth of the 'scape wheel slightly, and in a moment the wheel will be perfectly round, after which sharpen up the teeth that are too thick. L.

Male Centers. Conically pointed pins; the opposite of female centers.

CENTERING ATTACHMENT. The Potter patent self-centering lathe attachment shown in Fig. 49 will be found useful in rapidly bringing work to an accurate center, when pivoting, staffing, etc.

The attachment, which may be fitted to any make of American lathe, consists primarily of the side bed pieces R and D, the upright plate A, and the reversible anti-friction sliding jaws $o\ o\ o$. The upright plate A is attached to the slide D in such a way that it may be readily raised or lowered or adjusted in any other direction at pleasure; and may be set with either side facing the lathe head. Of the reversible sliding jaws *o o o*, which are made of Phospor Bronze Anti-Friction Metal, not requiring the use of oil, four sets of three in a set, are furnished with each attachment. These are of different form, as shown at *X V O U*, to adapt them to the various kinds of watch work, and are operated in radical grooves in the upright plate *A*, by means of the rotating lever *L*, which moves the three jaws in and out, to and from the center, or opens and closes them in perfect unison. One set of jaws may be withdrawn and another set substituted therefor in a few moments. With each change of the jaws, however, the plate *A* requires readjustment; but this, too, may be done in a few moments, as follows: Having previously provided yourself with a bit of straight wire or small steel rod, turned to run perfectly true in your lathe, and having fastened this in the chuch in your lathe, loosen the nuts *C C* so as to give freedom of movement to the plate *A*; then bring the attachment to proper position on the lathe bed and fasten it there; after which move the sliding jaws inward until they bind lightly on the bit of straight wire held in your chuck, and in this position again tighten the nuts *C C*. Once adjusted to accurate center in this way no further adjustment, whatever the size of work to be operated upon, is required, until another change of jaws.

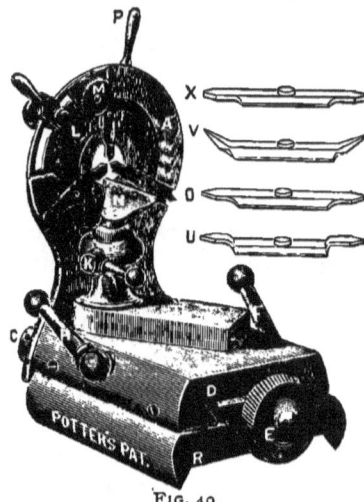

FIG. 49.

In use, the end of the work to be operated upon, is placed in an accurate split chuck in the lathe and the chuck tightened on it just sufficiently to hold it in place and to rotate it, the other end being supported in the centered bearing formed by the jaws *o o o*. In this position the jaws *o o o*, or such others as for the time may be in use, may be opened and closed as often as desired, and each time will instantly bring the work again to accurate center.

CENTERING INDICATOR. In centering quickly on the universal head, this tool is indispensible. It will also be found valuable for other work. It is not kept by dealers, and will have to be made by the watchmaker. The body of the indicator is made of sheet brass, and should be about five inches long by two inches in width at the larger end. The

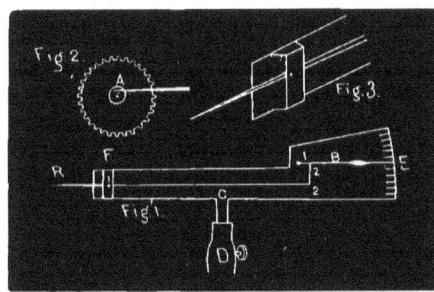

FIG. 50.

shank *C*, is made to fit in rest holder, and is either riveted or soldered to the body; *R* is steel or copper wire sharpened to a fine point, and balances on a pivot at 1; *B* is a clock hand pivoted to the body at 1; 2 and 2 are pivot joints only and do not go through the body; fig 3 will perhaps give a better idea of the end *R*. To center with this tool, unscrew your rest and remove it, then place the shaft *C*, fig 1, in rest holder and adjust it till the needle point *R* touches the top of hole as shown in fig. 2. The index hand will then note the variations as the head revolves. If too low, the hand will point above center and if high vice versa.

CENTER PUNCH. A punch having a sharp point, for

FIG. 51.

marking the center of work swung in a lathe, so that it may readily be removed and replaced without the trouble of finding the center each time.

CENTER OF GRAVITY. That point of a body about which all its parts are balanced, or which, being supported, the whole body will remain at rest, though acted upon by gravity. *Webster.*

CENTER OF GYRATION. That point in a body rotating around an axis, at which, if a given force were applied, it would produce the same angular velocity in a given time as it would if the whole mass of the body were collected at that point. *Webster.* Britten says that a circle drawn at seven-tenths of its radius on a circular rotating plate of uniform thickness would represent its center of gyration. The moment of inertia, or the controlling power of balances varies as their mass, and as the square of the distance of their center of gyration from their center of motion. Although not strictly accurate, it is practically quite near enough in the comparison of balances to take their weight, and the square of their diameter.

CENTER OF MOTION. That point which remains at rest while all the other parts of a body revolve around it.

CENTER OF OSCILLATION. That point at which, if the whole matter of a suspended body were collected, the time of oscillation would be the same. In a long cone suspended from its apex the center of oscillation is at four-fifths of its length from the apex, and in a bar suspended from one end that point is at two-thirds of its length. A pendulum being irregular in form it is difficult to calculate its center of oscillation, but it always is situated below its center of gravity. The following explanation may aid the student in locating the center of oscillation:

* All know that a simple theoretical pendulum is one where the whole weight is centered in one point, suspended from, and oscillating about, a fixed point, or center of suspension. A sphere of platinum, suspended by a fibre of silk, would probably be the nearest approximation to a perfectly simple pendulum. A compound pendulum is one where the weight is not centered in or about one point, but is extended for some distance up and down the rod. Suppose there are fixed upon the fibre, at equal distances, three platinum balls. From the

---

* *From the American Horological Journal.*

75 CENTER OF OSCILLATION.

well-known fact that a short pendulum vibrates quicker than a long one, the upper or short pendulum will *endeavor* to make its vibrations in the short time due to its length as a pendulum. The middle ball will *endeavor* to make its oscillations in the time its length of support demands, and the lower and longest will attempt the slow and regular vibrations of the long pendulum. Suppose that these three balls, representing three pendulums of three different lengths, be drawn aside from the perpendicular 5° and suddenly released, the consequence will be that the upper one will have made its full excursion by the time the middle one has descended to the perpendicular, and before the lower one has arrived there; the momentum of the three balls bending the fibre of silk into such a curve as will accommodate the *tendencies* of the three balls.

If the silk fibre be replaced by an inflexible rod, and the now rigid compound pendulum be drawn aside as before, the upper ball will *endeavor* to hasten forward the middle one to its own speed, and the middle and upper one will both combine to hasten the lower one. So also, the middle one will retard somewhat the rapidity of the upper one, and the slow-moving lower one will do its best to restrain the haste of both those above it, and the consequence of all these tendencies will be that the lower one will be somewhat accelerated, and the upper one proportionally retarded; the whole assuming a vibration which is the mean (middle ball) of the two extremes, provided the three masses are equal, thus compelling the whole to oscillate as a pendulum whose length is that of the middle ball. But if the lower ball be the largest, its control over those parts above it will be in proportion to its mass and the time of its vibrations will nearly coincide with those made by its center of gravity.

Suppose, again, the largest amount of matter to be in the upper ball. Then will its influence be more potent toward forcing the lower and longer pendulums to accommodate their rate to that of the upper one, and their vibrations will be thereby increased to a degree which will approximate the normal vibrations of that short pendulum. Thus you see the difficulty of exactly fixing upon the exact length of any compound pendulum by simple computation. Every particle of matter from the top of the rod to the lower extremity, which differs in its distance from the point of suspension, has its own time for making an oscillation about that point; and the greater the number of particles that have an equal distance from that point, the greater influence they possess in determining the time of vibration; in this case, as in republics, the mass rules. To obviate these counteracting influences that are constantly at work in the oscillations of the compound pendulum, it becomes necessary to concentrate, as far as possible, all the matter of the pendulum at such a distance from the point of suspension as will produce the number of vibrations desired, and this center of oscillation will always fall in a line produced through the center of gravity and the point of suspension, and will always be below the center of gravity.

The center of oscillation and suspension are convertible points; that is, a pendulum inverted and suspended from the center of oscillation will vibrate in the same time. Huygens, the Dutch scientist, discovered this remarkable fact, and it affords a ready means of determining experimentally the length of a compound pendulum, which may be measured by means of a platinum or lead ball, suspended by a fibre of silk from the same point, and in front of the pendulum to be measured, and of such a length that the vibrations will perfectly coincide in time. The distance from the point of suspension to the center of the ball (which is also the center of oscillation) is nearly the length of that compound pendulum.

It should be remembered that the *center of oscillation* is the point to be affected in all compensations for temperature. The difficulty in producing a perfect compensation pendulum is to harmonize and bring into coincidence the antagonistic tendencies of the center of gravity, center of oscillation and moment of inertia, all of which are properties and peculiarities of compound pendulums, and must be taken into consideration by those who are experimenting upon them with the expectation of producing any arrangement in advance of those in use at present.

CENTER SECONDS. See *Sweep Seconds*.

CENTER WHEEL. The wheel whose staff carries the minute hand.

CENTER STAFF. The arbor attached to the center wheel which carries the minute hand.

CENTRIFUGAL FORCE. The tendency that revolving bodies have to fly from the center. Britten says that that when balances are made too thin in the rim, they alter in diameter from this cause, in the long and short vibrations.

CHAIN HOOK. A small hook which is attached to each end of a fusee chain, to fasten the chain to the barrel and fusee.

CHAMFER. To groove. To cut a channel in. To cut or grind in a sloping manner anything originally right-angled. To bevel.

CHAMFERING TOOL. A tool for cutting a bevel or chamfer. A tool for cutting a furrow or channel is also known as a chamfering tool.

CHAMOIS. A soft leather used by watchmakers and jewelers, and so called because first prepared from the skin of a species of antelope known as chamois.

Chamois, to Clean. Many workshops contain a dirty chamois leather, which is thrown aside and wasted for want of knowing how to cleanse it. Make a solution of weak soda and warm water, rub plenty of soft soap into the leather, and allow it to remain in soak for two hours, then rub it well until quite clean. Afterward rub it well in a weak solution composed of warm water, soda and yellow soap. It must not be rinsed in water only, for then it will be so hard, when dry, as to be unfit for use. It is the small quantity of soap left in the leather that allows it to separate and become soft. After rinsing wring it well in a rough towel, and dry quickly, then pull it about, and brush it well, and it will become softer and better than most new leathers. In using a rough leather to touch up highly polished surfaces, it is frequently observed to scratch the work; this is caused by particles of dust, and even hard rouge, that are left in the leather, and if removed by a clean brush containing rouge, it will then give the brightest and best finish, which all good workmen like to see on their work.

CHARIOT. A brass bar screwed to the pillar plate of a cylinder watch to carry the lower pivot of the cylinder, and to afford a seat for the balance cock. Slight alterations in the intersection of the cylinder and the escape wheel are made by shifting the chariot. *Britten.*

CHIMES. A set of bells musically tuned to one another and sometimes attached to tower clocks, especially in Europe, such clocks being known as quarter clocks, or chiming clocks.

CHIMING BARREL. The cylinder in a chiming clock which raises the hammer in the chiming train by means of projections upon its surface.

CHRONOGRAPH. A recording time piece. In modern usage the term is applied to watches having a center seconds hand (driven from the fourth wheel), which generally beats fifths of a second. The hand is started, stopped or caused to fly back by manipulating a push on the side of the case.

CHRONOMETER. A portable time piece of superior construction, with heavy compensation-balance, and usually beating half seconds; intended for keeping very accurate time for astronomers, watchmakers, etc.

Marine Chronometer. A chronometer hung in gimbals for use at sea in determining longitude.

FIG. 52.   Pocket Chronometer. A pocket watch with chronometer escapement.

CHRONOMETER ESCAPEMENT. An escapement in which the escape wheel is locked on a stone carried in a detent, and impulse is given by the teeth of the escape wheel to a pallet on the balance staff once in every alternate vibration. The French claim the honor of the invention of the detached detent, or chronometer escapement, for Pierre Le Roy, while the English claim it for John Arnold. The first chronometer escapements were made with the small spring, or gold spring, attached to the roller on the balance staff. F. Berthoud made the escapement after this fashion, but Arnold transferred it to the detent. The detent as made by Arnold worked on a pivoted arbor, having a spiral spring around it to bring it back into position after it was released by the pallet. Earnshaw improved upon Arnold's construction by doing away with the arbor and making the detent and spring in one piece, as shown in Fig. 53. He also improved upon the escape wheel made by Arnold, whose wheel was made so that the unlocking took place inside the wheel, the acting curves of the teeth being raised from the plane of the wheel. Earnshaw made the teeth flat, and also changed the direction of the pressure during locking.

Saunier says of the chronometer escapement, that its mode of action is simple, but it does not admit of any error in the application of its principles, nor any inferior workmanship. It absolutely requires an isochronal balance spring and a compensation balance, and should never be employed in ordinary watches. Nevertheless, the chronometer escapement is adopted wherever the most reliable time is required, and among the best manufacturers in the world the good chronometer is considered as their finest production.

Britten says of the

ACTION OF THE ESCAPEMENT.

A tooth of the escape wheel is at rest on the locking pallet The office of the discharging pallet is to bend the detent so as to allow this tooth to escape. The discharging pallet does not press directly on the detent, but on the free end of the gold spring, which presses on the tip of the detent.

The balance, fixed to the same staff as the rollers, travels in the direction of the arrow around the rollers, with sufficient energy to unlock the tooth of the wheel which is held by the locking pallet. Directly the detent is released by the discharging pallet, it springs back to its original position, ready to receive the next tooth of the wheel. There is a set screw to regulate the amount of the locking on which the pipe of the detent butts. This prevents the locking pallet being drawn further into the wheel. It is omitted in the drawing, for clearness. It will be observed that the impulse roller is planted so as to intersect the path of the escape wheel teeth as much as possible, and by the time the unlocking is completed the impulse pallet will have passed far enough in front of the escape wheel tooth to afford it a safe hold. The escape wheel, impelled by the mainspring in the direction of the arrow, overtakes the impulse pallet and drives it on until the contact between them ceases by the divergence of their paths. The wheel is at once brought to rest by the locking pallet, and the balance continues its excursion, winding up the balance spring as it goes until its energy is exhausted. The balance is immediately started in its return vibration by the effort of the balance spring to return to its state of rest. You will notice that the nose of the detent does not reach to the end of the gold spring, so that the discharging pallet in this return vibration merely bends the gold spring without affecting the locking pallet at all. When the discharging pallet reaches the gold spring, the balance spring is at rest; but the balance does not stop, it continues to uncoil the balance spring until its momentum is exhausted, and then the effort of the balance spring to revert to its normal state induces another vibration; the wheel is again unlocked and gives the impulse pallet another blow.

Although the balance only gets impulse in one direction, the escape wheel makes a rotation in just the same time as with a lever escapement, because in the chronometer the whole space between two teeth passes every time the wheel is unlocked.

By receiving impulse and having to unlock at every other vibration only, the balance is more highly detached in the chronometer than in most escapements, which is a distinct advantage. No oil is required to the pallets and another

FIG. 53.

CHRONOMETER ESCAPEMENT.

a. Escape Wheel.
b. Impulse Roller.
c. Impulse Pallet.
(The Discharging Roller is underneath the Impulse Roller, and is indicated by means of dotted lines.)
d. Locking Pallet.
e. Foot of Detent.
f. Spring of Detent,
g. Blade of Detent.
h. Horn of Detent.
i. Gold Spring.

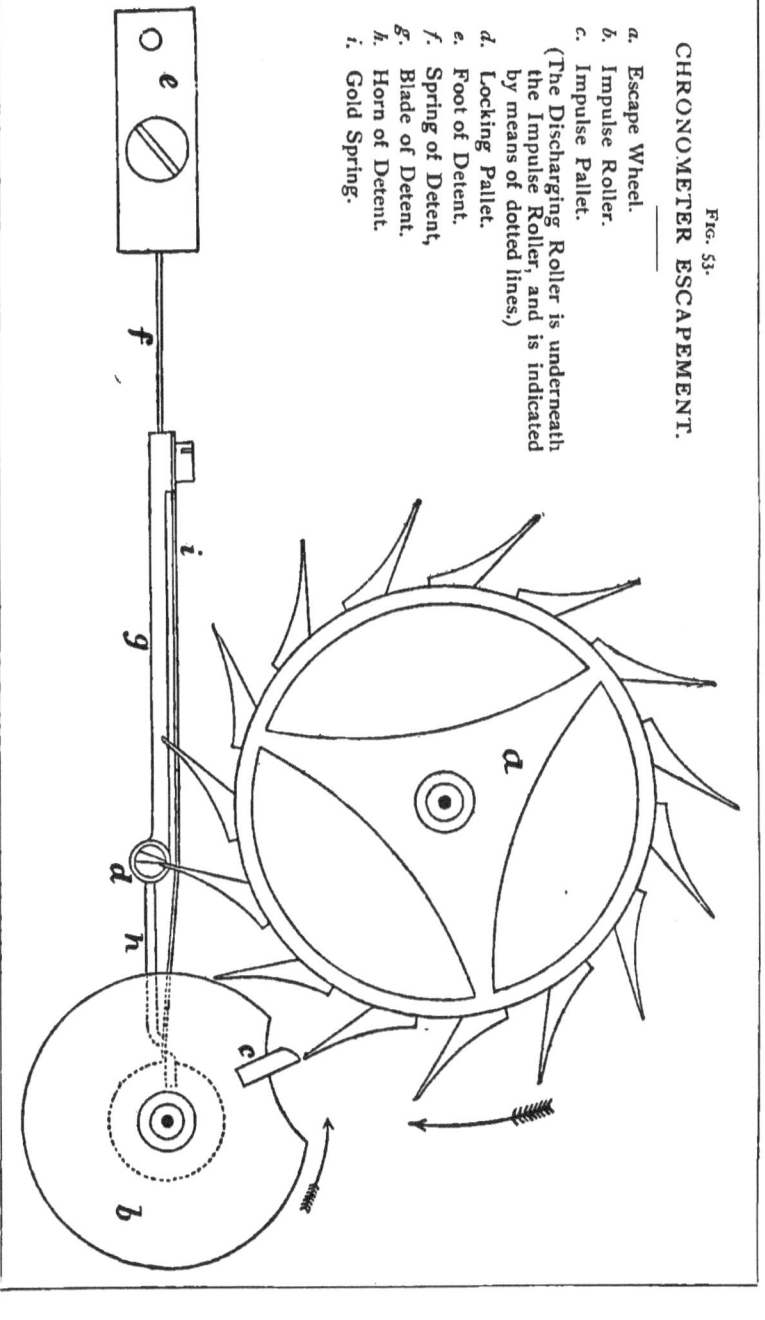

disturbing influence is thus got rid of. If properly proportioned and well made its performance will be quite satisfactory as long as it is not subjected to sudden external motion or jerks. For marine chronometers it thus leaves but little to be desired, and even for pocket watches it does well with a careful wearer; but with rough usage it is liable to set, and many watchmakers hesitated to recommend it on this account. It is much more costly than the lever, and would only be applied to very high-priced watches, and in these the buyer naturally resents any failure of action. Its use in pocket pieces is therefore nearly confined to such as are used for scientific purposes,

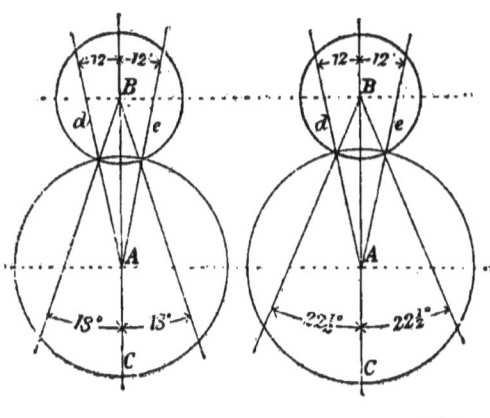

FIG. 54.   FIG. 55.

or by people who understand the nature of the escapement, and are prepared to exercise care in wearing the watch. There is another reason why watchmakers, as a rule, do not take kindly to the chronometer escapement for pocket work. After the escapement is taken apart, the watch does not so surely yield as good a performance as before. In fact it is more delicate than the lever.

CONSTRUCTION AND PROPORTION OF THE ESCAPEMENT.

For the ordinary 3-inch two-day marine chronometer movements, three sizes of escape wheels are used—viz.: .54, .56, and .58 of an inch in diameter; for eight-day marine chronometers the sizes are—.48, .50, or .52 of an inch. The escape wheel has fifteen teeth, and the diameter of the impulse roller is half that of the escape wheel. The roller is planted as close between two teeth of the escape wheel as possible, so that theoretically the roller intersects the path of the teeth for 24° of the circumference of the wheel. This gives theoretically a balance arc of 45°.* Practically it is less; there must be clearance between the roller and wheel teeth, an allowance must also be made for the side shake of the pivots. In Fig. 53, the impulse pallet is just opposite a tooth of the escape wheel when the discharging pallet is resting on the end of the gold spring. The balance moves through about 5° to accomplish the unlocking, and by the time that is done the impulse pallet will be 5° in advance of the tooth, and the tooth will drop through this space and more before it reaches the pallet, because after the wheel is unlocked it takes some time to get into motion at all, and at first its motion is slower than the motion of the pallet, which had not ceased to travel. The drop must be enough to allow the pallet to safely intersect the path of the tooth, and is arranged generally as shown, so that the pallet is 5° in advance of the tooth when the unlocking is completed. But many authorities insist on even more drop, so as to give the impulse more nearly on the line of centres. It is argued that the drop is not all mischievous loss of power, as it is in

---

*The balance arc is the amount that the edge of the impulse roller intersects the path of the wheel teeth, and is measured from the centre of the balance staff. Figs. 54 and 55 show a method of determining the relative size of the escape wheel and impulse roller for a given balance arc, which is taken from a report in the *Horological Journal* of a most excellent lecture on the chronometer escapement by Mr. Nelson. Fig. 54 (36° of balance arc) is an example of a usual proportion for pocket, and Fig. 55 (45° of balance arc) a usual proportion for marine chronometers. Through A B, the given centres of escape wheel and balance, draw the line C. From A set off by means of a protractor 12° (half the distance between two teeth of the escape wheel) on each side of the centre line, and draw *d e*. From B set off on each side of the centre line half the amount of the given balance arc and draw two other lines, as shown. The circles representing the tips of the escape wheel teeth and the impulse roller are drawn to cut the intersections of these four lines.

the lever escapement, for with a greater amount of drop the wheel attains a greater velocity when it does strike the pallet. However, most makers adhere to the 5°, although it may in some instances be advisable to vary it. If there is fear of over-banking, the arc of vibration may be reduced by giving more drop; and if the vibration is sluggish and the drop can be safely reduced, the vibration will be increased thereby.

The body of the escape wheel is thinned down to about one-half for lightness. The fronts of the wheel teeth diverge about 20° from a radial line so that the tips, being more forward, draw the locking stone safely in. The locking face of the stone is also set at a sufficient angle to to ensure perceptible draw. The edge of the impulse roller acts as a guard to prevent the wheel teeth passing in the event of accidental unlocking at the wrong time. There is a crescent-shaped piece cut out of the roller to clear the teeth of the wheel. It should be very little behind the pallet, and less than the distance between two teeth of the escape wheel in front of it to avoid the danger of running through or passing two teeth when such accidental unlocking occurs. It is important to see that there is enough cut out in front of the pallet to clear the wheel tooth at all times. When the balance is traveling very quickly—i. e., with an unusually large vibration—the pallet gets a long way in front of the tooth before the tooth starts, and then if the crescent is not cut far enough beyond the face of the pallet, the tooth would butt on the roller.

The radius of the discharging pallet is a trifle less than one-half that of the impulse pallet. If made too small the locking stone cannot return quick enough to catch the tooth.

The detent is made very light, and of about the proportion shown in the drawing. The spring of the detent is thinned down so that when the foot is fixed and it stands out horizontally, one pennyweight hung from the pipe deflects it about a quarter of an inch. If the spring is made too thin, it will cockle and give trouble. The detent may very easily be made too long from the point where it bends to the locking pallet, and would then be too sluggish and allow the wheel to trip by not returning quick enough after the unlocking to receive the next tooth of the wheel. The distance from the shoulder of foot to pipe to be equal to the diameter of the wheel is recommended by Mr. T. Hewitt as a very good rule.

The escape wheel is of hard hammered brass, the rollers of steel. The detent of steel, carefully tempered, with the point of the horn left softer to allow of bending. The pallets are all of sapphire or ruby, fastened in with shellac. A brass plug is fitted in to occupy the space in the pipe of detent not filled by the locking pallet. The gold spring is hammer-hardened.

POCKET CHRONOMETER.

The escape wheel for pocket chronometers varies from .28 to about .35 in diameter. The impulse roller is made larger in proportion to the escape wheel than in the marine chronometer, so as to lessen the tendency of the escapement to set. If the chronometer escapement is brought to rest by external motion just as the unlocking is taking place *it must set*, for the balance spring is then quiescent. In the lever escapement the tooth of the escape wheel is in the middle of the impulse plane of the pallet when the balance spring is quiescent, and in this respect the lever has the advantage. If the velocity of the balance in a chronometer is much reduced when the unlocking is completed, then a large impulse roller is of great assistance to the wheel in overcoming the inertia of the balance.

As the diameter of the roller is increased, the balance arc, and also the intersection of the path of the wheel teeth by the impulse pallet, is decreased. The velocity of the edge of the roller, too, more nearly approaches the velocity of the wheel tooth, so that less of the power is utilized. It is, therefore, not prudent to adopt a much less balance arc than 28° or 30°.

The tendency of pocket chronometers to set is also lessened by adopting a quick train; 18,000 is the usual train, but they are occasionally made with 19,200 by having sixteen teeth in the escape wheel instead of fifteen. This seems to be an objectionable way of getting the quick train. The teeth of the escape wheel being closer together, a smaller roller must be used to get the same intersection, and as there is less time for the detent to return there is great danger of mislocking.

For the convenience of getting the seconds hand to jump half-seconds, a 14,400 train is sometimes adopted in pocket chronometers. In this case the escape wheel has twelve teeth, the numbers of the rest of the train remaining the same.

The other parts of the pocket chronometer escapement are similar to those of the marine chronometer.

TO EXAMINE THE ESCAPEMENT.

See that the wheel is true and the teeth smooth and perfect, and that the rollers properly fit the staff. See that the end shakes and side shakes are correct. See that the "lights" between the wheel teeth and the edge of the roller are equal on both sides when the wheel is locked. If they are not, the foot of the detent must be knocked a trifle to or from the centre of the roller till the lights are equal. If the light is more than sufficient for clearance the roller must be warmed to soften the shellac, and the impulse pallet moved out a little. If the light is excessive there will be too much drop on to the locking after the wheel tooth leaves the impulse pallet, and with a large drop there is danger of tripping.

To ensure safe locking the detent should be set on so that when the banking screw is removed, and the locking pallet is free of the wheel teeth, it will just spring in as far as the rim of the wheel.

In pocket chronometer escapements it is especially necessary to see that the face of the locking stone is angled so as to give perceptible draw. Many pocket chronometers fail for want of it.

The gold spring should point to the centre of the roller. Bring the balance around till the discharging pallet touches the gold spring preparatory to unlocking, and notice how far from that point the balance moves before the gold spring drops off the face of the pallet. Then reverse the motion of the balance, and see if the same arc is traveled through from the time the *back* of the pallet touches the gold spring until it releases it. If not, the horn of the detent must be bent to make the action equal.

Bring the discharging pallet on to the gold spring, and let it bend the detent so that the locking stone is as much outside the wheel as it was within when the wheel was locked. The gold spring should then drop off the discharging pallet. Make it to length, sloping off the end from the side on which the pallet falls to unlock, and finish it with great care. The gold spring should be thinned near its fixed end as much as possible, and the detent spring thinned if it is needed. The judgment of the operator must determine the proper strength in both cases. The nose of the detent horn should be nicely flattened and the corners rounded off.

The locking pallet should not be perfectly upright. It should lean a little from the centre of the wheel, and a little toward the foot of the detent, so that the locking takes place at the root of the stone, and then the action of locking and unlocking does not tend so much to buckle the detent. The face of the impulse pallet, too, should be slightly inclined so that it bears on the upper part of the wheel teeth. By this means the impulse pallet will not mark the wheel in the same spot as the locking pallet.

Try if the escape wheel teeth drop safely on the impulse pallet by letting each tooth in succession drop on, and after it has dropped, turn the balance gently backward; you can then judge if it is safe by the amount the balance has to be turned back before the tooth leaves the pallet. If some teeth do not get a safe hold, the impulse roller must be twisted round on the arbor to give more drop.

If the escapement is in beat, the balance, when the balance spring is at rest, will have to be turned around an equal distance each way to start the escapement. When the balance spring is in repose, the back of the discharging pallet will be near the gold spring, and if the balance is moved around until the gold spring falls off the back of the pallet and then released, the escapement should start of itself; and in the other direction also, if the balance is released directly the wheel tooth leaves the face of the impulse pallet, the escapement should go on of itself.

CHRONOSCOPE. A clock or watch in which the time is indicated by the presentation of numbers through holes in the dial.

CHUCK. A mechanical contrivance for holding work in a lathe. True chucks are the most important adjuncts to a watchmaker's bench. A good lathe and untrue chucks will result in inferior work, while a cheap lathe with true chucks will permit of some good results.

FIG. 56.

Chucks hold the work truest that come the nearest fitting the hole in them. Trying to hold work too large or too small, will soon get them out of true, and often make the workman dissatisfied with his chucks, his work, himself and his lathe. Wax is the only sure thing for fine staff and pivot work

FIG. 57.

although there are many substitutes that do very well and with the aid of them a good workman can turn out a very fine job. With a good lathe, true chucks and sizes to suit, and a reasonable amount of practice first-class work can be done with split chucks. One chuck or tool of any kind seldom does all

FIG. 58.

kinds of work and does it all well. Fig. 56 is a good illustration of a modern Split Screw Chuck; Fig. 57 is a Moseley Shoulder Chuck, and Fig. 58 an Arbor Chuck, for holding saws, laps, etc.

Adjustable Chuck. The Hopkins patent adjustable chuck, shown in Fig. 59, is designed to grip and hold firmly and accurately any size of work from the smallest staff to the largest pinion, watch wheels of all sizes, mainspring barrels and other large work, and can be adjusted to any make of lathe by simply placing it friction tight, on a plug chuck fitted properly to the lathe. In using this chuck for staffs, pinions, wire, etc., fasten a V piece 7, of proper size, in the hole in attachment 6, taking

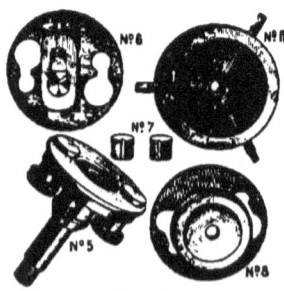

FIG. 59.

care that both the V and the seat in which it rests are free from chips, dirt, etc. Then lay your work in the V and fasten it there by means of the sliding jaw above it. This done, place the attachment on the face of the chuck body, with the disc slipped under the heads of the two spring bolts, and then spin the work to center, same as when using wax. After centering thus, fasten the disc to place by tightening the nuts on the back ends of the spring bolts.

For holding work by the web of the wheel, place the wheel under the screw cap on the face of attachment S and screw the cap down firmly on it, with the staff or pinion projecting outward through the center hole. This done, proceed the same as when using No. 6.

For main spring barrels and like work, use attachment 11, and place a bit of broken mainspring between the work and the ends of the three binding screws, and tighten the screws down on that instead of directly on the work.

Bezel Chuck. The Snyder Patent Bezel Chuck, shown in Fig. 60, was originally intended for holding bezels only, but it is now made so that it will hold watch plates, coins, etc., and is adjustable to any size. It can be fitted to any lathe and requires very little practice to use it, as it is extremely simple, and any one who uses a lathe can make or repair bezels in a workmanlike manner. It holds the work as in a vise, and no amount of turning or jarring will loosen the jaws, while it may be opened and closed instantly by simply turning the milled nut behind the face plate, thus enabling the operator to turn and fit a bezel perfectly by trying on the case as many times as as necessary. It holds the bezel by either groove, so that the recess may be turned out when too shallow or too small for the glass, or the bezel may be inverted and turned away when it rests too hard on the dial. It will be found especially useful in turning out the inevitable lump of solder from the recess in the bezel, after soldering and in fitting to case, as the process of soldering generally makes the bezel shorter and

FIG. 60.

consequently it will not fit on the case. It also renders the operation of polishing bezels after soldering, but a few minutes work. In turning out the recess for glass in bezels, especially heavy nickel bezels, it will prove a friend indeed, when for instance, you look through your stock of flat glasses and find none to fit, but have one that is just too large. All watchmakers know that if the groove in the bezel is imperfect it is apt to break the glass. The chuck is also useful as a barrel closer, holding work while engraving, and many other uses that will present themselves to the watch or case repairer.

Cement Chuck. The Spickerman patent cement chuck, shown in Fig. 61, is a very handy device, as it holds and centers accurately any wheel in a watch while drilling, polishing or fitting new staffs or pinions and all danger of injuring wheels is obviated. It fits all kinds of American or Swiss lathes.

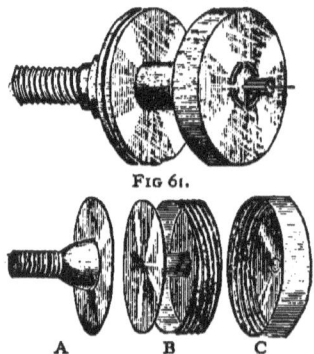

FIG 61.

A B C
FIG. 62.

The holder shown in Fig. 62 at *a*, is turned down to nearly the size of the screw for the lathe and the screw cut so the holder will set as close as possible to the lathe. The face of the holder is then turned perfectly true. Put wheel to be centered in cap *c*, as near to center as convenient and screw on *b*. Then place cement face of chuck *b* against face of holder *a* on the lathe and with a lamp, warm the cement between the surfaces, holding the chuck with a stick against the pivot of wheel in the cap, and it will move to an exact center as soon as warmed sufficiently. New cement should be added occasionally between the surfaces, as it hardens and burns away and does not center as well as when new. Fig. 61 shows chuck with wheel inside ready for drilling.

Dead Center Chuck.
By the use of this chuck,

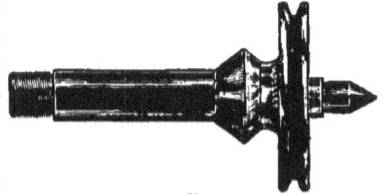

FIG. 63.

shown in Fig. 63, the work can be run on dead centers as well as by the bow or verge lathe, and the motion continuous.

Chuck Stepping Device. *A* rests in chuck slightly less than diameter of work. *B* tightens in rear end of draw-in-spindle. Turning *c* regulates depth of step. By the use of this tool any wire chuck will accurately serve as a step chuck. It is a device of great service to the watchmaker when used and understood. It enables him to make a step in any wire chuck of any depth he may wish, and will push out the work if desired. It is very useful many times for a stop for marking or cutting off when you want a number of pieces of the same length or kind. Many object to the stepped chuck for general use, objections which this device obviates.

Pivoting Chuck. The Gem patent pivoting chuck shown in Fig. 65, is intended as a substitute for wax for pivoting and like work.

By means of the ball *b*, placed between the two sliding sockets *c c*, with the several other parts as represented in Fig. 65, a combination of sliding and ball and

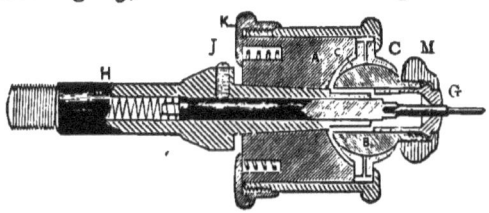

FIG. 65.

socket movements in connection with a spring pump center, is obtained. A set of ten or more, supplementary chucks *g*, with different sizes of center holes, and attachment *n*, for all sizes of wheels, are furnished with each chuck. The supplementary chuck *g*, in the form of a small split chuck, made to fit into a hole with taper mouth in the center of the ball *b*, and is drawn into place and the work fastened firmly in it by means of the binding nut *m*, which screws on to a projection extending outward from front side of the ball.

FIG. 64.

To use this chuck proceed as follows: Remove the nut m, and give freedom to the working parts by loosening the large back nut k. Then to bring the hole through the ball b, into line, spin the ball to center, first at the base of the projecting screw and then at the mouth of the hole through it, and in this position again fasten the parts, by tightening the nut k. Then give freedom to the pump center, by slightly loosening the set screw j. When doing this, hold your finger against

FIG. 66.

the front of the chuck, to prevent the center rod from shooting out of its place when freed. Then having placed a supplementary chuck g, of proper size, in its place in the chuck, and your work in it, with its back end resting properly in the countersink in the end of the pump center, fasten it there by screwing the cap m down snugly over it, using a small lever pin when necessary for this purpose, but not with undue force. Then again loosen the nut k and spin the work to center at its outer end; and then tighten both the nut k and set screw j. In tightening the set screw j, make sure it is so tightened as to prevent the pump center from slipping from place when working. If from tightening the screw j, it is found that the work has been thrown in any degree away from true center, loosen the nut k, leaving the pump center fast, and again spin to center, and fasten as before. All of which after a little practice may be done, and the work be brought to absolute truth in a few moments.

In using attachment n, for wheels, the nut m and chuck g are removed, and n substituted therefor; the work being held on the face of the attachment by flat headed screws that grip the arms of the wheel. For cylinder escape wheels a special attachment n is furnished. The best thing to use when spinning work to center in the chuck, is a bit of peg wood of wedge shape at one end. The countersinks in the ends of the pump center should in all cases be carefully tested, and if need be trued up in the lathe in which the chuck is to be used. In doing this, use a good, fine-pointed sharp graver, and make sure the countersink is perfectly true. The same rules in regard to truth in the countersink, and having the work rest properly in it, are to be observed in using this chuck as when using wax.

Step or Wheel Chucks. These chucks are usually made in sets of five, each chuck having nine steps, giving forty-five different sizes. These chucks are very useful in holding mainspring barrels, to fit in the cap of the barrel, should it become out of true. They are also valuable in trueing up barrels of English lever watches, that are damaged owing to the breakage of a mainspring. They are also very useful in holding almost any wheel in a watch, but particularly convenient in fitting a center wheel to a pinion, or in making sure that the hole in the wheel is in the center. These chucks are made by the various lathe manufacturers and are all similar to Fig. 67, and will hold wheels from .5 to 2.26.

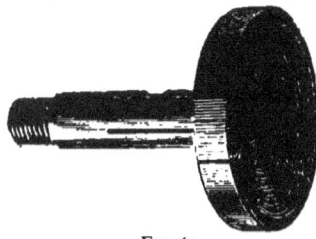

FIG. 67.

CHUCK BOX. A circular box with lid, for holding chucks. They are usually made of cherry or mahogany. By keeping your chucks in a box similar to that shown in Fig. 68, you can find a chuck of the desired size in a moment and the chucks are less liable to be damaged than when kept in a drawer with miscellaneous tools.

CLEANSING, PICKLING AND POLISHING.

To Clean Pendulums. Brass pendulum bobs are often found with black stains upon them that prove very obstinate to remove. Heat the bob moderately, touch the stains with a brush dipped in nitric acid, rub with a linen rag and again heat moderately.

CLEANSING, ETC.   94

To Clean Silver. Articles of silver, either solid or plated are quickly and easily cleaned by dipping in a moderate concentrated solution of potassium cyanide and then thoroughly rinsing in water. Jewelers will find it very convenient to have three stone jars, with tight fitting covers, to exclude all dirt. Label the jars " Cyanide," " 1st Water " and " Second Water." In these, large pieces of silverware can be cleaned with ease by dipping into the cyanide, then into jar number one and then jar number two. Dry with a soft linen rag and the articles will be found free from all stains.

FIG. 68.

To Clean Nickel. The nickel plates of watches are sometimes found to have rust stains upon them. These can be removed by rubbing the spot with grease, allowing them to stand for a few days, and rubbing thoroughly with a cloth moistened with ammonia. In obstinate cases, repeat the operation or touch the stains with dilute hydrochloric acid and rub thoroughly. Rinse in clean water and polish. A mixture of fifty parts of rectified alcohol and one part of sulphuric acid is also valuable for cleaning nickel plates. Immerse for ten or fifteen seconds, no longer, rinse in alcohol, and dry in sawdust.

To Clean Brass. To clean old brass, especially small figures, paper knives, etc., immerse them in a mixture of one part of nitric acid and half part of sulphuric acid. Allow them to remain a short time, rinse thoroughly in cold water, dry in sawdust and polish with Vienna lime, when they will appear like new.

Pickling of Metals. Metals are pickled for the purpose of removing the oxides and producing a lustrous surface. An excellent pickle for brass consists of ten parts of water and one of sulphuric acid. Dip into this pickle, wash, dry, and immediately dip into a second pickle consisting of two parts nitric acid and one of sulphuric acid and rinse thoroughly. This dissolves the zinc from the brass, and gives the metal a brilliant surface. All pickling operations with either hot or cold pickle should be carried on in the open air or in the draft of a well drawing chimney, as the vapors arising from the acids are very injurious. In order to retain the luster, a good transparent varnish should be applied.

Pickle for German Silver. To twelve parts of water add one part of nitric acid; immerse the article in this, quickly remove, and place in a mixture of equal parts of sulphuric and nitric acid, rinse thoroughly in water, and dry in sawdust. In all cases of pickling it is essential that all traces of acid be removed by frequent washings in clean water.

Pickle for Gold Alloys. Gold alloys especially those containing copper, assume an unsightly dark bown extrerior, owing to the copper oxide generated by the repeated glow-heating during work. In order to remove this, the object must be pickled, and either highly diluted sulphuric or nitric acid is used for the purpose, according to the color the article is designed to have.

If working with an alloy consisting only of gold and copper, either sulphuric or nitric acid may be used indefinitely, since gold is not attacked by any one of these acids, while copper oxide is easily decomposed thereby, and after having been pickled, the article will assume the color of pure gold, because its surface is covered with a layer of the pure metal.

If the alloy is composed of pure gold and silver however, only nitric acid can be employed, and the article is left immersed in it only for a short time; this acid dissolves a very small portion of the silver, and the article also assumes the color of pure gold.

When working with an alloy which, besides the gold, contains both copper and silver, the process of pickling may be varied in accordance with the color desired to be given to the article. If the pickling is performed in sulphuric acid, the copper alone is dissolved, the article assuming a color corresponding to a gold-silver alloy, which now constitutes the surface of the article.

If nitric acid is used, it will dissolve the silver as well as copper, and in this case a pure gold color is produced.

Pickling is done by first feebly glow-heating the article and cooling it; this operation is for the purpose of destroying any fat from the hands or other contamination adhering to the article. If it was soldered with some easily-flowing solder, this glow-heating must be omitted, but it may be cleansed from impurities by immersing it at first into very strong caustic lye, and rinsing it with water; it is then laid into the acid.

The acids are employed in a dilute state, taking forty parts water to one part concentrated sulphuric or nitric acid. If more articles than one, they had best be laid beside each other in a porcelain or stoneware dish, the diluted acid is poured over them, and some article is lifted out from time to time to watch the course of proceedings, whether it has assumed a yellow color.

When to satisfaction they are rinsed with clean water and dried. While pickling for the purpose only of causing the color peculiar to gold to appear, the process of coloring has for its object to lend the appearance of very fine gold to an article of an indifferent alloy. Various mixtures may be employed for the purpose, and we give two receipts below which are very appropriate:

Mix two parts saltpeter, 1 part table salt and 6 parts alum with 6½ parts water, and place in a porcelain dish for heating. As soon as you notice that the mixture begins to rise, add 1 part of muriatic acid, raise the whole to boiling and stir with a glass rod.

The article to be colored, and previously treated with sulphuric acid, as specified, is suspended to a hook, either of sufficiently thick platinum wire or glass; it is then introduced into the rather slow boiling bath, and moved around in it. It is to be taken out in about three minutes, and rinsed in clean water, inspecting its color at the same time. If not to satisfaction, it is returned to the bath, and this withdrawing or reintroducing is repeated until the desired color is obtained. By the latter immersions the article is left only one minute at a time in the fluid.

When sufficiently colored, the article, after rinsing, will be of a high yellow and mat color; it is washed repeatedly in water to remove the last traces of the bath, and then dried between soft and heated sawdust.

In place of drying in sawdust the article may also be dipped in boiling water, leaving it in for a few seconds; the adhering water will evaporate almost instantaneously.

The second coloring method consists in pouring water over a mixture of 115 parts table salt and 230 nitric acid, so that the salt is dissolved; it is then to be heated until a dry salt residue is again present. This residue is mixed with 172 parts fuming muriatic acid and heated to boiling, for which purpose a porcelain vessel is to be used.

As soon as the pungent odor of chlorine gas begins to evolve, the article to be colored is immersed, and left for about eight minutes in the fluid for the first time; in other respects, a similar treatment, as specified above, is also used for this method; if the article colored was polished previously, a subsequent polishing is unnecessary.

On account of the vapors evolved by the coloring baths, which are very dangerous to health, the operations should be performed either under a well-drawing flue, or what is still better, in open air.—*Goldsch Miedekunst.*

Polishing Agents. Various polishing agents are used by watchmakers, jewelers, gold and silversmiths, a few of which are here described. Where the article will admit of it, the best results are obtained by polishing in the lathe. For this purpose the watchmaker should not use his regular lathe, but should have for the purpose what is known as a polishing lathe, fitted with its various attachments in the shape of scratch-brushes, buffs, etc.

Ferric Oxide. This material is used in its natural state and also prepared artificially under various names, such as crocus, red stuff and rouge. It is used for polishing fine articles of steel, gold, silver, copper and bronze.

Tin Putty is an artificial compound prepared from glowing oxalate of tin, which is obtained by decomposing tin-salt with oxalic acid.

Tripoli. A gray-white or yellowish powder, which is made from the shells of microscopic organisms. It is used for polishing soft metals, first with oil, and then dry.

Lime. This material is used in the burned and unslaked state. A popular variety is known as Vienna lime. See that heading.

Belgian Polishing Powder. This powder is used for polishing articles of silver and silver plated ware. It consists of a mixture of 250 parts of whiting, 117 parts elutriated pipe-clay, 62 parts white lead, 23 parts white magnesia, and 23 parts rouge.

English Silver Soap. This mixture which is used for polishing silverware is prepared as follows: Dissolve 2 parts of castile soap in 2 parts of soft water over a fire; when melted, remove and stir in 6 parts of fine whiting, pour into moulds and allow it to cool. A little rouge may be added as coloring matter if desirable.

English Silver Paste. Three parts of perfumed vaseline, 5 parts of whiting, 1 part of burnt hartshorn, and one of pulverized cuttle bone. Stir well and put up in tin boxes.

Gold Polishing Powder. Mix together 4.3 parts of alumina, 17.4 of chalk, 4.3 of carbonate of lead, 1.7 of carbonate of magnesia, and 1.7 of rouge.

Polishing Paste for Brass. Dissolve 15 parts of oxalic acid in 120 parts of boiling water and add 500 parts of pumice powder, 7 of oil of turpentine, 60 of soft soap, and 65 of fat oil.

The polishing agent is usually mixed with oil, alcohol or water to prevent scattering, and is then applied by the polishing tool in the shape of cloth and leather buffs, polishing files, etc. Either the work or the tool should revolve with great velocity in order to secure good results. Many articles are brought to a high degree of polish by the use of the burnisher, after subjecting them to the action of the ordinary polishing agents. See *Burnisher*, also *Buff*.

Scratch Brushing. Articles in relief which do not admit of the use of the burnisher are brightened by the aid of the scratch brush. The shape of the brush varies according to the article to be operated upon. Hand scratch brushes are sometimes made of spun glass, with fibres of extreme fineness and elasticity, and are used for scouring only very delicate objects. They are also made of numerous wires of hardened brass and are prepared in similar form to the glass brushes, except when purchased the ends of the wires are not cut off, the operator being expected to do so before using them. The object in leaving the wires connected being to prevent them becoming damaged. Circular scratch brushes, like that shown in Fig. 69, in which the wires are arranged radially, are used for scouring articles which will admit of their use. They are attached to the spindle of a polishing lathe, and the wires consequently all receive a uniform motion in the same direction. Scratch brushes are seldom if ever used dry, the tool and the work being constantly wet with a decoction of soap-root, marshmallow, cream of tarter, alum or licorice root. With small articles the scratch

FIG. 69.

brush is held as you would a pencil, and is moved over the article with a backward and forward motion. The brushes must be carefully looked after and the wires kept straight and in good order. If they become greasy they are cleansed in caustic potash, and if they become rough they are sometimes dipped into nitric acid. With circular brushes it is well to reverse them occasionally in order to change the direction of the wires. Dirty polishing leathers should be cleaned by soaking them for an hour or two in a weak solution of soda in warm water, first rubbing the leather thoroughly with soap. Rinse thoroughly and wash in soap and water. The soap in the water will keep the leather soft and pliable. Dry it in a towel and rub it thoroughly and your leather will be much better than any new one you can buy.

CIRCULAR ERROR. The difference of time in a clock caused by the pendulum following a circular instead of a cycloidal path. *Britten.*

CLAMPS. Movable pieces of brass, lead, leather or cork attached to the jaws of a vise while holding objects that would be injured by the vise jaws.

CLEAT. A narrow or thin piece of metal used to fasten two pieces of metal together by the aid of solder, screws or rivets.

CLEPSYDRA. A water clock. A machine used anciently for measuring time by means of the discharge of water through a small aperture.

CLICHE. The forming of metal objects by means of forcing a die into heated metal.

CLICK. A pawl or dog which falls into a ratchet wheel and prevents it from turning backward, and is usually held in position by means of a spring known as the click spring. A ratchet wheel with click is fixed to the barrel arbor of watches and clocks to maintain the mainspring after being wound.

Click Spring. The spring which holds the click in position on a ratchet wheel's tooth.

To Mount a Click Spring. When the old click spring has been taken down from the bridge, find a new one, which, in length from click to foot, into which the holes are drilled for fastening, is suited to the shape and length of the bridge. With three claws fasten this latter in an uprighting tool, placing the centering center into the screw hole of the bridge, which serves for screwing on the click spring. When the bridge has in this manner been mounted well upon the plate of the uprighting tool, raise up the centering center and lay the new click spring exactly as it is to be located in its place upon the bridge, carefully preventing the claws from covering that part of the bridge to which the spring is fastened. The upper face of the spring must, by so much as will be lost afterwards in grinding and polishing, protrude beyond the surface of the barrel bridge. Then retain the spring in its place by applying a finger, and lower the point of the uprighting tool upon the click spring, making a dot by applying a gentle pressure exactly at the true spot. This dot is enlarged by punching, and a hole is then drilled exactly to suit the size of the screw. The burr is next removed, and the spring finished suitable to shape and length. If the bridge contains a foot-pin hole, bush it by firmly driving into it a brass pin, file off its projecting part level with the bridge, and screw the spring in place. Then drill, as closely as possible to the extreme end of the spring, a small hole for the pin, clear through into the bridge. Harden the spring, anneal it, chamfer and polish the edges, grind and polish the surface; fit the foot pin.

FIG. 70.

CLUB TOOTH. The form of tooth shown in Fig. 70 and for lever escape wheels having a part of the impulse angle on the tooth. See *Lever Escapement*

COCK. The horizontal bracket which holds the end of a staff. A vertical or hang-down bracket is called a potance. See *Balance Bridge.*

COLLET. A collar or band of metal. 2. A small collar fitted friction tight to the balance staff, and which is slotted to receive the lower end of the hairspring. 3. The part of a ring in which a stone is set. 4. The under side of a brilliant cut stone.

COLLET WRENCH. A tool for twisting a hairspring collet to position, which consists of a metal handle, hollow at the extremity for the reception of the pivot, and having a minute wedge-shaped projection from its face, which enters the slit in the collet, allowing it to be turned readily.

COLORING GOLD ARTICLES. See *Cleansing, Pickling aud Polishing*.

CLUTCH. A mechanism for connecting two shafts with each other or with wheels in such a manner that they may be readily disengaged.

COMPASS. An instrument consisting of a magnetized needle turning freely on a point, used to determine horizontal directions in reference to the cardinal points.

COMPASSES. An instrument for measuring figures, describing circles, etc., consisting of two pointed limbs, usually pivoted together at the top.

CONCAVE. The internal surface of a hollow rounded body. The reverse of convex.

COMPENSATION BALANCE. A balance for a watch or chronometer which compensates the effect of variations of temperature on the vibrations of the balance. See *Balance*.

COMPENSATION PENDULUM. A pendulum in which the effect of changes of temperature on the length of the rod is so counteracted that the distance of the center of oscillation from the center of suspension remains invariable.

COMPENSATION CURB. A bar composed of two metals, usually brass and steel, free to act at one end but retained at the other, the free end carrying the curb pins that regulate the acting length of a hairspring. Not used in American watches and found only in old watches of European make.

CONICAL PENDULUM. A revolving pendulum. A pendulum used only on fancy and equarorial clocks, whose bob revolves in a horizontal circle.

One revolution of a conical pendulum, says Britten, is performed in the same time that a vibrating pendulum, whose length is equal to the vertical height of a conical pendulum, makes two revolutions. If extra impulse is given to a conical pendulum, the circle described is enlarged, the vertical height lessened, and the time of its revolution decreased.

CONICAL PIVOT. A pivot whose shoulders are of conical form, used only in pivots having end stones. See *Balance Staff.* pp. 49.

FIG. 71.

CONOIDAL. Having the form of a cone.

CONTRATE WHEEL. A crown wheel. A wheel whose teeth set at right angles to its plane and used ordinarily as a gear wheel for transmiting power from one shaft to another, standing at right angles to it. The escape wheel of the verge escapement.

CONVERSION. A term in watch-making signifying that a change of escapement is made, as a movement originally having a duplex escapement is changed to a lever escapement.

CONVEX. Rising or swelling into a rounded body. The reverse of concave.

CONVEXO-CONCAVE. Convex on one side and concave on the other.

CONVEXO-CONVEX. Convex on both sides.

COPPER. A metal of a reddish color, malleable, ductile and tenacious. It fuses at 2,000° Fah. and has a specific gravity varying from 8.8 to 8.9. It has a breaking strain of 48,000 lbs. per square inch. In horology it is employed as a backing for enameled watch dials, in the construction of grid-iron compensation pendulums, in the manufacture of compensation balances, etc. When mixed with tin it forms bell-metal and bronze and with zinc it forms brass and other alloys. See *Alloys*.

CORUNDUM. The earth alumina, as found native in a crystalline state, including sapphire, which is the fine blue variety; the oriental ruby, or red sapphire; the oriental amethyst, or purple sapphire. It is the hardest known substance next to the diamond. The non-transparent variety, dark-colored and granular is known as Emery. *Dana.*

CORUNDUM-WHEELS. Wheels faced with corundum, (emery) or made of a composition of corundum and cement. See *Emery Wheels*.

COUNTER BALANCE. A mass of metal placed on the opposite side of a wheel to that to which a crank is attached to compensate for the weight of the latter.

COUNTERMARK. A mark attached to gold and silver-ware of English make to attest its standard. See *Hall Mark*.

COUNTERSINK. To enlarge the outer end of a hole for the reception of the head of a screw, bolt, etc. A tool used to turn out or countersink. Fig. 72 illustrates Happers-

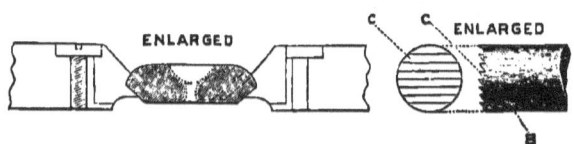

FIG. 72.

berger's patent, flat bottomed countersinks, which are designed for making or deepening flat-bottomed countersinks

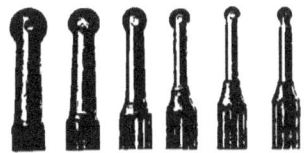

FIG. 73.

for screw heads of any kind. The screw-thread or hole will not be injured in using these tools. Fig 73 illustrates a set of wheel countersinks made with cutters on one end and burnishers on the other. Countersinks are also made of steel in the form of drills and from emery in the form of a cone, with metal handle for revolving. The emery countersink will be found very useful for large holes and for trimming the edges of holes in enamel dials.

CRANK. The bent portion of an axis serving as a handle or connection for communicating circular motion, as the crank on a steam engine. To twist or distort, as applied to metals.

CRESCENT. The concave formed in the roller of the lever escapement to allow the passage of the safety pin.

CROWN-WHEEL. A wheel whose teeth are set at right angles to its plane. A contrate wheel. The escape wheel of the verge escapement is a crown wheel.

CRUCIBLE. A melting pot capable of enduring great heat, without injury and used for melting metals. It is made of clay or clay compounded with black lead and other materials.

CRYSTAL. A term applied to the glass of a watch case.

CURB PINS. The two brass pins that stand on either side of the hairspring near its stud attachment, and are attached to the regulator. They effect the time of the vibration of the balance according as they are shifted by means of the regulator to or from the point of attachment of the spring. Some authors advise timing in positions by the curb pins. This should never be attempted. The regulator should always stand as near the center of the index as possible. The curb pins should never be far from the stud and should be just wide enough apart to let the spring move between them and no more. Instead of disturbing the curb pins when timing in positions, add to or take from the weight of the balance. See *Balance Screw Washers.*

CYCLOID. A curve generated by a point in the plane of a circle, when the circle is rolled along a straight line, keeping always in the same plane. *Webster.*

The path through which a pendulum travels, to secure uniformity in the time of its vibration through arcs different in extent should be cycloidal.

CYLINDER ESCAPEMENT. The cylinder escapement was invented by George Graham about 1700, and was

FIG. 74.

a. Escape Wheel.
b. Cylinder.
c. Entering Lip of Cylinder.
d. Exit Lip of Cylinder.

e. Passage for Escape Wheel.
f. Tooth removed, showing Stalk on which Teeth are supported.
g. Collet for Balance.

an improvement upon and a development of an idea conceived by Tompion, who had prior to this time invented an escapement somewhat similar. It is a frictional dead beat escapement as distinguished from a detached escapement. It was, at the time of its introduction, considered of but little value, as its principles were not thoroughly understood, it was difficult to manufacture, and above all the tendancy to excessive wear of the acting surfaces. The Swiss solved the problem by making both the cylinder and wheel of escape, steel and hardening them.

The balance with this escapement is mounted on a hollow cylinder large enough in the bore to admit a tooth of the escape wheel. Nearly one-half of the cylinder is cut away where the teeth enter, and impulse is given to the balance by the teeth, which are wedge-shaped, rubbing against the edge of the cylinder as they enter and leave. The teeth of the verge escapement lie in a vertical plane in the plan of a watch, and the term horizontal, therefore, fairly distinguished the cylinder escapement when it was introduced, but now that all the escapements in general use answer to the title, "cylinder escapement" appears to be the more suitable description.

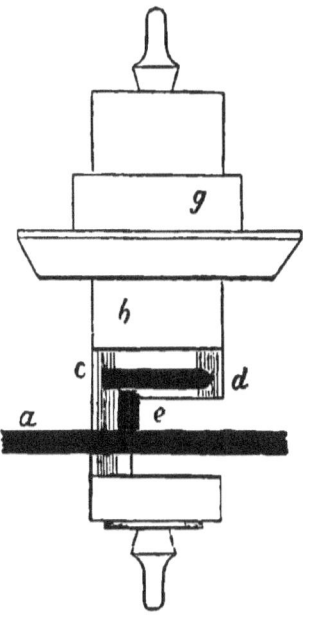

FIG. 75.
Elevation of Cylinder and One Tooth of Escape Wheel therein.

Britten gives the following in regard to the

ACTION OF THE ESCAPEMENT.

Fig. 74 is a plan of the cylinder escapement, in which the point of a tooth of the escape wheel is pressing against the outside of the shell of the cylinder. As the cylinder, on which the balance is mounted, moves round in the direction of the arrow, the wedge-shaped tooth of the escape wheel pushes into the cylinder, thereby giving it impulse. The tooth cannot escape at the other side of the cylinder, for the shell of the cylinder at this point is rather more than half a circle; but its point rests against the inner side of the shell untill the balance completes its vibration and returns, when the tooth which was inside the cylinder escapes, and the point of the succeeding tooth is caught on the outside of the shell. The teeth rise on stalks from the body of the escape wheel, and the cylinder is cut away just below the acting part of the exit side, leaving only one-fourth of a circle in order to allow as much vibration as possible. This will be seen very plainly on examining Fig. 75, which is an elevation of the cylinder to an enlarged scale.

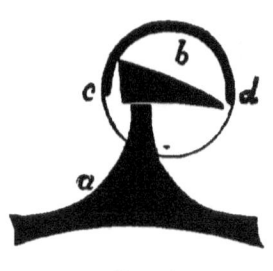

FIG. 76.

PROPORTION OF THE ESCAPEMENT.

The escape wheel has fifteen teeth formed to give impulse to the cylinder during from 20° to 40° of its vibration each way. Lower angles are as a rule used with large rather than with small sized watches, but to secure the best result either extreme must be avoided. In an escapement with very slight inclines to the wheel teeth, the first part of the tooth does not work, as the tooth drops onto the lip of the cylinder some distance up the plane. On the other hand, a very steep tooth is almost sure to set in action as the oil thickens. The diameter of the cylinder, its thickness, and the length of the wheel teeth are all co-related. The size of the cylinder with relation to the wheel also varies somewhat with the angle of impulse, a very high angle requiring a slightly larger cylnder than a low one. If a cylinder of average thickness is desired for an escapement with medium impulse, its external diameter may be made equal to the extreme diameter of the escape wheel × .115.

109 CYLINDER ESCAPEMENT

Then to set out the escapement, if a lift of say 30° be decided on, a circle on which the points of the teeth will fall is drawn within one representing the extreme diameter of the escape wheel at a distance from it equal to 30° of the circumference of the cylinder. Midway between these two circles the cylinder is planted. (See Fig. 77.) If the point of one tooth is shown resting on the cylinder, a space of half a degree should be allowed for freedom between the opposite side of the cylinder and the heel of the next tooth. From the heel of one tooth to the heel of the next=24° of the circumference of the wheel ($\frac{360}{15}$ = 24), and from the point of one tooth to the

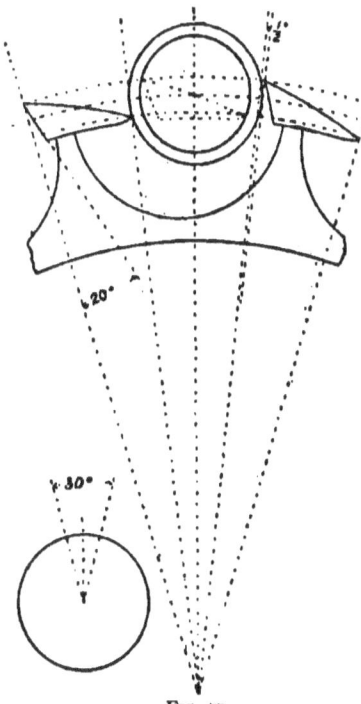

FIG. 77.

point of the next also=24°, so that the teeth may now be drawn. They are extended within the innermost dotted circle to give them a little extra substance, and their tips are rounded a little, leaving the points of the impulse planes the most advanced. The backs of the teeth diverge from a radial line from 12° to 30° to give the cylinder clearance; a high angled tooth requiring to be cut back more than a low one. A curve whose radius is about two-thirds that of the wheel is suitable for rounding the impulse planes of the teeth. The internal diameter of the cylinder should be such as to allow a little freedom for the tooth. The acting part of the shell of the cylinder should be a trifle less than seven-twelfths of a whole circle, with the entering and exit lips rounded as shown in the enlarged plan, Fig. 76, the former both ways, and the latter from the inside only. This rounding of the lips of the cylinder adds a little to the impulse beyond what would be given by the angle on the wheel teeth alone. The diameter of the escape wheel is usually half that of the balance, rather under than over.

Britten says of the

EXAMINATION OF THE ESCAPEMENT.

See that cylinder and wheel are perfectly upright. Remove the balance spring, and put the cylinder and cock in their places. Then with a little power on, and a wedge of cork under the balance to check its motion, try if all the escape wheel teeth have sufficient drop, both inside and out. If the drop is sufficient inside with none outside, the wheel is too small; if the reverse the wheel is too large—that is, provided the cylinder is planted the correct depth. If some of the teeth only are without necessary freedom, make a hole in thin sheet brass of such a size that one of the teeth that has proper shake will just enter. Use this as a gauge to shorten the full teeth by. For this purpose use either steel and oilstone dust or a sapphire file, polish well with metal and red stuff, and finish with a burnisher. Be careful to operate on the noses of the teeth only, and round them both ways so that a mere point is in contact with the cylinder. If the inside drop is right, and there is no outside drop with any of the teeth, although it would indicate a wheel too small, it may be prudent to change the cylinder for one of the same inside diameter but thinner, rather than remove the wheel, for it often happens that a larger wheel would not clear the fourth pinion.

If the teeth of the escape wheel are too high or too low in passing the opening of the cylinder, the wheel should be placed on a cylinder of soft brass or zinc small enough to go inside the teeth, with a hole through it and with a slightly concave face. A hollow punch is placed over the middle of the wheel while it is resting on the concave face of the brass or zinc cylinder, and one or two light taps with a hammer

111 CYLINDER ESCAPEMENT

will bend the wheel sufficiently. In fact, care must be taken not to overdo it. It rarely happens that the wheel is free neither of the top nor bottom plug, but should this be the case, sufficient clearance may be obtained by deepening the opening with a steel polisher and oilstone dust or with a sapphire file. A cylinder with too high an opening is bad, for the oil is drawn away from the teeth by the escape wheel.

If a cylinder pivot is bent, it may very readily be straightened by placing a *bouchon* of a proper size over it.

When the balance spring is at rest, the balance should have to be moved an equal amount each way before a tooth escapes. By gently pressing against the fourth wheel with a peg this may be tried. There is a dot on the balance and three dots on the plate to assist in estimating the amount of lift. When the balance spring is at rest, the dot on the balance should be opposite to the centre dot on the plate. The escapement will then be in beat, that is, provided the dots are properly placed, which should be tested. Turn the balance from its point of rest till a tooth just drops, and note the position of the dot on the balance with reference to one of the outer dots on the plate. Turn the balance in the opposite direction till a tooth drops again, and if the dot on the balance is then in the same position with reference to the other outer dot, the escapement will be in beat. The two outer dots should mark the extent of the lifting, and the dot on the balance would then be coincident with them as the teeth dropped when tried in this way; but the dots may be a little too wide or too close, and it will, therefore, be sufficient if the dot on the balance bears the same *relative* position to them as just explained; but if it is found that the lift is unequal from the point of rest, the balance spring collet must be shifted in the direction of the least lift till the lift is equal. A new mark should then be made on the balance opposite to the central dot on the plate.

When the balance is at rest, the banking pin in the balance should be opposite to the banking stud in the cock, so as to give equal vibration on both sides. This is important for the following reason: The banking pin allows nearly a turn of vibration, and the shell of the cylinder is but little over half a turn, so that as the outside of the shell gets around toward the center of the escape wheel, the point of a tooth may escape and jamb the cylinder unless the vibration is pretty equally divided. When the banking is properly adjusted, bring the balance around until banking pin is against the stud; there should then be perceptible shake between the cylinder and the plane of the escape wheel. Try this with the banking pin, first against one and then against the other side of the stud. If there is no shake the wheel may be freed by taking a little off the edge of the passage of the cylinder where it fouls the wheel, by means of a sapphire file, or a larger banking pin may be substituted at the judgment of the operator. See that the banking pin and stud are perfectly dry and clean before leaving them; a sticky banking often stops a watch. Cylinder watches and timepieces, after going for a few months, sometimes increase their vibration so much as to persistently bank. To meet this fault a weaker mainspring may be used, or a larger balance, or a wheel with a smaller angle of impulse. By far the quickest and best way is to *very slightly* top the wheel by holding a piece of Arkansas stone against the teeth afterward polishing with boxwood and red stuff. So little, taken off the wheel in this way as to be hardly perceptible will have great effect.

Fitting New Cylinder and Plugs. In most cases of broken cylinders the upper half is left while the lower and most important part is missing. Take total length over all first, the same as in replacing staff, which can be done by the use of the Staff Length Gauge, (see *Gauges*), and then measure the length of the old cylinder from the under side of the hub to the end of the top pivot, and the difference between the two measurements will give the length of the lower part of cylinder and pivot, and this will serve as a guide in selecting an unfinished cylinder of proper length. The cylinders and also cylinder plugs can be purchased from material houses so cheaply that it will scarcely pay the watchmaker to make them. See *Cylinder Plugs*. Having selected a cylinder proceed to center it in the lathe in a finely centered chuck,

113 CYLINDER ESCAPEMENT

leaving the lower end exposed. Turn the lower pivot first; then finish off the lower plug, and if necessary, turn off any surplus body of shell from the lower part of the cylinder as occasion demands. For obtaining the requisite measurements for the work, the little tool shown in Fig. 15 and the Staff or Cylinder Height Gauge shown under *Gauges* will be found useful. Saunier advocates the use of experimental cylinders like that shown in Fig. 78, and suggests that the workman will do well to make two or three different sizes during his leisure moments. They can be made from the cylinders kept in stock by material dealers. The cylinder and lower plug are better to be in one piece to increase the strength; the slot shallow and in different positions, (for the position of the banking slot is the most difficult to ascertain), and the cylinder only perforated where the top plug is inserted. The top plug should be removed, the hole tapped, and a new plug, somewhat longer, screwed in. The action of this tool is similar to the Staff Height Gauge mentioned above.

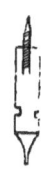

FIG. 78.

After the lower end is finished the wax is turned away and the cylinder turned true and finally cut off at the proper length, preserving as fine a center as possible, after which the cylinder is reversed and finished.

In pivoting, it is very seldom necessary to drill the cylinder, as the upper and lower pivots are generally the extremity of plugs closely fitting in each end. In most cases the top pivot may be replaced by resting the cylinder on a stake, the hole of which is of a sufficient diameter to allow of the entrance of the plug, and too small to allow the cylinder to pass through. A knee punch and a few light taps of a hammer are generally sufficient to drive the plug out far enough to admit of the turning of a new pivot. The lower plug must be driven out entirely (being too short to admit of turning a new pivot) and a new plug inserted. The plugs must be made to fit tightly without taper, as with a taper plug there is great danger of splitting the cylinder. Should the plug be very tight and difficulty is encountered in driving it out, a few light taps all around the cylinder will generally stretch it enough to remove the plug easily.

CYLINDER HEIGHT TOOL. See *Gauge*.

CYLINDER PLUGS. Steel plugs fitted to the ends of a cylinder and on the ends of which the pivots are formed. Cylinder plugs can be obtained ready made from material dealers; assorted sizes in neat boxes.

DAMASKEEN. To decorate a metal by the inlaying of other metals, or by etching designs upon its surface. The embelishment of the surface of metals with rings or bars is snailing and is not damaskeening, although improperly called so by watch makers and watch factory employes particularly. See *Snailing*, also *Electro Plating*, *Bronzing* and *Staining*.

DEAD BEAT ESCAPEMENT. An escapement in which, except during the actual impulsion, the escape wheel remains stationary and does not recoil. See *Graham Escapement*.

DECANT. To pour off a liquid from its sediment; as the decanting of diamond powder, prepared chalk, etc. Saunier advises the watchmaker to prepare all his smoothing and polishing materials by decantation, as he will by this means free them from hard or large particles and obtain a uniform grain. At the present time the watchmaker can however obtain diamond dust, prepared chalk, etc., ready for use, that are supposed to be have been properly decanted. There are however many poor concoctions that have not gone through the proper treatment, and if the watchmaker is desirous of doing fine work and having reliable materials always at hand it is well to decant these preparations even though they be labeled "prepared." The operation is a very simple one and takes but little time. The material being reduced to a powder is placed in a vessel filled with water, oil, or other liquids, according to the the nature of the material to be operated upon, and after being thoroughly stirred it is allowed to partially settle. The liquid is then poured into another vessel, the heavy portion remaining in the bottom of the first vessel. This residue is only fit for use in the very coarsest work. The liquid is then stirred, allowed to settle partially again and is then poured into another vessel. The powder left should be labeled 1. By successive operations, each time increasing the interval of time allowed for settlement, finer deposits can be obtained which may be labeled respectively 2, 3, 4, etc. In decanting diamond powder or oilstone dust, oil should be used; for tripoli, rottenstone, or chalk, water; and for hartshorn and some other materials, alcohol is used. Diamond powder as purchased from the material dealer can rarely be improved upon by manipulation unless the operator is expert.

DEMAGNETIZER. A machine or tool used to remove magnetism from parts of watches. There are several demagnetizers upon the market. In some of these machines the arc and incandescent electric light wires are attached to generate the magnetism, while in the Ide demagnetizer it is generated by the use of horseshoe magnets.

The Greaves demagnetizer, shown in Fig. 79, is intended to be used either with a battery or electric light wire. The method of demagnetizing with this machine is as follows: turn the handle of cylinder with the right hand very slowly—the slower the better, say about forty revolutions a minute; place the watch immediately over the magnets with, the left hand holding the mainspring and heavy stem winding parts over the magnets so they shall be the last to pass over, and in the center of space dividing the magnets, but not touching them; hold it still for a few seconds and then slowly move it forward and around the edge of the magnets, approaching the front and against it in a circular line as indicated at No. 1, Fig. 80, preserving the same face toward the magnets, as in No. 2, and when a point indicated by a horizontal line in No. 1 is reached, withdraw from magnet in a straight line. If not successful in removing all the magnetism, repeat the operation, only a little further away, as indicated by the dotted lines

FIG. 79.

in No. 1. The case springs need not be removed to demagnetize them; by passing them in the same manner as the watch, keeping the heavy part nearest the center line between the magnets, the result will be obtained.

It is well to observe the following directions in caring for the battery: take one pound Bichromate of Potassiun, (poison) and one pint of Commercial Sulphuric Acid and mix in an earthen vessel. Pour the acid over the Bichromate; about a half an hour afterwards pour over it about one gallon of water, stir well and let stand for ten or twelve hours. Get two one gallon straight earthen or glass jars for battery. Divide the

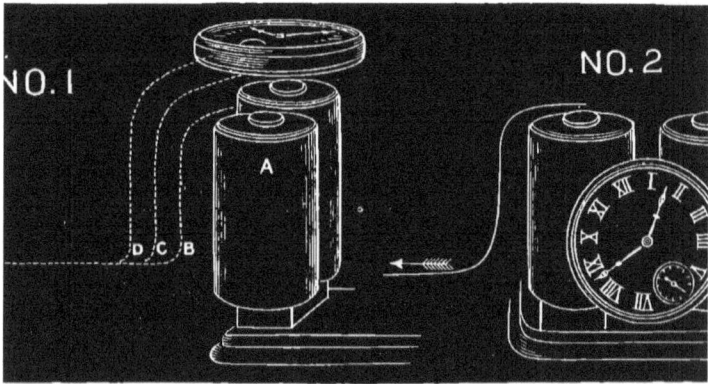

FIG. 80.

solution between them; place the zinc carbons into them and add enough water to immerse them about two-thirds, and put in water to replace evaporation whenever necessary. Never leave the zincs in the solution longer than necessary as they

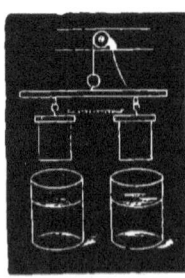

FIG. 81.

weaken the solution, but remove them as soon as the operation of demagnetizing is complete. It is well to construct a box that will hold the two jars, and by means of a pulley and two hooks attached as shown in Fig. 81, you can with very little trouble remove the zincs at any time when not in use. Connect the battery to the demagnetizer by attaching to the two binding posts one end of each of two long copper wires, and be careful to see that you have metallic contact, by scraping the ends of the wires with a knife where they go into the posts, and the other two ends are to be attached, one to the zinc pole and the other to the carbon pole of the two zinc carbons.

Connect the two zinc carbons with a short piece of copper wire, as shown in Fig. 81, attaching one to the carbon pole and the other to the zinc pole. To test if the circuit is

FIG. 82.

perfect, place a piece of steel on the magnets and it will be attracted very strongly to them; on turning the roller a little, the current will alternate from one pole to the other, relieving the steel and attracting it alternately.

The Berlin Demagnetizer, shown in Fig. 82, is constructed on a principal similar to the Greaves, and like it, gives best results when used with electric light wires. Procure an. attachment plug and fasten to the end of the flexible cord accompanying machine. Insert in lamp receptacle and turn on the current. Press down key and turn handle of commutator, about 150 revolutions a minute. Insert the watch or part to be demagnetized into the opening of magnet, and revolve very slowly, keeping it in a straight line with center of magnet until at a distance of two or three feet. Keep turning commutator at regular speed. Release key before ceasing to turn. It is not necessary to remove the movement from the case nor to let it remain in the magnet. While the current is on and the handle being turned with key down, insert the watch into the opening and proceed as above.

DEPTH. The contact point between a wheel and pinion.

DEPTHING TOOL. A mechanical device for transferring the depthing of a wheel and pinion to a plate. Britten advises that before using a new depthing tool the centers be turned end for end, also transposed, and assertaining after each change if there is any deviation in a circle described by the points, in order to test the truth of the tool. The tool should be held in the left hand, with the adjusting screw pointed to the right. Place the pinion in the centers on the left, and the wheel on the right, first opening the tool sufficiently for the teeth of the wheel to clear the teeth of the pinion. The teeth of the wheel and pinion are then brought into contact by means of the regulating screw, shown at the bottom in Fig. 83. When the pinion and wheel are in right contact, the tool may be secured with the screws furnished for that purpose. Then hold the tool so that you may observe the contact of wheel and pinion. After you are satisfied that the depthing is correct and that the teeth do not butt, the depth may be marked off by loosening the binding screws, taking the wheel and pinion out of the tool, and while one center is kept tight and inserted in the hole from which the depth is to be taken, the loose center is brought down until it touches the plate. If the tool is found to be perfectly upright and all is satisfactory, tighten the loose center and mark the plate where the wheel or pinion is to be planted. The mark can then be made permanent by the use of a center punch or graver.

FIG. 83.

DETACHED ESCAPEMENT. The escapement of a time piece in which the balance or pendulum, during a portion of its vibration, is detached from the train.

DETENT. That which locks or unlocks a movement; the piece of steel that carries the stones that lock and unlock an escape wheel.

DIAL. The graduated face of a time piece. The greater majority of American dials are what is known as enamel dials, which consist of a copper plate for a base and an enameled face. The process of making these dials, as carried on in our factories is as follows: The copper is shaped and holes punched in one operation. The feet are then brazed on after, which the enamel is applied to both the back and face, after which it is fired. After smoothing they are again fired, and, if perfect, they are sent to the painter. For many years after most of the other work in our factories was done by machinery, the painting of dials was hand work. The Waltham company, after experimenting for a number of years, finally brought to perfection a process by means of which the dials are lettered, the numerals, minute and second marks are printed by photography. Various processes are used in other factories, among them being the transfer process, which is effected by rubbing the enamel paint into a steel plate into which the lettering of the dial is countersunk, taking an impression from this plate upon a rubber platten and then transferring this impression to the dial. After painting the dials are again fired.

Dials of gold, silver and other metals are extensively used, particularly in the Spanish-American countries.

To Drill an Enamel Dial. Select a piece of soft copper wire of the diameter you wish the hole, file off the end perfectly flat, and hammer into the copper a small quantity of fine diamond power. This form of drill will be found to perforate the enamel of a dial quite rapidly. Broaches made in the same manner give excellent results. These tools can be used either by revolving in the fingers or in the lathe. Emery countersinks will be found very useful for trimming the edges of holes in enamel'dials.

To Remove a Name from Dial. Apply a little fine diamantine to the end of your forefinger and gently rub the name until it disappears. The finish can be restored by polishing the place carefully with a small quantity of diamantine mixed with oil and applied by means of a small piece of cork. An agate burnisher is also used for the same purpose.

To Remove Stains from Enamel Dials. Enamel dials sometimes have black or cloudy stains upon their faces, caused usually by the tin boxes in which they are shipped. These can be removed with a piece of soft tissue paper previously dampened with nitric acid. Wipe the stained places, carefully avoiding the painted portions as much as possible, for in some very cheap dials the painting is not well fired and may be injured by the acid. Wash the dial thoroughly in clean water and dry in sawdust.

To Reduce the Diameter of a Dial. Rest the dial in an inclined position and file the edge with a half-smooth file, dipping the file in turpentine occasionally, and finish with a fine emery stick.

To Repair a Chipped Dial. Gently heat the surface of the dial and fill the hole with a compound of white lead and white resin heated over the flame of a spirit lamp. It is better to heat the blade of a knife rather than the wax and run no risk of discoloring the wax. Cut off a small piece of the wax and press firmly into the hole, allowing it to project a little above the dial. When cold, scrape down even with the dial and finish by holding it close to the flame, when the patch will gloss over nicely. Be careful and do not get it too close to the flame or you may turn the enamel yellow. A mixture of white lead and white wax applied and polished by friction is also used, but it is not as handy and is not as capable of a high polish.

To Clean Metal Dials. Silver and gold dials can be restored by gently heating the back over a spirit lamp and dipping the dial in diluted nitric acid. If the figures are painted however they will be removed and it will be necessary to repaint them, but if they are enameled on, the enamel, will not be injured. If the figures are painted the dial may be cleaned by brushing with powdered cream of tarter either dry or in the form of a paste mixed with water. Avoid all the painted portions and work the paste in between the painted portions with a pointed peg wood. Wash with warm water and dry by carefully patting with a soft linen rag.

To Grind Enamel from the Back of Dial. It is sometimes necessary to remove a portion of the enamel from the back of a dial to allow room for the motion work, etc. The most convenient method is to grind the back with emery, preferably in the shape of a wheel. Water should be applied to the work from time to time to prevent heating.

DIAMANTINE. This polishing agent is used extensively for polishing steel, and is a preparation of crystallized boron. It is not applicable to brass or copper work. Rubitine and Sapphirine are similar chemical preparations; they act quicker but do not yield as good results.

DIAMOND DRILLS. Pieces of copper wire, in the end of which are imbedded fragments of diamond in the shape of triangular prisms and held in place with shellac. They are used for drilling jewels, etc. They may be purchased, ready made, from material dealers.

DIAMOND GRAVERS. These are very similar to diamond drills and are mounted in the same manner, but usually consist of larger, though shorter and stronger diamond fragments, and are used for shaping jewels, etc. They may also be obtained from material dealers.

DIAMOND LAPS OR MILLS. These are of two kinds, one for grinding and the other for polishing. The grinding mills are copper discs from an inch to an inch and a half in diameter, into the surface of which diamond powder of various grades has been hammered or rolled. The polishing mills are made of box-wood, vegetable ivory, etc., and the powder is applied to their surfaces in the shape of a paste mixed with olive oil. These mills are useful for cutting and polishing ruby-pallets, and other hard stones, for flattening stones to be used as jewels and for manipulating hard steel.

DIAMOND FILES. Strips of copper into the face of which diamond powder of various degrees of coarseness has been hammered or rolled. Used for working ruby-pallets and other hard stones and hard steel.

DIAMOND POWDER. A cutting and polishing agent prepared from the crushed chips from the diamond cutter's table, black, brown, and other inferior stones known as bort and small diamonds. After pulverizing thoroughly the powder is decanted in olive oil to various degrees of fineness. To be had of material dealers generally. Used for charging the face of mills or laps for grinding and polishing hard stones, etc. It is also used for drilling by being applied to the end of small taper piece of steel, flattened on the end for the reception of the powder, which is moistened with olive oil.

DIPLEIDOSCOPE. An instrument invented by J. M. Bloxam in 1843, used for determining the time of apparent noon. It consists of two mirrors and a plane glass disposed in the form of a prism, so that, by the reflection of the sun's rays from their surfaces, two images are presented to the eye, moving in opposite directions, and coinciding at the instant the sun's center is on the meridian.

DISTRIBUTOR. Among European workman a countershaft is called a distributor.

DIVIDING PLATE. See *Index*.

DOG SCREWS. The screws with half heads by which a movement is held in its case.

DOG. A clutch. An adjustable stop to change the motion of a machine tool.

DOUBLE ROLLER ESCAPEMENT. A form of the lever escapement in which a separate roller is employed for the guard action.

DOUBLE SUNK DIAL. A dial having two sinks, one for the hour and another for the seconds hand.

DOUZIEME. A unit of measurement, indicating $\frac{1}{12}$ of a line or $\frac{1}{144}$ of an inch. See *Gauge*.

DRAW. The angle of the locking faces of the pallets, as in the lever escapement.

DRAW PLATE. A plate of very hard steel for drawing wire of various shapes and diameters. They are made for drawing round, half-round and square wire. The plates are sometimes formed in jewel for working steel wire, etc. These plates are very handy for readily reducing wire to any desired diameter, and may also be employed for reducing the diameter of bouchons.

DRIFTING TOOL. A tool for punching holes in mainsprings, etc. It consists of a frame to be held in the vise, through which a screw passes, and to the end of which a handle is attached. It is used but little in this country, as the mainspring punch has superceded it, being simpler and quicker to operate.

DRILLS AND DRILLING. Drilling may be effected in two ways, by rotating the drill and holding the work stationary, or *vice versa*. The most satisfactory results, however, are obtained by revolving the work and gradually bringing the drill into contact with it. Although it is not always possible to do this owing to the shape of the article to be drilled. A drill of the shape shown in Fig. 84 is preferable for drilling hardened steel, while the shape shown in Fig. 85 is best suited for drilling soft steel, brass, etc. Oil or glycerine diluted with alcohol is the best lubricant for the

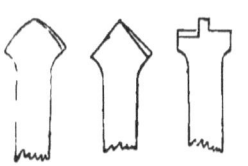

FIG. 84.   FIG. 85.   FIG. 86.   FIG. 87.

softer metals, but when drilling hard steel turpentine should be used. Drills of the form shown in Fig. 86 are used for drilling flat bottomed holes for countersinking screw heads, etc. See also *Countersinks*. The twist drill shown in Fig. 87 is desirable when drilling deeply, as this form of drill heats slowly and the particles are carried to the surface of the work. Pivot drills, like those shown in Fig. 88, can be purchased from material dealers, mounted on cards, and ready for use at such small cost that it will scarcely pay the watchmakers to make them.

Drills of a form indicated by Fig. 89 are recommended highly by Saunier and are known as semi-cylindrical drills. They are made from cylindrical steel rods, rounded at their ends and filed down to a trifle less than half their thickness. The length of the point should be greater or less according to the nature of the metal to be operated upon, but under no circumstances must the point itself be sharp. This form of drill should be shapened on the round side and not on the flat surface. It possesses, says Saunier, the advantage that when placed in a drill-chuck it can be turned exactly round, of the required diameter and finished; so that whenever replaced in the chuck, one can be certain beforehand that the hole drilled will be of a definite diameter. With such a drill the hole is smoothed immediately after it is made by one or the other cutting edges.

FIG. 88.

FIG. 89.

DRILL REST. In using the lathe for drilling, a great saving in both time and drills can be effected by using a drill rest similar to that shown in Fig. 90. It is well to have a half dozen different sizes, starting at ¼ inch and increasing by ⅛ inch, for various classes of work. These rests are not kept by material dealers, but can be made by the watch-

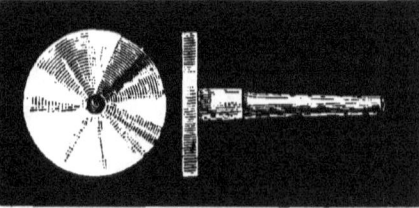

FIG. 90.

maker. Saw from a piece of rolled sheet brass, say 1/16 inch thick, the circles required, leaving metal enough to finish nicely. Place a steel taper plug in the taper chuck of your lathe and turn down a recess, leaving a shoulder on the taper. Drill a hole through the brass plate to fit the steel taper tightly. Place the end of the taper on a lead block and proceed to rivit the brass plate on the taper, making sure that it is true. Replace the taper in the lathe-chuck and proceed to turn the face and edge of the brass plate perfectly true and to the proper size. Those who have tried to drill a straight hole through an object by holding it in the fingers know just how difficult it is to do, but by placing one of these drill rests in the spindle of the tail stock, placing the article to be drilled against it and bringing it up against the drill, you can drill the hole perfectly upright and avoid all danger of breaking the drill.

DRILL STOCK. A tool used for holding drills, the more modern variety having a small chuck on one end for centering and holding the drill. These tools are made in various forms, but the design shown in Fig. 91 is one of the best.

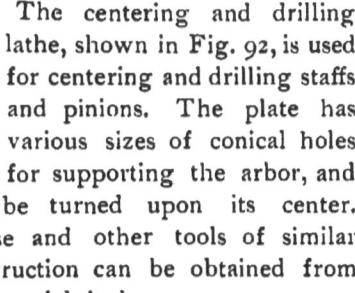

FIG. 91.

DRILLING LATHE. The centering and drilling lathe, shown in Fig. 92, is used for centering and drilling staffs and pinions. The plate has various sizes of conical holes for supporting the arbor, and can be turned upon its center. These and other tools of similar construction can be obtained from all material dealers.

FIG. 92.

DROP. The distance which the escape wheel travels before touching on the pallet.

DRUM. The barrel of a turret clock on which the driving cord is wound. There is a variety of escapement, known as the Drum Escapement, which is met with but little in this country. Britten says this variety of escapement in a continual source of trouble to English repairers. It receives impulse at every other vibration only, and the idea of the escapement appears to be, that by providing a long frictional rest on one of the pallets, the extra pressure of the escape wheel tooth, when the mainspring is fully wound, will be sufficient to prevent any considerable increase in the arc of vibration of the pendulum. Clocks with this escapements, however, often stop from the diminished power when the spring is nearly run down, again, when it is fully wound, because the small and light pendulum has not the energy to unlock the pallet.

DUPLEX ESCAPEMENT. An escapement invented by Pierre Le Roy about 1750. As first constructed, this escapement had two escape wheels, (from whence its name is derived), one used for giving impulse, and the other to lock or or check the wheel when the impulse tooth escaped from the pallet. This form was afterwards simplified by changing to that shown in Fig. 93. Britten says of this escapement, that like the Chronometer, it is a single beat escapement, that is, it receives impulse at every other vibration only. The escapement has two sets of teeth. Those farthest from the centre lock the wheel by pressing on a hollow ruby cylinder or roller fitted round a reduced part of the balance staff, and planted so that it intercepts the path of the teeth. There is a notch in the ruby roller, and a tooth passes every time the balance, in its excursion in the opposite direction to that in which the wheel moves, brings this notch past the point of the tooth resting on the roller. When the tooth leaves the notch, the impulse finger, fixed to the balance staff, receives a blow from one of the impulse teeth of the wheel. The impulse teeth are not in the same plane as the body of the wheel, but stand up from it so as to meet the impulse finger. There is no action in the return vibration. In the figure the detaining roller traveling in the direction of the arrow is just allowing a locking tooth of the wheel to escape from the notch, and the pallet is sufficiently in front of the tooth from which it will receive impulse to ensure a safe intersection.

The balance is never detached, but the roller on which the wheel teeth rest is very small and highly polished, so that there is but little friction from this cause, and the alteration in its amount is, therefore, not of such consequence as might be imagined. A very usual proportion is for the diameter of the roller to be one-fifteenth of the diameter of the largest part

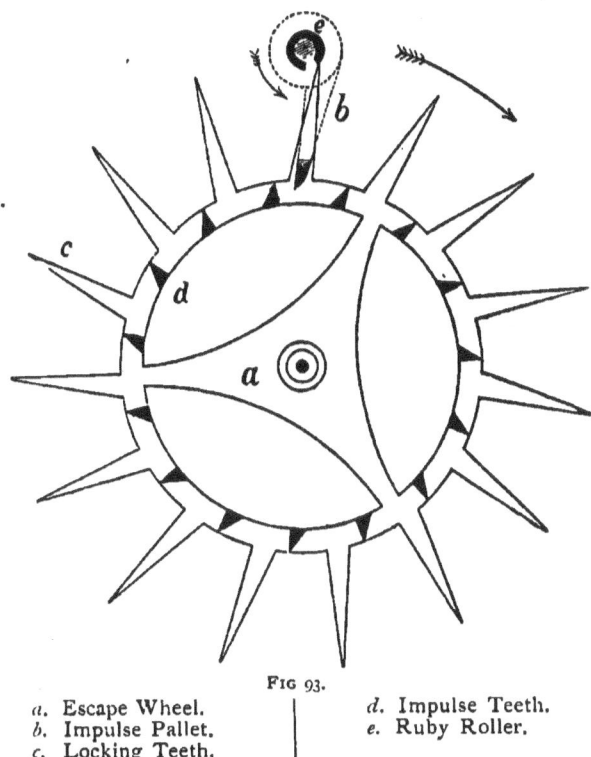

FIG 93.

a. Escape Wheel.
b. Impulse Pallet.
c. Locking Teeth.
d. Impulse Teeth.
e. Ruby Roller.

of the escape wheel, which it intersects about 30° measured from the centre of the roller. The impulse teeth should have considerable drop on to the pallet. Ten degrees is not an unusual amount. The escape wheel is made as light as possible, of hard hammered brass of very fine quality. The points of the impulse teeth are usually two-thirds the distance of the points of the locking teeth from the centre of the wheel. The impulse pallet is sometimes jeweled.

The staff requires to be planted with great exactness, and one of the most frequent causes of derangement of the Duplex Escapement is the wearing of the balance pivots. In such cases, the pivots having been re-polished, new holes, or at all events a new bottom hole, should be put in. See also that the point of each locking tooth is smooth and nicely rounded, and that every impulse tooth falls safely on the pallet; if some are shallow, twist the impulse pallet round so as to give more drop. Or if the roller depth is also shallow, carefully make the teeth of equal length by topping, and then, supposing it to a full-plate watch, very slightly tap the cock and the potance towards the wheel until the escapement is made safe. In a three-quarter plate the recess for the jewel setting may be scraped away on one side and rubbed over on the other. The extra amount of intersection of the impulse pallet in the path of the wheel teeth thus made can be easily corrected by polishing off the surplus amount, if any.

It is of the utmost consequence in this escapement that all the jewel holes should fit accurately, and that the balance staff should have very little end shake, otherwise the pivots will be found to wear away very quickly.

A loose roller is occasionally the cause of stoppage. The staff and roller should be carefully cleaned from oil which would prevent the shellac from sticking, and if the staff is polished where the roller fits, it may be grayed for the same reason. Then warm the roller and fix with shellac.

It sometimes happens that the impulse pallet, in running past, just catches on the impulse tooth, and when the balance leans towards the escape wheel, the continual recurrence of this causes the vibration to fall off, and gradually stops the watch. If the locking teeth are already the right depth, the fault should be corrected by polishing a very little off the corner of the pallet with a bell-metal polisher if the pallet is of steel, or with an ivory polisher and the finest diamond powder if it is jeweled. But the greatest care must be taken not to overdo it.

A small drop of oil should be applied to the notch and nowhere else, except to the pivots.

When the escapement is in beat, the notch in the roller is between the locking tooth resting on it and the line of centers, or a little nearer the latter; out of beat is a cause of stoppage.

The idea of this escapement is seductive; it conforms to the requirement of giving impulse across the line of centres, and at one time it was considered an excellent arrangement, but it has proved to be quite unreliable. The best proportion of its parts and the finest work are insufficient to prevent it setting. On the introduction of the Lever it declined, and is rarely made now.

DUPLEX HOOK. The impulse pallet in the Duplex Escapement.

DUPLEX ROLLER. The ruby roller of the Duplex Escapement.

DUST BANDS. Thin metal bands or guards which are inserted between the upper and lower plates of a movement to exclude all dust.

ELECTRO-PLATING, BRONZING AND STAINING. When Dynamo-electric machines are not used, Bunsen's battery is the most suitable for the execution of galvanic depositions. Each element is composed of a glass vessel which is half filled with nitric acid at 36° or 40° Bé, and which receives a hollow cylinder of pulverized coke, molded and cemented at a high temperature by sugar, gum or tar. At the upper end of this cylinder, where it does not dip into the acid, a copper collar is fixed, which may be tightened at will by means of a screw. A copper band or ribbon is fixed to the collar, and may be connected with the zinc of another element. A porous porcelain sell is placed inside the coke cylinder, and contains a dilute solution of sulphuric acid, (1 part acid and 9 parts water), into which is put a bar or cylinder of zinc, strongly amalgamated or covered with mercury. When a battery of several elements is to be formed, the coke of the first element is connected with the zinc of the second, and so on, and the apparatus is completed at one end by coke communicating with the anode, and at the other by a zinc connected with the cathode or object to be electro-plated·

A modification of Bunsen's battery, which is preferred by gold and silver electro-platers, is as follows: Each element is composed of an exterior vessel or pot, most generally of stoneware; a cylinder of zinc, covered with mercury, provided with a binding screw or with a copper band, whether for a single element or for the end of a combination of elements in a battery, or to connect the zinc with the carbon of another element; a porous cell of earthenware pipe or porcelain; a cylinder of graphite, made from the residue found in old gas retorts. The graphite is bound by a copper band fixed to it by means of a wire of the same metal, all the binding being afterwards covered with a thick varnish to protect it from the acid fumes of the battery; notwithstanding the varnish, the acid may rise by capillary attraction and corrode the copper band between the carbon and the wire; therefore binding screws of various shapes and sizes should be used to connect the carbon or zinc, by means of ribbons or wires. Use conducting wires of pure copper, covered with silk, cotton, india rubber or gutta-percha, and preventing the metal at their extremities in order to effect the connections. Other batteries, such as Daniell's, Grove's, Smee's, etc., are used, but for a description of these and the dynamo-electric machines the readers is referred to works on this subject.

Batteries should be placed in a room where the temperature does not vary greatly. Frost arrests their action, and great heat increases it too much.

No matter what battery be used, there are several preliminary conditions that must be complied with in order to produce satisfactory results, *i. e.* that the deposition may adhere firmly and take place uniformly. It is absolutely necessary that the pure metallic surface of the article be exposed, and that it be perfectly free from grease. The articles to be plated, if lustrous surfaces are desired, must first be ground and polished. The grease must be removed from the surface by boiling in potash or caustic soda, and this is followed by scouring with freshly burnt lime, pulverized thoroughly and free from all grit. If the article will not stand heat, cleanse with benzine. In order to free the surface of non-metallic substances, if the article be of iron, steel or silver, dip it in a mixture of 1 part by weight of sulphuric acid to 15 of water; if copper or brass, the articles are first dipped in dilute sulphuric acid, and then in a mixture of 100 parts, by weight, of nitric acid, 50 of sulphuric acid, 1 of common salt and 1 of soot. As soon as the surface of the article assumes a bright appearance, it is washed in clean water once or twice, avoiding handling with the fingers or greasy cloths. Wooden plyers, kept clean, serve well for handling.

Avoid the injurious fumes produced by the acids, by operating in the open air or in the draft of a chimney. In order to determine whether the article is entirely free from grease, dip it into water, and if all grease is removed, the water will adhere uniformly, if, however, lines and spots appear, the article is not thoroughly clean, and must again be put through the cleansing process.

Gold Baths. Both warm and cold baths are used, the former being preferable as they yield denser depositions, require less strength of current and need not be so rich in gold as cold baths. Baths often differ with the tastes of the electroplater so that it is difficult to state what is the best. However, the bath prepared with potassium cyanide is very extensively used by the trade and is considered the most profitable. In purchasing your chloride of gold where possible, get the brown neutral variety as it is preferable to others as it contains less acid.

A good warm bath, Brannt says, is prepared as follows: Neutral chloride of gold, 0.35 oz.; 99 per cent potassium cyanide, 0.7 oz.; and water 1 quart. Dissolve the potassium cyanide in one-half of the water and the chloride of gold in the other half; mix both solutions and boil for half an hour, replacing the water lost by evaporation. An excess of potassium cyanide in the gold bath must be avoided, as it causes a pale color in the gilding. As anodes it is best to use sheets of fine gold, which gradually dissolve, and thus convey fresh metal to the bath. The current must not be so strong that a formation of bubbles is perceptible; it is best to use a current of such strength only that deposition takes place slowly, a coating of the greatest density being thus obtained. Avoid using cheap and inferior chemicals as the difference in price is more than offset by the loss of time and damage that often results from inferior grades. To obtain good results always use as pure water as possible, filtered rain water being the most desirable. The best temperature for cold baths is 66° F. Care should also be taken to see that the baths are covered with cloths to exclude dust and where it does penetrate, the baths should be skimmed off.

Only copper, brass and bronze, can be directly gilded, other metals must first be coppered or brassed; this applies to good work. In gilding parts of watches, gold is seldom directly applied upon the copper, there is generally a preliminary operation called graining by which a slightly dead appearance is given to the articles. They are thoroughly finished, all grease removed as described above,—threaded upon a brass wire, cleansed in the compound acids for a bright luster and dried in sawdust. The pieces are fastened upon the flat side of a piece of cork by means of brass pins and the parts are thoroughly rubbed over with a clean brush dipped in a paste composed of fine pumice stone powder and water. The brush is moved in circles in order to rub evenly. Thoroughly rinse in clean water in order to remove every particle of pumice stone, both from the article and the cork. Place the whole in a weak mercurial solution, composed of nitrate of mercury $\frac{1}{16}$ oz.; water $2\frac{1}{4}$ gal.; sulphuric acid $\frac{1}{2}$ ι .; which will slightly whiten the copper. Pass quickly through this solution and then rinse. After the parts are grained in the manner described, they may be gilded the same as ordinary work. For the production of a thick deposit frequent scratch-brushing of the articles is absolutely necessary, the brush being moistened with a decoction of soap-root or solution of tartar.

Red Gold. To obtain red gold, a solution of copper cyanide in potassium cyanide are added in small portions until the desired tone is obtained; it may also be obtained by suspending a few copper anodes beside of the gold anodes.

Green Gold. To obtain green gold add cyanide or chloride of silver dissolved in potassium cyanide, or suspend silver anodes beside of the gold anodes.

Dead Luster. This is affected by various means. The article to be plated, may by the means of acids, be given a dead luster surface before plating or it may be effected by the slow deposit of a large quantity of gold. The latter is the more desirable but most expensive. If the article be of brass it may be dipped in a mixture of 3 parts of nitric acid, containing 1 part of zinc in solution, with 8 parts of pure, strong, nitric acid and 8 parts of boiling sulphuric acid. After the effervescence has ceased the brass is taken out and is found to have assumed a dead brown surface. After being drawn through strong nitric acid it assumes a lustrous surface.

Imitation Damaskeen in Gold and Silver. A beautiful effect is produced on iron and steel objects by imitation damaskeen in gold or silver. First copper the entire surface of the articles and by means of liquid asphalt trace upon their surfaces the figures or lines to appear in gold or silver. By then dipping the articles into a solution of chromic acid, the coppering is dissolved where it is not protected by the asphalt. The asphalt is then removed by the application of oil of turpentine, and the gilding executed in the usual manner. The same result is achieved with platinum articles by substituting nitric for chromic acid.

Silver Baths. Brannt says, that for ordinary galvanic silvering 0.35 oz. of fine silver (= 0.56 oz. of nitrate of silver, or 0.47 oz. of chloride of silver), is dissolved in a solution of 0.7 oz. of 98 per cent potassium cyanide in 1 quart of water. For heavy silvering of knives, forks, etc., a stronger bath is used: 0.88 oz. of fine silver, (= 1.17 oz. of chloride of silver, or 1.03 oz. of cyanide of silver,) is dissolved in a solution of 1.75 oz. of 98 per cent. potassium cyanide in 1 quart of water. No accurate statement can be made in regard to the content of potassium cyanide in the bath, as it depends on the strength of the current used. With a very weak current, and consequently slow precipitation, somewhat more potassium cyanide may be used than with a stronger current and more rapid precipitation. The anodes, for which fine silver is used, will indicate by their appearance whether the bath contains too much or too little potassium cyanide. They should become gray during silvering, and gradually reassume their white color after the interruption of the current. If they remain white during silvering, the bath contains too much potassium cyanide, and, if they turn black, and retain this color after the interruption of the current, potassium cyanide should be added.

The articles to be silvered should be moved constantly to avoid the formation of streaks. Before silvering the metals must be prepared by amalgamation. This is done by dipping the articles, previously freed from grease, as explained above, in a dilute solution of mercurous nitrate (30 to 150 grains per qt.); allowing them to remain in the solution only long enough to become uniformly white. Rinse them in water, brush off with a clean soft brush, and immediately place in the silver bath. Steel, iron, zinc, tin, nicked and Britannia ware must first be coppered and then amalgamated before being placed in the bath.

The articles remain in the bath from ten to fifteen minutes, when they show a uniformly white surface; they are then taken out, scratch-brushed with a brass brush to see that the deposit adheres, all grease removed, and then placed in the bath. After the current is shut off, the articles should be left in the bath a few seconds to prevent the deposit from turning yellow.

If the articles are not to be burnished, but are to be left with a mat as they come from the bath, they must be thoroughly rinsed in water without coming in contact with the fingers or the sides of the vessel, then dipped in clean hot water and hung up to dry. They then should be coated with a colorless laquer to prevent turning yellow. If the articles are to have a polished surface, they are to be finally scratch-brushed with frequent moistening with soap-root, dried in warm sawdust and burnished with a steel or stone burnisher.

Nickel Baths. Iron and steel must be prepared by immersing in a hot solution of caustic soda or potash, thoroughly brushed, rinsed in water and dipped in a pickle of 1 part sulphuric acid, 2 parts hydrochloric acid and 10 parts of water, again rinsed, thoroughly rubbed with fine well washed pumice stone or Vienna lime, again rinsed and put in the bath. If finely polished tools, they may be brushed with whiting or tripoli instead of pumice stone. Copper wire should be tightly wound around all metal articles. Small articles may be suspended from copper hooks. The battery or dynamo is placed in action before immersing the articles, which remain in the bath until they have acquired a white appearance, which will be in from five to thirty minutes, depending on the strength of the current and the size of the article. In case the article assumes a gray or black color, or feels rough and gritty, the current is too strong, or if it assumes a yellowish white appearance, it is too weak. The simplest nickel bath consists of a solution of pure double sulphate of nickel and ammonium 8 to 10 parts by weight in 100 parts of distilled water. Boil the salt in a corresponding quantity of water, say 8 to 10 parts of nickel salt to 100 of water, depending on the temperature. With this bath cast nickel anodes and a strong current should be used. The article after its removal from the bath should be dipped for a few seconds in boiling water, drained and dried in warm sawdust. They may then be polished, but cannot be burnished. The luster on nickel-plated objects depends greatly on the polish given them before plating. The composition of nickel baths depends greatly upon the metals to be operated on which can best be determined by experiment. The anodes should be suspended by strong hooks of pure nickel wire, and the articles should be placed at a distance of from $3\frac{1}{4}$ to $4\frac{1}{4}$ inches from them. If the article is to receive a thick deposit it should be turned in the bath from time to time, from end to end, so that these portions which were down come up. Small articles which cannot be suspended are placed in a sieve, it being preferable to use a heated bath for the purpose. Iron, steel, copper, brass and bronze are usually nickeled directly, but Britannia ware, zinc and tin are coppered or brassed before nickeling. In case a freshly prepared bath yields a dark deposit it can generally be remedied by working the bath for two or three hours.

Doctoring. This term is applied to plating defective places which occurred either by accident or negligence on the part of the operator. It is equally applicable to gold, silver or nickel plated articles. Take a piece of the anode, be it gold, silver or nickel, about the size of your little finger, and connect it with the positive pole by a thin copper wire. Around this anode wrap a piece of ordinary muslin several times; hold the defective article on the top of the positive pole, and after dipping the anode in the solution until the muslin is thoroughly soaked, move it to and fro over the defective place, and a coating is thus formed.

Aluminum Baths. Reinbold's formula for an aluminum bath which is said to give excellent results is as follows: In 300 parts, by weight, of water, dissolve 50 parts of alum, and to this add 10 parts of aluminum chloride. Heat to 200° F. and when cold, add 39 parts of cyanide of potassium. Use a feeble current. Aluminum is one of the most difficult and uncertain of metals to deposit electrically.

Brass Baths. Carbonate of soda 10½ ozs.; water 10 qts.; neutral acetate of copper 4¼ ozs.; chloride of zinc 4¼ oz.; bisulphate of soda 7 ozs.; potassium cyanide, 98 per cent, 14 oz., arsenious acid 30¾ grs. Dissolve the carbonate of soda in 5 qts. of the water, and then add gradually the bisulphate of soda. Now stir together the acetate of copper and chloride of zinc with 2 qts. of the water, and slowly and with constant stirring, pour the mixture into the solution of the soda salts. Add the solution of potassium cyanide in 3 qts. of water, then the arsenious acid, and boil the whole for a few hours, replacing the water lost by evaporation; when cold filter the solution.

Copper Baths. The composition of these baths must depend on the purposes for which they are to be used. The acid copper bath is used for plastic deposits of copper, but cannot be used for the electro-positive metals, zinc, iron, tin, etc., as they decompose the solution and separate from it pulverulent copper, while an equivalent portion of zinc, iron, etc. is dissolved. Alkaline baths are therefore exclusively employed with these metals.

A good bath is prepared by Brannt as follows: Water, 10 qts.; crystallized bisulphate of soda, 7 oz.; crystallized carbonate of soda, 14 oz.; neutral acetate of copper, 7 oz.; potassium cyanide, 75 per cent, 7 ozs.; spirit of sal-ammoniac 4.4 ozs.

In order to get a good copper deposit on wax figures, etc., brush the figure with alcohol, and then brush with finely pulverized plumbago with a soft hair brush, until the plumbago is thoroughly incorporated into the surface of the object. Place a copper wire in the wax figure and work the plumbago thoroughly over it with the brush, so as to make a perfect electric connection between the wire and the wax coating. A saturated solution of sulphate of copper, (blue vitriol), and water is then made, stirred frequently and left to stand for 24 hours before using. A copper anode is used and is attached to the carbon or copper pole of the battery and the wax object, by means of its wire is attached to the zinc pole.

Recovery of Gold from Bath. To recover gold from bath evaporate the bath to dryness, mix the residue with litharge and fuse the mixture. A lead button is thus formed in which all the gold is contained. Dissolve the button in nitric acid, and the gold will remain behind in the form of small flakes. Filter off and dissolve the flakes in aqua regia.

Recovery of Silver from Bath. To recover silver from cyanide bath; evaporate the bath to drynesss, mix the residue with a small quantity of calcined soda and potassium cyanide and fuse in a crucible, and the metal will be found in the form of a button in the bottom of crucible.

Recovering Gold From Coloring Bath. Dissolve a handful of sulphate of iron in boiling water, and add it to your "color" water; it precipitates the small particles of gold. Now draw off the water, being very careful not to disturb the auriferous sediment at the bottom. You will now proceed to wash the sediment from all traces of acid with plenty of boiling water; it will require three or four separate washings, with sufficient time between each to allow the water to cool and the sediment to settle, before passing off the water. Then dry in an iron vessel by the fire and finally fuse in a covered skittle pot with a flux.

A Grained or Matted Surface on Brass. Dissolve a little table salt in a mixture of equal parts of nitric and sulphuric acids. The articles are to be well ground and thoroughly cleaned. They are then suspended by a horsehair in the solution for a few seconds. They are then withdrawn and afterwards dipped into hot water, after which they are scratch brushed with beer, for which operation you can use a brush of brass or German silver. This being done the parts are silvered with ease, and again scratch brushed and then gilt. In this manner an equally grained surface of a uniform and desirable color is obtained. This method is equally applicable to articles of copper or German silver. A coarser grain can be obtained by the addition of a little more salt.

Gilding Steel. Steel may be gilded by means of a solution of gold and ether. To do this a quantity of gold is dissolved in nitro-muriatic acid, and then boiled until the liquid evaporates, when the residue is dissolved afresh in water, to which is added 3 times as much sulphuric ether. The liquid is then left for 24 hours in a bottle, tightly corked, after which time it will be seen to float on the surface of the water. If the steel is then dipped into it, it will become gilded immediately, and if designs have been painted on the surface of the metal with any varnish, a beautiful specimen of a steel and gilded surface is obtained. For other metals the galvanic process is employed.

Nickel Plating Without a Battery. The article to be plated must be free from rust or greasy matter, and the chemicals be pure. Prepare a weak solution of chloride of zinc containing about 5 to 10 per cent. of the salt—say 1 to 2 ounces of the chloride to 98 or 99 ounces of water. To this add enough sulphate of nickel to turn the solution a deep green color; the solution is then heated to the boiling point in a Wedgewood or other porcelain vessel. Next suspend the object in the water for half an hour, when a brilliant white coating will be formed; then wash the article and carefully dry it. Articles thus plated will bear light cleaning with whiting. The solution may then be poured off, filtered, and used again with a small addition of the chloride of zinc and the sulphate of nickel. In like manner, a covering of cobalt may be obtained by using sulphate of cobalt in place of sulphate of nickel. The color of the cobalt is very nearly like that of polished steel, with a slight rose tint, but it does not rust.

Nickel Plating by Boiling. Prepare a bath of pure granulated tin, tartar and water, which heat to the boiling point, and add a small quantity of pure red hot nickel oxide. A portion of the nickel is soon dissolved, as is shown by the green color assumed by the liquid which stands upon the grains of tin. If articles of copper or brass are plunged into the bath, they become covered in a few minutes with a white, beautiful silvery metalic coating, which consists almost entirely of pure nickel. If a little carbonate or tartrate of cobalt is added to the bath, a bluish shade, either light or dark, may be given to the coating, which becomes very brilliant when it is properly polished with chalk or dry sawdust.

Aniline Bronzing Fluid. A bronzing fluid which is said to be very brilliant, and appliable to all metals, as well as to other substances, is prepared as follows: Take 10 parts of aniline red, and 5 parts of aniline purple, and dissolve in 100 parts of 95 per cent alcohol, accelerating the solution by placing the vessel in a sand or water bath. Solution having been effected, add 5 parts of benzoic acid, and boil for from 5 to 10 minutes, until the greenish color of the mixture has been converted into a fine, light-colored bronze, which is applied with a brush and dries quickly.

Antique Bronze. The green stain of verdiris can be given to bronze by covering the spots to be discolored with ground horse radish saturated with vinegar, and keeping the mixture wet with vinegar, until the stain has become fixed. This will require some days, for though the discoloration will show after a few hours, it will be superficial and vanish by wiping. Three or four days will, however, turn your bronze into an antique, so far as appearances go.

Antique Green. An imitation of antique bronze can be applied to new articles by the following process: Dissolve 3 parts of common salt, 1 part of sal-ammoniac and 3 parts of powdered tartar in 12 parts of boiling water. Add 8 parts of a solution of cupric nitrate, and coat the articles with the liquid.

Black Bronze for Brass. 1. Dissolve 1 oz. of copper carbonate in $8\frac{3}{4}$ fluid ounces of spirit of sal-ammoniac. Add one pint of water an stir constantly. The articles to be colored should be suspended in the liquid by means of brass or copper wires for a short time. The coating adheres better if the articles are polished with coarse emery paper.

2. Brush the brass with a diluted solution of nitrate of mercury, and then several times with a solution of liver of sulphur.*

Black Stain for Gun Barrels. Polish the barrel thoroughly and coat by means of a woolen rag, with a very thin layer of olive oil, and then dust over with hardwood ash. Heat over glowing coals and allow it to cool slowly; when cool brush over with water containing a few drops of hydrochloric acid to the pint and then quickly wash in water. The iron portions of the damaskeened barrels will appear black while the steel portions will come out white. The barrel is then dried and finally rubbed with oil.

Blue Bronze. Cleanse the metal from all grease by dipping in boiling potash lye and afterwards treat it with strong vinegar. Wipe and dry the article thoroughly and

---

*Fused sulphuret of potassium, so called from its resemblance to liver in color.

rub it with a linen rag, moistened with hydrochloric acid. Allow the coating to dry for a quarter of an hour, and then heat the article on a sand bath, until it assumes the desired color, when it should be removed.

Blue Stain for Iron and Steel. Make a mixture of hydrochloric acid 16 parts, fuming nitric acid 8, and butter of antimony 8. The hydrochloric acid should be added to the other ingredients a drop at a time to avoid heating. Apply the mixture to the metal (after thoroughly polishing with lime) with a rag, and rub with a piece of green young oak wood until the desired color is produced.

Bronze for Copper. In 100 parts of acetic acid of moderate concentration, or in 200 parts of strong vinegar dissolve 30 parts of carbonate or hydrochlorite of ammonium and 10 parts each of common salt, acetate of copper and cream of tarter. Rub the object with the solution and allow it to dry for forty-eight hours. The object will then be found entirely covered with verdigris. Brush with a waxed brush and especially the relieved portions.

Bronze for Small Brass Articles. Oxide of iron, 3 parts; white arsenic, 3 parts; hydrochloric acid, 36 parts. Clean the brass thoroughly and apply with a brush until the desired color is obtained. Oil well and finish by varnishing or lacquering.

Bronze Liquid. Dissolve sal-ammoniac, 1 oz.; alum, ½ oz.; arsenic, ¼ oz.; in strong vinegar, 1 pt. The compound is immediately fit for use, and, where the metal is good, is seldom found to fail.

Bronze for Medals. The following process of bronzing is carried on in the Paris mint. Powder and mix 1 pound each of verdigris and sal-ammoniac. Take a quantity of this mixture, as large as a hen's egg, and mix into a dough with vinegar. Place this in a copper pan (not tinned), boil in about 5 pints of water for 20 minutes, and then pour off the water. For bronzing, pour part of this fluid into a copper pan, place the medals separately in it upon pieces of wood or glass, so that they do not touch each other, or come in contact with the copper pan, and then boil them in the liquid for a quarter of an hour.

Bronze for Steel. Methylated spirit, 1 pint; gum shellac, 4 ounces; gum benzoine, ½ ounce. Set the bottle in a warm place, with occasional agitation. When dissolved, decant the clear part for fine work, and strain the dregs through muslin. Now take 4 ounces powdered bronze green, varying the color with yellow ochre, red ochre and lamp black, as may be desired. Mix the bronze powder with the above varnish in quantities to suit, and apply to the work, after previously cleansing and warming the articles, giving them a second coat, and touching off with gold powder, if required, previous to varnishing.

Brown Bronze. Brown bronze is prepared the same as blue bronze, but the blue bronze is finally rubbed over with a linen rag saturated with olive oil, which will change the blue color into brown.

Brown Stain for Copper. To produce a dark-brown color upon copper, take the white of an egg, beat it into froth, add a little boiled or rain water, and add to this mixture *caput mortuum* (red oxide of iron); rub them well together in a mortar, and sufficiently thick until the color covers, and may be applied. The copper articles are to be pickled and simply washed; no sand must be used, else the color adheres badly. The latter is next applied with a brush until it covers the surface; it is then dried by a fire, the article is gently rubbed with a soft rag and *caput mortuum* powder, and finally hammered with a hammer with polished face.

Brown Stain for Gun Barrels. Mix 12 parts of a solution of sulphate of iron, 16 parts of sulphate of copper, 16 parts of sweet spirit of nitre and 12 parts of butter of antimony. Let the mixture stand in a well corked bottle for twenty-four hours and then add 500 parts of rain water.

Thoroughly polish and clean the barrels, wash with fresh lime water, dry thoroughly and apply the mixture evenly with a piece of cotton. After drying for twenty-four hours, brush with a scratch brush and repeat the coating. Do this twice, the last time using leather moistened with olive oil in lieu of the scratch brush, rubbing thoroughly. After standing for ten or twelve hours, repeat the polishing with sweet oil and leather until a beautiful polish is obtained.

Chinese Bronze. Small articles bronzed by this process possess a peculiar beauty, and lose none of their lustre, even when exposed to atmospheric influences and rain. Powder and mix thoroughly 2 parts of crystalized verdigris, 2 parts of cinnabar, 2 of sal-ammoniac, 2 of bills and livers of ducks, and 5 of alum. Moisten the mixture with water or spirit of wine, and rub it into a paste, cleanse the article to be bronzed thoroughly, and polish it with ashes and vinegar. Then apply the paste with a brush. Heat the article over a coal fire, and wash the coating off. Repeat this operation until the desired brown color is obtained. By adding blue vitriol to the mixture, a chesnut brown color is produced, while an addition of borax gives a yellowish shade.

Gold Bronze for Iron. Dissolve 3 ounces of finely powdered shellac in $1\frac{3}{4}$ pints of spirit of wine. Filter the varnish through linen and rub a sufficient quantity of Dutch gold with the filtrate to give a lustrous color to it. The iron, previously polished and heated, is brushed over with vinegar, and the color applied with a brush. When dry the article may be coated with copal lacquer to which some amber lacquer has been added.

Gold Tinge to Silver. A bright gold tinge may be given to silver by steeping it for a suitable length of time in a weak solution of sulphuric acid and water, strongly impregnated with iron rust.

Gold-Yellow Color on Brass. A gold like appearance may be given to brass by the use of a fluid prepared by boiling for about 15 minutes, 4 parts caustic soda, 4 parts milk sugar, and 100 parts water, after which 4 parts of a concentrated solution of sulphate of copper is added with constant stirring. The mixture is then cooled to 79° C., and the previously well cleaned articles are for a short time laid into it. When left in it for some time they will first assume blueish and then a rainbow color.

Gray Stain for Brass. Many black and gray pickles possess the defect that they give different colors with different copper alloys, while in the case of certain alloys they refuse to act altogether. For instance, carbonate of copper, dissolved in ammonia, gives to brass a handsome, dark-gray color, while it does not whatever attack various other alloys; therefore it is little suitable for instruments. A dark-gray pickle, which almost indiscriminately stains all copper alloys a handsome gray, resembling in color the costly platinum, is composed by dissolving 50 grams arsenic in 250 grams hydrochloric acid, and adding to the solution 35 grams chloride of antimony and 35 grams finely pulverized hammer scales. The articles to be pickled are rinsed in a weak, warm soda solution, prior to as well as after immersion, to be followed by continued rinsing in water. The recipe is simple, and has been repeatedly tested with uniformly good results.

Green Bronze for Brass. Add to a solution of $8\frac{1}{2}$ drachms of copper in 1 ounce of strong nitric acid, $10\frac{1}{2}$ fluid ounces of vinegar, $3\frac{1}{2}$ drachms of sal-ammoniac, and $6\frac{3}{4}$ drachms of aqua-ammonia. Put the liquid in a loosely corked bottle, and allow it to stand in a warm place for a few days, when it may be used. After applying it to the articles, dry them by exposure to heat, and when dry, apply a coat of linseed oil varnish, which is also dried by heat.

Imitation of Antique Silver. The article is dipped in a bath of water containing about 10 per cent. of sulphide of ammonium, and then scratch-brushed with a brush made of glass threads or bristles. When afterward burnished with an agate tool its surface becomes a beautiful dark brown color.

Oxidizing Silver. 1. Place the silver or plated articles in a solution of liver of sulphur diluted with spirit of sal-ammoniac. They are then taken out, washed, dried and polished. This process produces a blue-black tint, while a solution of equal quantities of sal-ammoniac and blue vitriol in vinegar gives a brown shade.

2. Sal-ammoniac, 2 parts; sulphate of copper, 2 parts; saltpeter, 1 part. Reduce these ingredient to a fine powder, and dissolve in a little acetic acid. If the article is to be entirely oxidized, it may be dipped for a short time in the boiling mixture; if only in parts, it may be applied with a camel-hair pencil, the article and the mixture both being warmed before using.

3. There are two distinct shades in use, one produced by chloride, which has a brownish tint, and the other by sulphur, which has a bluish-black tint. To produce the former it is only necessary to work the article with a solution of sal-ammoniac; a much more beautiful tint, however, may be obtained by employing a solution composed of equal parts of sulphate of copper and sal ammoniac in vinegar. The fine black tint may be produced by a slightly warm solution of sulphate of potassium or sodium.

Silvering for Copper or Brass. 1. Mix 1 part of chloride of silver with 3 parts of pearl ash, 1½ parts common salt, and 1 part whiting; and well rub the mixture on the surface of brass or copper (previously well cleaned), by means of a piece of soft leather, or a cork moistened with water and dipped in the powder. When properly silvered, the metal should be well washed in hot water, slightly alkalized, then wiped dry.

2. Mix three parts of chloride of silver with 20 parts finely pulverized cream of tartar, and 15 parts culinary salt. Add water in sufficient quantity, and stir until the mixture forms a paste, with which cover the surface to be silvered by means of blotting paper. The surface is then rubbed with a rag and powdered lime, washed, and rubbed with a piece of soft cloth. The deposited film is extremely thin.

Silvering Small Iron Articles. The small iron articles are suspended in dilute sulphuric acid until the iron shows a bright clean surface. After rinsing in pure water, they are placed in a bath of a mixed solution of sulphate of zinc, sulphate of copper, and cyanide of potassium, and there remain until they receive a bright coating of brass. Lastly they are transferred to a bath of nitrate of silver, cyanide of potassium, and sulphate of soda, in which they quickly receive a coating of silver.

Silver Plating Without a Battery. 1. The process consists in exposing the article, which has previously been well cleansed with a potash solution and dilute hydrochloric acid, to the operation of a silver bath, which is prepared in the following manner: Form a solution of 32 grams (1 oz., 13.8 grains) nitrate of silver, 20 grams silver (12 dwts., 20.6 grains) in 60 (1 oz., 18 dwts., 13.9 grains) grams nitric acid, the silver is precipitated as silver oxide with a solution of 20 grams solid caustic potash in 50 grams (1 oz., 12 dwts., 3.6 grains) distilled water, carefully washed, and the precipitate taken up by a solution of 100 grams (3 oz., 4 dwts., 7.2 grains) cynide of potassium in 500 grams distilled water. The fluid, distilled through paper, is finely diluted with distilled water to 2 liters (4½ pints). The thus prepared silver bath in gently warmed in the water bath, and the article to be silver plated laid in it and kept in motion for a few minutes, and after taking out it is dried in sawdust, and then polished with Vienna chalk for giving luster.

2. For rapid silver plating, prepare a powder of 3 parts of chloride of silver, 20 parts carefully pulverized cream of tartar, and 15 parts pulverized cooking salt; mix it into a thin paste with water, and rub it upon the well cleaned metallic surface with blotting paper. After you are certain that all parts of the article have been touched alike, rub it with very fine chalk powder or dust upon wadding or other soft cloth. Wash with clean water and dry with a cloth.

3. Dissolve 1 oz. nitrate of silver, in crystals, in 12 oz. soft water; then dissolve in the water 2 oz. cynide of potash, shake the whole together, and let it stand until it becomes clear. Have ready some half-ounce vials, and fill half full with Paris white, or fine whiting, and then fill up the bottles with the

liquid, and it is ready for use. The whiting does not increase the coating power, it only helps to clean the article, and save the silver fluid, by half filling the bottles.

4. Make a solution of 4 ounces lunar caustic (equal to a solution 2½ ounces silver in 7½ ounces nitric acid); the silver of this solution is precipitated as oxide of silver by the addition of a solution of 2½ ounces of caustic potash in 6½ ounces distilled water; and the precipitate, after being washed, is added to a solution of 12½ ounces of cynide of potassium in one quart of water. This solution is then filtered and water added to bring it to 4 quarts. In this solution, which is heated on the water bath, the pieces to be silvered are left for a few minutes. Being agitated, they are taken out, and put to dry in fine sawdust and then polished.

Steel-Blue on Brass. Dissolve 1½ drachms of antimony sulphide and 2 ounces of calcined soda in ¾ pint of water. Add 2¾ drachms of kermes, filter, and mix this solution with another of 2¾ drachms of tartar, 5½ drachms of sodium hyposulphite and ¾ pint of water. Polished sheet brass placed in the warm mixture assumes a beautiful steel-blue.

To Give Copper a Durable Luster. Place the copper articles in a boiling solution of tartar and water for fifteen minutes. Remove, rinse off with cold water and dry.

EMERY. The dark colored and non-transparent variety of corundum. See *Corundum.*

EMERY COUNTERSINKS. See *Countersinks.*

EMERY FILES, PENCILS AND STICKS. Emery files are to be had ready made from all material dealers and consist of wooden handles to which emery cloth is glued. Emery pencils are kept by some dealers and will be found very useful for grinding the inside of metal objects, and also on small work of various kinds, being easy to handle, clean and light. Emery sticks are of two kinds, solid square sticks and round and square sticks of wood to which emery paper or cloth is glued. Emery paper and cloth may be had from most material dealers, varying from 0000 to No. 4.

EMERY WHEELS. Wheels of solid emery or wooden wheels, to the surface of which emery paste has been applied. The best wheels for watchmakers use are the solid wheels in which vulcanite is the cementing medium. They may be had from material dealers generally or from dental supply houses, in sizes varying from ½x⅛ in. to 3½x¾ in. A set of three or more of these wheels will prove very valuable adjuncts to the watchmakers bench for grinding dials to allow freedom of motion for wheels in fitting new dials; for grinding milling cutters, drills, gravers, etc. As purchased from dealers these wheels have a central hole, by means of which they can be mounted for use by the watchmaker as follows: Turn down a piece of No. 30, Stubs' steel wire, to the size of the opening in your wheel and rivit your wheel firmly upon it, as shown in Fig. 94. It can then be used in your lathe very handily, either with or without water. The best sizes for watchmakers use are ½ in., 1 in. and 1½ in. diameter. *L.*

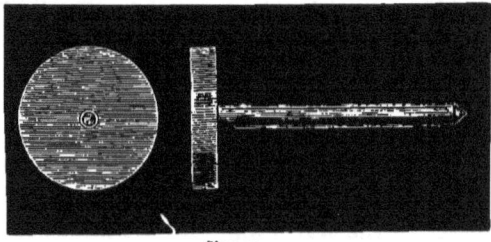

FIG 94.

END STONE. The small stone disc on which a watch pivot rests, applied principally to escapement and balance pivots. Jewels with end stones are known as capped jewels.

ENGINE TURNING. The wavy, curved lines used as decorations for watch cases.

ENGRAVING BLOCK. A mechanical device for holding coins, jewelry, silverware, etc., while engraving. Fig. 95 is the usual form given to engraving blocks and is known as the flat base variety. Fig. 96 has what is known as the cannon-ball base, but the holding devices are similar to the flat base. Various attachments are furnished for holding rings, spoons, coins, etc.

EPICYCLOID. A curve generated by a point in the circmference of a movable circle, as it rolls upon another circle. *Webster.* The teeth of driving wheels are usually of this form.

EQUATION OF TIME. The difference between mean and apparent time. *Webster*

ESCAPEMENT. The mechanical device in a watch or clock by which the motion of the train is controlled so that the power may be dispelled uniformly. Saunier divides

FIG. 95.   FIG. 96.

escapements into three principal classes; Recoil, Dead Beat and Detached. I. Recoil escapements are so classed, because at a certain period of this action, the wheel moves backward or recoils in a manner more or less marked. The verge escapement in watches and certain forms of the anchor in clocks, may be used as examples.

II. Dead Beat escapements are so called because except during the actual impulsion, the wheel remains stationery, a point being supported either against the axis of the balance itself, or against the accessory piece, concentric with this axis, which catches it in its movement of rotation. The cylinder and duplex escapements in watches and the pin and Graham escapements in clocks are examples of this class.

III. Detached escapements may be called Dead Beat escapements, but their principal characteristic consists in the fact that the balance performs its vibration in absolute independence of the wheel, except during the very brief periods of impulse and unlocking. The wheel, then, does not rest on the axis of the balance, but on an intermediate and distinct piece. The lever escapement in watches, the detent escapement in chronometers, as well as several forms of escapements employed in clocks, come under this head. See *Anchor, Chronometer, Cylinder, Dead Beat, Duplex, Graham, Pin Pallet, Pin Wheel and Verge.*

ESCAPE PINION. The pinion on the escape wheel staff.

ESCAPING ARC. Twice the angular distance a pendulum has to be moved from its point of rest, in order to allow a tooth of the escape wheel to pass from one pallet to the other. *Britten.*

EYE GLASS. Eye glasses for watchmaker's use are mounted in many different styles. Some have horn, others have vulcanite and still others cork mountings. The vulcanite mounted glass with a light spring attached to sustain it in place is very popular with apprentices. The Clark patent glass, shown in Fig. 97, is becoming very popular in this country. It is provided with an annular reflector, with a central opening and corrugations, and so seated in the outer end of the glass as to reflect the rays of light falling on the outside of it in front of the glass, and concentrating them upon the object being viewed. It is especially useful in examining the inside of watches, as it often occurs that it is difficult to get light sufficient to do so.

FIG. 97.

FERRULE. The small pulley or wheel around which the string of a bow is wound when giving motion to a piece of work. See also *Collet.*

FILES. Files for watchmakers use are made in every conceivable shape, and in sizes from that of a fine cambric needle to 1 x ¼ in. The various styles are known as flat, pillar, joint, three-cornered, knife, round, half round, oval, square, smooth cut, barrette, warding, conical, slitting, pivot, ratchet, screwhead, escapement, etc. Escapement files are usually put up in sets of twelve assorted shapes as shown in Fig. 98, and are chiefly used by finishers in watch factories. The average American has a tendency to be extravagant, and in no trade or calling is this extravagance better exemplified than in that of the watchmaker and particularly in the matter of files. Many watchmakers benches will be found, in the drawers of which, from one to two dozen files will be found, and out of all that number, not to exceed six will be in anything like respectable shape for good work. This is not occasioned by the poor quality of the goods used in this country, because eight out of every ten files used by watchmakers, are French, Swiss or English manufacture, and cost the American more money than his European brother, but rather from a careless handling of these tools, from a want of training.

FIG. 98.

The skilled European watchmaker serves a long apprenticeship to a master who insists that he first becomes proficient in the use of the file, then the graver, etc., before he is allowed to work upon a clock or watch. In this way he acquires a proficiency in the use of tools which the average young American watchmaker is a stranger to. The American watchmaker will employ a new file upon steel work, whereas, the European first employs a new file in working brass or copper and even then handles it very carefully. He would no more think of using a new file upon steel work than he would of flying. A new file is carefully used, and gradually advanced from a soft to a hard metal, will at the end of six months, be a much better file for steel work than a new one, and will last four times as long.

When the surface of a file becomes choked with particals of steel, iron or brass, Saunier advises that it be cleaned as follows: Place the file for a few seconds in hot potash and water, and on withdrawal, dry it before the fire and brush the surface with a stiff brush. If the file has a tendancy to fill up, slightly oil the surface by means of a linen rag.

FILING BLOCK. A contrivance made to take the place of the filing rest, which was made of boxwood or bone. It consists of a cylinder of hardened steel which revolves upon a staff which in turn enters a split socket. The surface of the steel cylinder is grooved with various sizes of grooves for the different sizes of wire, or to suit any work, as shown in Fig. 99. The cylinder is revolved until the desired size groove is brought uppermost, when the split socket is placed between the jaws of a vise, and the vise closed, thus holding the cylinder in the desired position. Fig. 99 illustrates Mr. Ide's patent block which is well made and of superior material.

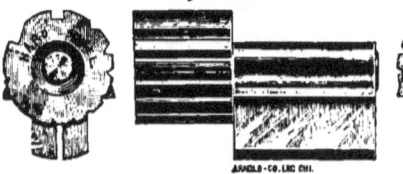

FIG. 99.

FILING FIXTURE OR REST. These rests will be found very convenient in squaring winding arbors, center squares, etc. There are several makes of these tools, but they are all built upon the same principle, that of two hardened steel rollers on which the file rests, and Fig. 100 is a fair example. One pattern is made to fit in the hand rest after the T is removed, while the other is attached to the bed of the lathe in the same manner as the slide rest. The piece to be squared is held in the split or spring chuck in the lathe, and the index on the pulley is used to divide the square correctly. Any article can be filed to a perfect square, hexagon or octagon as may be desired. The arm carrying the rollers can be raised or lowered as required for adjustment to work of various sizes.

FIG. 100.

FLUX. A mixture or compound to promote the fusion of metals; used in assaying, refining and soldering, as alkalies, borax, etc.

FLY OR FAN. A fan having two blades used for preserving the uniformity of motion, as in music boxes and the striking mechanism of clocks. The resistance of the air on the fan blades prevents the train from accelerating.

FOLLOWER. Where two wheels are toothed together the one that imparts the power is known as the driver, and the one receiving the power is called the follower.

FOOT WHEEL. In the selection of a foot wheel the workman must be governed by his own experience and taste, for like cigars the variety that exactly suits one person is very distasteful to another. Some workman prefer a treadle having a heel and toe motion, while others prefer a swing treadle like that shown in Fig. 101.

FOURTH WHEEL. The wheel that imparts motion to the escape pinion, the second hand being attached to its staff.

FRICTION. The resistance which a moving body meets with from the surface of the body on which it moves and is caused by the unevenness of the surfaces, combined with some other causes, such as natural attraction, magnetism,

FIG. 101.

etc. It varies as does the weight or pressure applied and is independent of surfaces in contact, but if the surfaces are disproportionate to the pressure, rapid abrasion will be the result, which in its turn produces uneven surfaces and tends to increase the friction. In order to prevent the abrasion of the surfaces a lubricant is applied, either in the shape of oil or plumbago, which spreading itself over the surfaces of the bodies interposes a film between the two acting surfaces, and this film, especially in light bodies, has a greater retarding influence than mere friction itself. In such cases the acting surfaces are made very minute, as in balance, staff-pivots, etc. In these pivots the resistance arising from the lubricant is usually greater than that of the friction proper, and it gradually increases as the lubricant become viscid. For this reason plumbago is advocated as a lubricant in large machines, as it does not become viscid and is an excellent lubricant. It is not applicable, however, for watch or clock work. From the above it is apparent that a light bodied or thin lubricant is desirable on small bearings, such as balance pivots, while as the barrel or power is approached and larger surfaces used the lubricant should be of a heavier body, or thicker. The nearer that a revolving surface is to its center of motion the less the friction. It is therefore essential when extra surface is desired that the surfaces be *increased in length*, and that the *diameter* of a pivot *be not increased* for if the *diameter* be doubled the resistance is doubled, as the acting surface is twice the distance from the center of motion.

FRICTIONAL ESCAPEMENTS. Those escapements in which the balance is never free or detached from the escapement. In contradistinction to the detached escapement, the duplex, cylinder or verge are examples of frictional escapements.

FROSTING. The matted or rough surface sometimes given to work before gilding or silvering. See *Electro-Plating*, *Bronzing and Staining*. The gray surface produced on steel work of watches is also known as frosting, though more commonly called graying.

FULL PLATE. A term applied to movements having a full top plate and the balance above the plate.

FUSEE. A brass cone, as shown in Fig. 102, having a spiral groove cut on it to hold the chain, and interposed between the barrel and the center pinion of a watch for the purpose of equalizing the pull of the mainspring and converting it into a constant pressure at the center pinion, for the pull of the mainspring is greater when wound around the barrel arbor than when it has expanded to the circumference

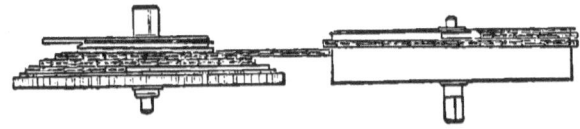

FIG. 102.

of the barrel. The principal of its construction is that by winding the fusee chain upon its cone the mainspring is wound, and the greatest pull comes upon the smaller end of the cone, and as the pull becomes less by the unwinding of the mainspring, the leverage (by means of the chain unwinding from a smaller to a larger cone) increases, and the rate of its increase constitutes a perfect adjustment of the mainspring. The fusee is held in great esteem by English watchmakers and possesses many excellent points, although not employed in any American made watch.

Repairing Watch Fusee Top Pivot.* First file up and re-polish the square, taking off the corners sufficiently to prevent them standing above the pivot when it is re-polished. Put the square into an eccentric arbor and get the fusee quite true. Now put a screw ferrule on to the fusee back arbor, and place the whole piece in the turns with the eccentric in front, using the bow on the ferrule at back. If the pivot is much cut it should be turned slightly with the point of the graver. Polish first with steel and coarse stuff, afterwards with bell-metal and fine stuff, and finish with the glossing burnisher.

---

*H. B. in Britten's Hand Book.

To put in a Watch Fusee Top Hole.* Put the pillar plate in the mandril and peg the bottom hole true, then turn out the top hole to the required size for stopping. The stopping (a hollow one) should be small, and no longer than just sufficient to form the rivet. If there be danger of bending the plate, the stopping should be softened slightly (the hammering will re-harden it), and the ends turned hollow to facilitate the riveting. The top hole is now to be turned to nearly right size for the pivot, testing it frequently for truth with the peg, as much broaching is especially to be avoided. In finishing the stopping use polished cutters, take off the corners of the hole, and polish the cup or chamfer for the oil with peg and redstuff. The same procedure is to be followed with ¾-plate fusee, and it will be found best to finish the stopping in fusee piece before screwing the steel on to the brass. Be careful to give the fusee but little end shake; if it be at all excessive the stop work and the maintaining work will become uncertain, and either or both may fail.

GAS HEATER. This heater, shown in Fig. 103, is to take the place of a forge in heating and tempering small articles. With a full pressure of gas, a piece of steel half an inch in diameter can be heated sufficiently to harden in about six minutes. It does not heat to a degree that will injure the quality of steel; which makes it very valuable for heating small pieces. Watchmakers will find in its use great convenience as well as economy of time and fuel; and also, that tools heated by it will be tougher than when heated in a forge in the usual way.

FIG. 103.

Put on sufficient gas to prevent the flame from descending into the tube. For heating larger pieces the flame should be nearly three inches wide. The upper ends of the curved side pieces should not be more than one quarter of an inch apart. The article to be heated should be held in the upper

---

*H. B. in Britten's Hand Book.

part of the flame above the central blue part and parallel with it. The larger the piece to be heated the further it should extend into the flame. The heater should be located in a dark place, and supports may be provided for greater convenience in heating heavy articles.

GAUGE. An instrument for determining dimensions or capacity. The watchmaker cannot be too careful in the selection of his measuring instruments, as accuracy and perfection in watchmaking is an essential element to success. Accuracy is more essential than finish, though both are desirable; still a movement that is accurate may be a fine timekeeper, although it may be lacking in finish and not artistic to look upon. Measuring instruments of all kinds should be handled with care, and in the more delicate ones cleanliness also plays an important part. You cannot expect accurate results from a fine Vernier caliper that is recklessly thrown into a heap of other tools upon the bench. It should be carefully handled, and when you are through using it you should carefully wipe it and place it in some drawer in your bench where it will not be mutilated by being jambed against other tools.

Dennison's Standard. There are few tools so useful to practical watchmakers as the Dennison Standard Gauge, shown

FIG. 104.

in Figs. 104 and 105. Aside from the mistakes it often enables the workman to avoid, it is useful, inasmuch as the habit of measurement once acquired, he will seldom rely on guess. Nos. 1 and 3 are intended for measuring the width of mainsprings. It is very important to know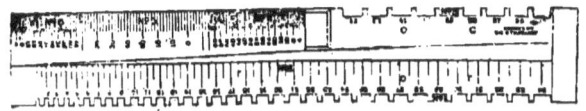

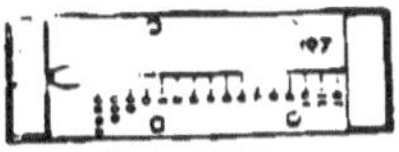

FIG. 105.

that a mainspring is of the right width, and also whether it is equal in its measurement. No. 2 is for diameters of pinions, wire, etc. No. 4 is for diameters of wheels, 5 diameters of crystals, 6 verges, etc., and 7 is a steel thickness gauge, which fastened to the back and will measure the smallest pivot.

Douzieme. A measuring tool having two limbs hinged together similar to a pair of scissors. One of the limbs terminates in a pointer that indicates upon a scale the extent to which the jaws are opened. The true Douzieme gauge has a scale divided into twelfths, though some patterns are now made that have a scale divided into tenths and hundreds of an inch, and again there are others that measure the fractions of a millimeter. This tool is useful for taking measurements of all kinds. For example, we will suppose that the watchmaker is putting in a new balance staff; we will take it for granted that the upper part of the staff is entirely finished and that he is ready to find the total length that the staff should be. He takes the top plate with the balance cock and potance attached, and measures the distance from the top of cock hole jewel to top of potance hole jewel by means of this gauge. He places the jaw *a* on potance jewel and *b* on cock jewel, and notes the number on the scale that the pointer is opposite, which is generally 30 for an 18 size full plate American movement.

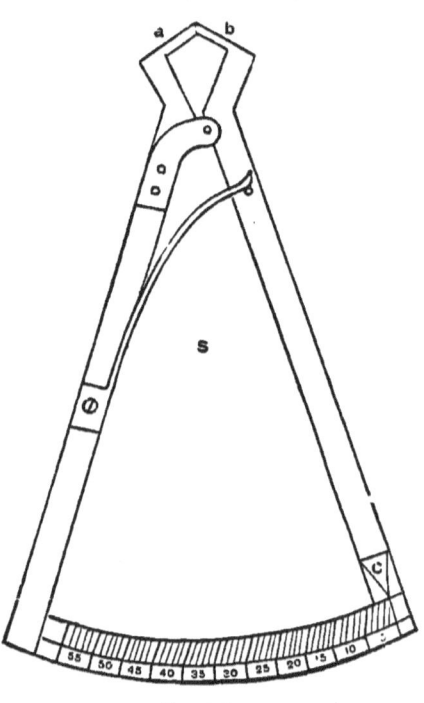

FIG. 106.

Micrometer Caliper. Fig. 107 is a full size cut of the Brown & Sharp Mfg. Co.'s micrometer caliper. It measures from one-thousandth of an inch to one-half inch. It is graduated to read to thousandths of an inch, but one-half and one-quarter thousandths are readily estimated. This instrument is also graduated to hundredths of a millimeter, but when so graduated the table of decimal equivalents is omitted. They are also made to read to ten-thousandths of an inch. The edges of the measuring surfaces are not beveled, but are left square, as it is more convenient for measuring certain classes of work. It will gauge under a shoulder, or measure a small projection on a plain surface. Watchmakers will especially appreciate micrometers of this form. This tool will be found very useful for gauging mainsprings, pinions, etc. In the caliper, shown by cut, the gauge or measuring screw is cut on the concealed part of the spindle C, and moves in the thread tapped in the hub A; the hollow sleeve or thimble D is attached to the spindle C, and covers and protects the gauge screw. By turning the thimble, the screw is drawn back and the caliper opened.

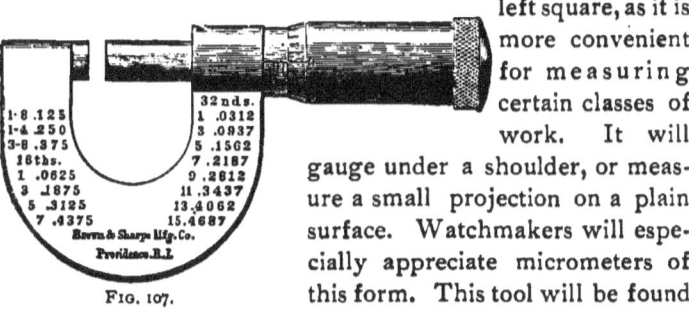

FIG. 107.

The pitch of the screw is 40 to the inch. The graduation of the hub A, in a line parallel to the axis of the screw, is 40 to the inch, and is figured 0, 1, 2, etc., every fourth division. As the graduation conforms to the pitch of the screw, each division equals the longitudinal distance traversed by the screw in one complete rotation, and shows that the caliper has been opened 1-40th or 0.25 of an inch. The beveled edge of the thimble D is graduated into 25 parts, and figured every fifth division 0, 5, 10, 15, 20. Each division, when passing the line of graduation on Hub A, indicates that the screw has made 1-25th of a turn, and the opening of the caliper increased 1-25th of 1-40th, or a thousandth of an inch.

GAUGE.

Hence, to read the caliper, multiply the number of divisions visible on the scale of the hub by 25, and add the number of divisions on the scale of the thimble, from zero to the line coincident with the line of graduations on hub. For example: as the caliper is set in the cut, there are three whole divisions visible on the hub. Multiplying this number by 25 and adding 5, the number of divisions registered on the scale of the thimble, the result is eighty-thousandths of an inch. (3×25=75+5=80.) These calculations are readily made mentally.

TABLES FOR USE IN CONNECTION WITH MICROMETER CALIPERS

DIMENSIONS OF WIRE GAUGE SIZES IN DECIMAL PARTS OF AN INCH.

No. of Wire Gauge.	Size of each No. in decimal parts of an inch of the American Wire Gauge.	Size of each No. in decimal parts of an inch of the Birmingham Wire Gauge.	No. of Wire Gauge.	Size of each No. in decimal parts of an inch of the American Wire Gauge.	Size of each No. in decimal parts of an inch of the Birmingham Wire Gauge.
0000	.460	.454	19	.03589	.042
000	.40964	.425	20	.03196	.035
00	.36480	.380	21	.02846	.032
0	.32486	.340	22	.02535	.028
1	.28930	.300	23	.02257	.025
2	.25763	.284	24	.0201	.022
3	.22942	.259	25	.0179	.020
4	.20431	.238	26	.01594	.018
5	.1×194	.220	27	.01419	.016
6	.16202	.203	28	.01264	.014
7	.14423	.180	29	.01126	.0.3
8	.12849	.165	30	.01002	.012
9	.11443	.148	31	.00893	.010
10	.10189	.134	32	.00795	.009
11	.09074	.120	33	.00708	.008
12	.08081	.109	34	.0063	.007
13	.07196	.095	35	.00561	.005
14	.06408	.083	36	.005	.004
15	.05707	.072	37	.00445	
16	.05082	.065	38	.00396	
17	.04525	.058	39	.00353	
18	.0403	.049	40	.00314	

GAUGE.

DECIMALS EQUALING PARTS OF AN INCH.

$\frac{1}{64}=.0156$	$\frac{11}{64}=.1718$
$\frac{1}{32}=.0312$	$\frac{3}{16}=.1875$
$\frac{3}{64}=.0468$	$\frac{13}{64}=.2031$
$\frac{1}{16}=.0625$	$\frac{7}{32}=.2187$
$\frac{5}{64}=.0781$	$\frac{15}{64}=.2343$
$\frac{3}{32}=.0937$	$\frac{1}{4}=.2500$
$\frac{7}{64}=.1093$	$\frac{17}{64}=.2656$
$\frac{1}{8}=.1250$	$\frac{9}{32}=.2812$
$\frac{8}{64}=.1406$	$\frac{19}{64}=.2968$
$\frac{5}{32}=.1562$	$\frac{5}{16}=.3125$

Pinion and Wire Gauge. The jewelers' gauge shown in Fig. 108 will be found very useful in measuring pinions, wire or flat metal. The slot is graduated to thousandths of an inch. If in measuring a pinion it passes down tale slot to number AO, then the pinion is $\frac{70}{1000}$ of an inch in diameter.

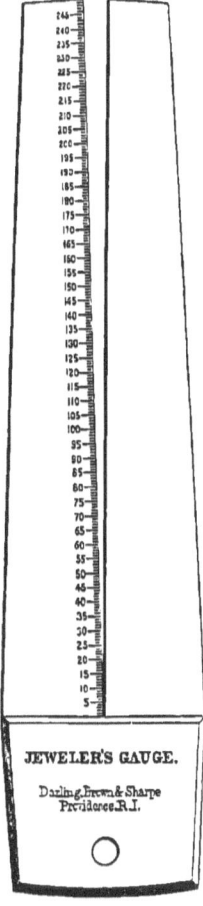

FIG. 108.

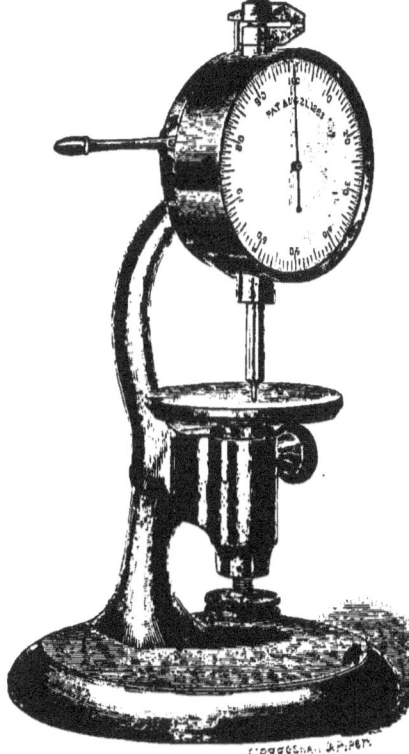

FIG. 109.

Registering Gauge. The registering gauges shown in the illustrations are two of the best examples of this class of tools. They are manufactured by A. J. Logan, Waltham, Mass., and are very accurate and nicely finished. Fig. 109 is an upright and jaw gauge, and Fig. 110 is designated as a jaw and

FIG. 110.

depth gauge. They are both made to gauge one one-thousandth of a centimeter or one one-thousandth of an inch. Fig. 110 shows the piece of work marked A, being gauged, while B represents a stationary spindle to get the depth of a hole or recess or the thickness of any piece of work which will be indicated on the dial.

Staff Gauge. The tool shown in Fig. 111, the invention of Mr. E. Beeton, is designed for measuring the height of the balance staff from the balance seat to the end of the top pivot. The illustration is enlarged to give more distinctness.

E E' is a piece of curved steel about $\frac{1}{20}$ of an inch thick, and $\frac{1}{8}$ of an inch wide. On the lower side from E' to the end the arm is filed down in width and thickness to correspond to an ordinary balance arm; C is a slot in the upper arm E, which allows A, B, D, A' to be moved backward and forward. *D D'* is a round brass post drilled and tapped; the part *D'* has a thread cut on it, and the part shown in the slot *C* fits with easy friction. *B* is a locknut, drilled and tapped to fit the thread on *D'*. It is for the purpose of clamping *D D'* against the arm *E*. *A A'* is a small steel screw with milled head, and is made to fit the tapped hole in *D D'*.

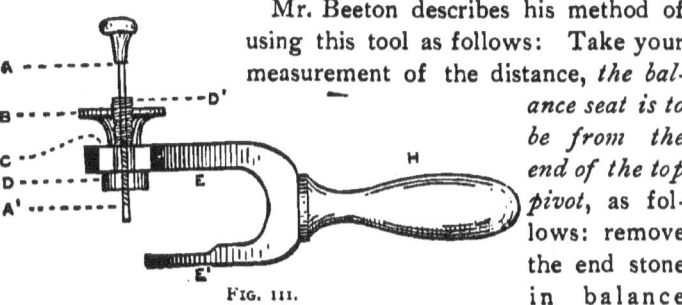

FIG. 111.

Mr. Beeton describes his method of using this tool as follows: Take your measurement of the distance, *the balance seat is to be from the end of the top pivot*, as follows: remove the end stone in balance cock, and screw the cock on the top plate, (18-size full plate movement) then taking the plate in your left hand, and tool (shown is Fig. 111) in your right, place *H* in position, so that the end of the screw *A'* rests on the jewel in the balance cock, and notice the position of the arm *E'* which corresponds to the balance arm, between the top plate and under side of balance cock. If the distance between the arm *E'* and end of screw *A'* is too great, the arm *E'* will be too low and touch the plate; if not enough, it will be too high and touch the regulator pins. Therefore, all that is necessary to do is to move the screw *A A'* up or down as the case may be, sufficiently to ensure that the arm *E'* will assume the position the *arm of the balance* is to have. Take an 18-size balance with oversprung hairspring, the arm is at the bottom of the rim, in that case, when measuring, the screw *A'* is adjusted so as to bring the arm *E'* close to the plate, when *A'* is resting on the balance jewel; if the balance is old style with under sprung hair-spring, the balance arm is at top of rim, in which case *A'* is adjusted so that the arm *E'* is close to the balance cock; if the balance arm is in the center of the rim, as in some English and Swiss balances, the screw *A'* is adjusted so that the arm *E'* is midway beween the plate and cock.

The reason the part A, B, D, A', is arranged to move laterally in slot C is, because all balance shoulders are not the same distance from the center, and where, in some cases, the screw A' would be in a line with the center of the staff when the arm E' was resting on the balance seat, in other cases it would reach past the center, of course, short of it; and, therefore, it is made adjustable to suit all cases.

Staff Length Gauge. Another form of staff gauge, which is very simple, and which any watchmaker can manufacture is made as follows: Procure a small tube of steel, or make one from steel wire, thread it on the inside, and screw into each end a small steel plug as shown in Fig. 112, until the ends of the plug meet, cut off the outer end of plugs so as to leave the total length that of a short staff; harden, draw to a blue, place in a split chuck, plugs and all, and turn a pivot of good length on each plug. Flatten the sides of the plugs at the base of the pivots, so that they may be readily turned in or out by the aid of tweezers. By inserting this tool in the place of the balance, and screwing the plugs to the right position, screwing bridge down, and adjusting until the right end-shake is obtained, you can ascertain in a moment the exact length that the staff should be over all, which can easily be transferred to calipers and thence to the new staff.

FIG. 112.

Staff or Cylinder Height Gauge. The obvious advantage of this tool, which is shown at Fig. 113, is the automatic transfer of the measurement so that it may be readily applied to the work in hand. The tool, as the illustration shows, consists of a brass tube terminating in a cone-shaped piece. To the bottom of this cone is attached a disc through which a needle plays. Around the upper end of the tube is a collar upon which is fixed a curved steel index finger. A similar jaw, which is free to move, works in a slot in the tube. The movable jaw is tapped and is propelled by a screw that terminates in the needle point. This tool is very useful in making the necessary measurements required in putting in a staff. To use it in this work, set the pivot of the gauge through the foot hole, and upon the end-stone project the needle such a distance as you wish the shoulder to be formed above the point of the pivot. Next set the gauge in the foot hole as before, and elevate the disc to a height that shall be right for the roller, which is done by having the lever in place, the little disc showing exactly where the roller should come. Finish the staff up to that point, then take the next measurement from the end-stone to where the· shoulder should be, for the balance to rest upon. This point being marked, the staff can be reversed and measurements commenced from the upper end-stone, by which to finish the upper end of the staff. Distances between the shoulders for pinions and arbors can be obtained with the same facility, a little practice being the only requisite.

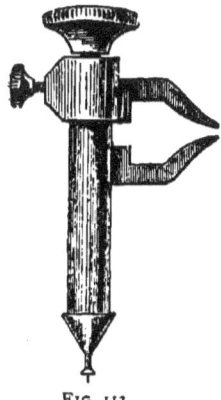

FIG. 113.

Twist Drill and Steel Wire Gange. This gauge which is shown in Fig. 114 will be found very useful in

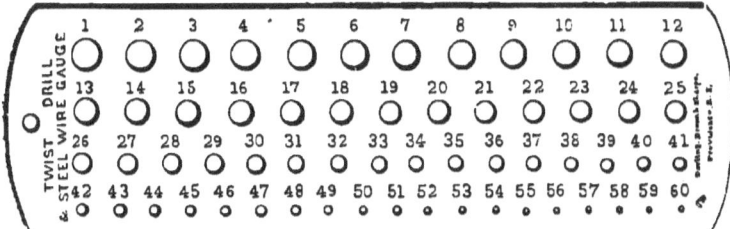

FIG. 114.

determining the diameter of twist drills and steel wire, and is very accurately and nicely made.

Vernier Caliper. Fig. 115 is an illustration of the Vernier Caliper, a light, convenient and valuable instrument for obtaining correct measurements. The side represented in the illustration is graduated upon the bar to inches and fiftieths of an inch, and by the aid of a Vernier is read to thousandths of an inch, (see description below). The opposite side is graduated to inches and sixty-fourths of an inch. The outside of the jaws are of suitable form for taking inside measurements, and when the jaws are closed, measure two hundred and fifty thousandths of an inch in diameter.

These instruments can be furnished with millimetres, (in the place of sixty-fourths of an inch), and provided with a Vernier to read to one-fiftieth of a millimetre.

On the bar of the instrument is a line of inches numbered 1, 2, 3, each inch being divided into tenths, and each tenth into five parts, making fifty divisions to one inch. Upon the sliding jaw is a line of divisions, (called a Vernier, from the

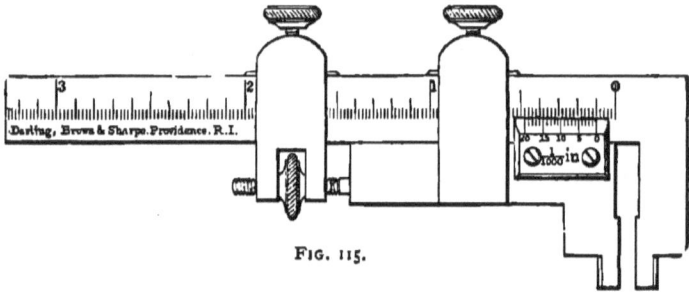

FIG. 115.

inventor's name), of twenty parts, figured 0, 5, 10, 15, 20. These twenty divisions on the Vernier correspond in extreme length with nineteen parts, or nineteen-fiftieths on the bar, consequently each division on the Vernier is smaller than each division on the bar, by one thousandth of an inch. If the sliding jaw of the caliper is pushed up to the other so that the line 0 on the Vernier corresponds with 0 on the bar, then the next two lines to the left will differ from each other one thousandth of an inch, and so the difference will continue to increase one thousandth of an inch for each division till they again correspond on the twentieth line on the Vernier. To read the distance the caliper may be open, commence by noticing how many inches, tenths and parts of tenths the zero point on the Vernier has been moved from the zero point on the bar. Then count upon the Vernier the number of divisions until one is found which coincides with one on the bar, which will be the number of thousandths to be added to the distance read off on the bar. The best way of expressing the value of the divisions on the bar is to call the tenths one hundred thousandths (.100) and the fifths of tenths, or fiftieths, twenty thousandths (.020). Referring to the accompanying cut it will be seen that the jaws are open one tenth of an inch, which is equal to one hundred thousandths (.100). Suppose now, the sliding jaw was moved to the left, so that the first line on the Vernier would coincide with the next line on the bar, this would then make twenty thousandths (.020) more to be added to one hundred thousandths (.100), making the jaws then open one hundred and twenty thousandths (.120) of an inch. If but half the last described movement was made, the *tenth line on the Venier* would coincide with a line on the bar, and would then read, one hundred and ten thousandths (.110) of an inch.

GILDING. (See *Electro-Plating*.)

GIMBALS. A contrivance for securing free motion while in suspension of a ship's chronometer, compass, etc., so that it may not be affected by the motion of the ship. It is virtually a universal joint. It was invented by Cardan and first applied to timepieces by Huygens.

GORING BARREL. A barrel having teeth around its circumference for driving the train. All American watches are of the goring barrel type.

GORING FUSEE. A fusee having the maintaining power attachment. All modern fusees have a maintaining power which drives the train while the fusee is being wound. Examples of old fusees are, however, occasionally met with which have no maintaining power and the watch is stopped during the operation of winding.

GOLD ALLOYS. (See *Alloys.*)

To Distinguish Genuine from Spurious Gold. Genuine gold dissolves in chlorine water and the solution has only a slightly yellowish color. Hence chlorine is a safe agent to distinguish genuine from spurious gold. To test the genuineness of gilt articles, rub a tiny drop of mercury on one corner of the surface to be examined; it will produce a white, silvery spot if the gold is pure, or if there is gold in the alloy. If this silvery spot does not appear there is no gold in the surface exposed. To prove the correctness of this result a drop of the solution of nitrate of mercury can be dropped on the surface, when a white spot will appear if the gold is counterfeit, while the surface will remain unaltered if the gold is genuine. After the operation, heating the article slightly will volatize the mercury and the spots will disappear. Pure gold can be distinguished from its alloys by a drop of chloride of gold or of nitrate of silver. If the gold is pure there will be no stain, but if mixed with other metals the chloride of gold will leave a brownish stain upon it and the nitrate of silver a gray stain. The simplest means of distinguishing genuine gold from a gold-like alloy consists in running the article to be tested against an ordinary flint until a lustrous metallic coloring remains upon the latter. Now hold a strongly sulphurated burning match against the coloring; if it disappears from the flint the article is not gold. *Brannt.*

GOLD SPRING. A very thin spring made of gold attached to the detent of a chronometer escapement. *See Chronometer Escapement.*

GRAHAM ESCAPEMENT. A dead beat escapement or one in which the escape wheel does not recoil. It was invented by George Graham early in the eighteenth century, and is used in regulators and fine clocks. For regulators and other clocks with seconds pendulum, says Britten, this escapement, which is shown in Fig. 116, is the one most generally approved. The only defect inherent in its construction is that the thickening of the oil on the pallet will affect the rate of the clock after it has been going some time. Notwithstanding this it has held its own against all other escapements on account of its simplicity and certainty of action. The pallets of the Graham escapement were formerly made to embrace fifteen teeth of the wheel, and until recently ten, but now many escapements are made as shown in the drawing, with the pallets embracing but eight. This reduces the length of the impulse plane and the length of run on the dead face for a given arc of vibration, and consequently the relative effect of the thickening of the oil. The angle of impulse is kept small for the same reason. There is not much gained by making the pallets embrace a less number of teeth than eight, for the shake in the pivot holes and inaccuracies of work cannot be reduced in the same ratio, and are therefore greater in proportion. This involves larger angles and more drop. It is purely a practical question, and has been decided by the adoption of eight teeth as a good mean for regulators and fine clocks where the shakes are small. For large clocks of a rougher character, ten teeth is a good number for the pallets to embrace.

TO SET OUT THE ESCAPEMENT.

Draw a circle representing the escape wheel to any convenient size, and assuming the wheel to have 30 teeth and the pallets are to embrace eight of them, set off on each side of a centre line, by means of a protractor, 45°. Lines drawn from the centre of the escape wheel through these points will pass through the centre of impulse faces of the pallets; thus, 360 (number of degrees in the whole circle) divided by 30 (proposed number of teeth) = 12, which is the number of degrees between one tooth and the next. Between 8 teeth there are seven such spaces and 12 × 7 = 84, and 84 + 6 (half of one space = 90), the number of degrees between the centres of the pallets. The proper position for the pallet staff centre will be indicated by the intersection of tangets to the wheel circle drawn from the centres of the pallets. But it happens that a tangent of 45°=the radius, and, therefore, the practical method adopted is to make the pallet arms from the staff

GRAHAM ESCAPEMENT. 170

hole to the center of impulse face equal to the radius of the escape wheel. If we take the radius of wheel to be $= 1$, it will be found that with the pallet arms this length, the height of the pallet staff hole from the centre of the wheel will be 1.41, and the horizontal distance between the impulse faces of the pallets will be 1.41 also.

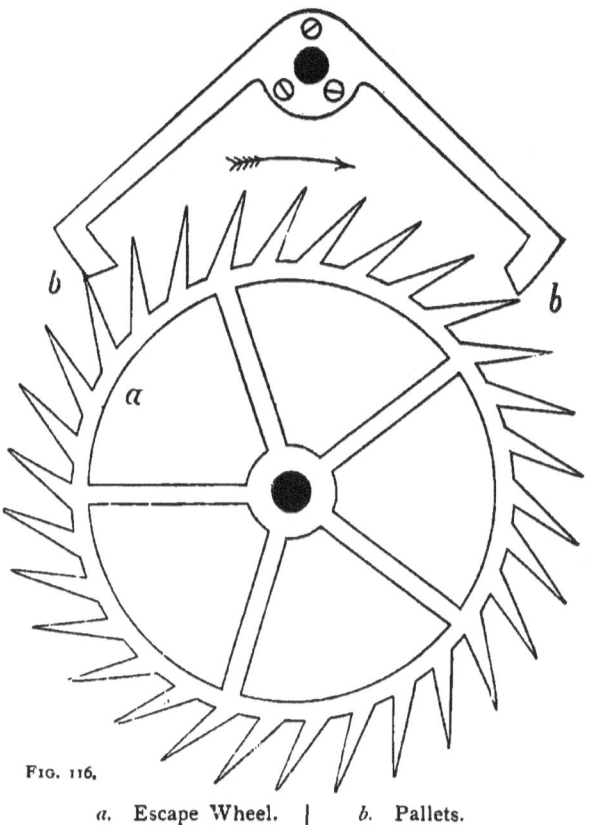

FIG. 116.

a. Escape Wheel. | b. Pallets.

The width of each pallet is equal to half the distance between one tooth and the next, less drop, which need not be much if the escape wheel teeth are made thin as they should be. The dead faces of the pallets are curves struck from the pallet staff hole. The escaping arc = two degrees, is divided into $1\frac{1}{2}°$ of impulse and $\frac{1}{2}°$ of rest; $1\frac{1}{2}°$ of impulse is quite enough if the escapement is properly made, and if increased beyond 2°, it will be at the cost of the time keeping properties of the clock from the effect of the thickening of the oil aready referred to.

From the centre of the wheel set off two radial lines barely 3° on each side of the radial lines already drawn to mark the centre of the pallets. Then strike the curved dead faces of the pallets just touching the radial lines last drawn.

Now from the pallet centre draw lines through the spot where the curved locking face of each pallet cuts the wheel circle. If you look at the engraving you will see that a wheel tooth is resting on the left-hand pallet. The amount of this rest is $\frac{1}{2}°$, as already stated. Mark off this $\frac{1}{2}°$, which gives the position of the locking corner of the pallet, and then set off another line $1\frac{1}{2}°$, below it, which will mark the spot for the other corner of the pallet. On the right-hand pallet, the line already drawn marks the extreme corner, and it is only necessary, in order to get the locking corner, to set off a line $1\frac{1}{2}°$ ABOVE it.

The wheel teeth diverge from a radial line about 10°, so that their tips only touch the dead faces of the pallets.

For escaping over ten teeth, the distance between the centre of the wheel and the centre of the pallet staff should be equal to the diameter of the wheel; with this exception the preceding directions are applicable for setting out.

The wheel is of hard hammered brass, and for regulators is made from an inch and a half to two inches in diameter, and very light. The pallets are usually of steel, nicely fitted to the arbor, and, in addition, screwed to a collet thereon as shown. In the best clocks the acting faces are jeweled. Sometimes the pallet arms are cast of brass, and the pallets formed of solid jewels. Many good clockmakers put two banking pins in the plate, one on each side of the crutch, to prevent the pallets from being jammed into the wheel by careless handling.

GRAVER.   172

The Graham escapement requires a heavy pendulum especially if the train is comparatively rough. The clock weight must be sufficient to overcome increased resistance arising from inaccuracy of work; consequently, when the train runs freely, so much extra pressure is thrown upon the dead faces of the pallets that a light pendulum has not enough energy to unlock, and the clock stops. For clocks with shorter than half-seconds pendulums the pallets are generally made "half dead," that is the rests, instead of being curves struck from the pallet staff hole, are formed so as to give a slight recoil to the wheel.

GRAVER. A steel cutting tool used for engraving, turning, etc. The "Guaranteed" engravers, shown in Fig. 117, are unique from the fact that they cut at both ends; the handle (which is patented) is so adapted that it will accommodate the reverse end of innumerable size and shapes of gravers. The various angles of points of the gravers are very excellent and cover the entire field as used both for turning and engraving.

FIG. 117.

Use of the Graver.* The beginner should first practice on hard wood, then brass, iron, steel and hardened and tempered steel, progressing from one material to the other as his ability warrants. He should turn for a long time with the *point* of a square or lozenge-shaped graver, the end of which is ground off on a slope; this is the only possible method of learning to turn *true*, and it enables the workman to acquire great delicacy of touch. Owing to carelessness or to the fact that when first beginning they were set to work on metal that was too hard or rough, most beginners turn with gravers that are ground to very blunt points; as the graver bites less they are obliged to apply a proportionately increased pressure, and only succeed in tearing the metal away, subjecting it to a kind of rolling action and rendering the hand heavy. If a pupil will not practice turning with the graver point so as to preserve it intact for some time, dependent on the nature of the metal, he will never be able to turn perfectly true. Irregular and sudden depressing of the graver point, or engaging it too deeply, causes its frequent rupture.†

When sufficient experience has been gained in turning with the graver point and a trial is made with the cutting edge, do not attempt much at a time by pressing heavily, but take the metal sideways so as to remove a continuous thread, using all the points of the edge in succession. The metal will thus be removed as a thin ribbon or shaving. When the hand has had some experience, it will be found easy to remove long strips.

Hardened steel that has been drawn down to a blue temper requires certain precautions. If the graver is found not to cut cleanly, it must at once be sharpened, and no attempt should be made to remove more metal by increasing the pressure of the hand, because the steel will burnish and become hard under a point or edge that is blunt, and the portions thus burnished are sometimes so hard as to resist the best gravers. The only way of attacking them is to begin at one

---

* The directions apply to the use of the graver as a turning tool only. For directions for engraving on gold, silver, copper, etc., the reader is referred to an excellent work by G. F. Whelpley entitled "General Letter Engraving," price $1.25, Geo. K. Hazlitt & Co., Chicago.

† See illustrations and directions for holding graver, under heading *Making Balance Staff*.

side with a fine graver point which must be sharpened frequently; at times it becomes necessary to temper the metal afresh before it will yield. It is well to moisten the point of the graver with turpentine.

Apprentices and even watchmakers themselves are frequently careless as to the proper sharpening of their gravers, and think that they can hasten their work by the application of considerable pressure; in this way they sometimes produce bright spots that require several hours work before they can be removed. A majority of Swiss workmen turn indifferently with the right or left hand. This is a very useful accomplishment, easily acquired when young.

GRAVIMETER. An instrument for ascertaining the specific gravity of liquid or solid bodies.

GRAVITY. The tendancy which a body has towards the center of the earth.

Specific Gravity. The ratio of the weight of a body to the weight of an equal volume of some other body taken as the standard or unit. This standard is usually water for solids and liquids, and air for gasses. Thus 19, the specific gravity of gold, signifies that gold is 19 times heaver than water. *Webster.*

GRAVITY ESCAPEMENT. An escapement in which the train raises a lever a constant distance, and the weight of the lever when returning to position gives impulse to the pendulum. The double three-legged variety was invented by E. B. Denison in 1854. Gravity escapements are particularly applicable to turret clocks.

GREAT WHEEL. The wheel on the fusee arbor which drives the center pinion. The largest wheel in a watch or clock. *Britten.*

GUARD PIN. See *Safety Pin*.

GYRATE. To revolve around a central point. See *Center of Gyration.*

HAIR SPRING. The spring that determines the time of vibration of the balance. The term hair spring is distinctively American, as all other nations use the more fitting appellation of Balance Spring. The different forms of hair springs are illustrated in Fig. 118. The most common form is the volute or spiral spring, shown at A. B. is a helical spring used in chronometers. C. is a Breguet spring, which is a flat spiral with its outer end bent up above the plane of the body of the spring, and carried in a long curve towards the center, near which it is fixed. The advantage of the Breguet spring is that it distends when in action, on each side of the

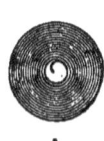

ELEVATION   PLAN
A   B   C
FIG. 118.

center, thus relieving the balance pivots of the side pressure which the ordinary flat spring tends to give, and it also offers opportunities of obtaining isochronism by varying the character of the curve. Glasgow says that a hair spring, of whatever form, to be isochronous must satisfy the following conditions: its center of gravity must always be on the axis of the balance, and it must expand and contract in the vibrations concentrically with that axis. Immish contends that mere length of spring has nothing to do with isochronism. Mr. Glasgow contends that the whole question of isochronism resolves itself into the adoption of a spring of the correct length, and recommends for a lever watch fourteen turns if a flat, and twenty turns if a Breguet spring is used, if a cylinder watch use from eight to twelve turns. He argues that if a spring is too short, the short vibrations will be fast and the long vibrations slow, and that all bending and manipulation of the spring with a view to obtain isochronism are really only attempts to alter the effective length of the spring. Mr. Britten contends that the position of the points of attachment of the inner and outer turns of a hair spring in relation to each other has an effect on the long and short vibrations quite apart from its length. For instance, a very different performance may be obtained with two springs of precisely the same length and character in other respects, but pinned in so that one has exactly complete turns, and the other a little under or a little over complete turns. He argues that a short spring as a rule requires to be pinned in short or complete turns, and a long one beyond the complete turns. In duplex and other watches with frictional escapements, small arcs of vibration and short springs, it will be found that the spring requires to be pinned in nearly half a turn short of complete turns.

HAIR SPRING STUD INDEX. Wathier's Self-adjusting Hair Spring Stud Index, shown in Fig. 119, is a very useful device, and by its use the watchmaker can save much time and can obtain better results than by following the regular methods of determining when a movement is in beat. Place the lower part of balance staff in round cleat A. Turn balance until ruby pin comes over oblong hole at B. Now let the balance down until roller table rests on steel center plate. The balance will then be ready for the spring. Place the hair spring on the staff, with the stud in exact line with the line on the index corresponding in name with the movement you wish to put in beat. Now fasten the hair spring collet on the staff, and you will find movement in beat. At a glance, the watchmaker may be lead to believe that this tool is only applicable to the fourteen movements shown on the index, but in reality it serves for almost every movement that comes into the hands of the repairer. For example, the line marked E. Howard & Co., not only serves for that make of watches, but also for Waltham 14 and 16 sizes. Directions accompany each tool.

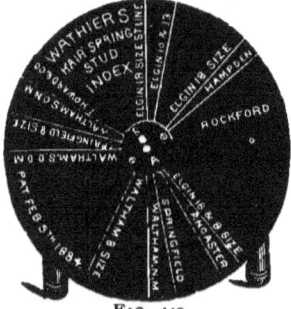

FIG. 119.

HALF PLATE. A watch in which the top pivot of the fourth wheel pinion is carried in a cock, so as to allow of the use of a larger balance than could otherwise be used. *Britten.*

HALL MARKS.

HALL MARK. The stamp placed upon articles of gold or silver after being assayed by government officials. The United States government does not employ hall marks, but articles can be assayed by the proper officers, and a certificate of their standard given upon payment of a small fee. The hall marking of watch-cases is not compulsory in Switzerland, unless they contain some stamp indicating their quality, and the English and other hall marks are recognized. In Great Britain, with few exceptions, the hall marking of jewelry is optional with the maunfacturer, but all gold or silver cases made in Great Britain and Ireland must be marked. The hall marks for Switzerland are shown in Fig. 120,

GOLD. SILVER.

18k OR .755. 14k OR .583. STERLING OR .935 .800.
FIG. 120.

Hall marks are not alone useful for determining the quality of goods, but are also a great aid in determining the age of watches, etc. The hall mark of Great Britain consists of several impressions in separate frames or shields; the quality

FIG. 121.

mark, the office mark, which designates where it was stamped year mark, and if duty is chargable, the head of the reigning sovereign. The standard or quality mark for London and Birmingham is, for gold, a crown, as shown in Fig. 121, and 18 or some other figures to designate the carat. The standard mark for 22 carat gold prior to 1845 was a lion passant, which is now used as the quality mark for sterling silver. The quality mark for 15k. gold is 15 or .625, for 12k. is 12 or .5 and for 9k. is 9 or .375. The decimals indicate the proportions of pure gold of 24k. in the alloys. The office or location mark for London is a Leopard's head in a shield, as shown in Fig 121. The leopard's head was crowned prior to 1823.

HALL MARKS. 178

FIG. 122.

Watch cases have been exempt of duty in Great Britain since 1798, but all foreign cases are stamped, the die for silver being an octogon with the word foreign and for gold a cross. These dies also contain a mark to show where marked, that of London having a sun or full moon.

In Great Britain, from 1697 to 1823, the standard mark for silver was a lion's head, and the office mark a figure of Britannia, but from the latter date, to the present time, a lion passant and a leopard's head have been used. The date marks shown in Fig 122, will prove very valuable in fixing the dates of watches made in Great Britain as in most cases, the case was made at a date coinciding pretty closely with the manufacture of the watch.

HANDS. An index or pointer used in indicating minutes and hours on a watch, clock or similiar dial. The watch hand remover shown in Fig. 123, is a very nice pattern and can also be used as a roller remover and for several other purposes.

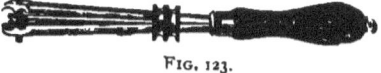

FIG. 123.

The action of the tool can be readily understood by examining the illustration. The threaded wire in the center extends through the entire tool and is raised or lowered by the milled nut at the end of handle. This tool can also be used for holding hands while broaching the hole or the tool shown in Fig. 124, and known as the nine-hole, sliding tongs and many other patterns, for sale by material dealers, may be used for the same purpose.

FIG. 124.

Fig. 125, shows a second-hand holder, with hand in position ready to broach. This tool can also be used as a screw head tool. In order to broach out a new hand, if the boss of the old hand has been preserved, place a small slip of cork upon the end of the broach and insert it in the old hand as far as it will go, and the new hand may then be broached until the cork is reached before trying it for fit. The holes in hands may be closed by forcing them into a conical hole in a steel plate, first turning off the metal around the edge of the hole, so that it is left rather thin, or it may be contracted after reducing the edge, by means of the stake.

HORIZONTAL ESCAPEMENT. (*See Cylinder Escapement.*)

HOUR GLASS. An instrument for measuring the hours, consisting of a glass vessel having two cone-shaped compartments, from the uppermost of which a quantity of sand, water, or mercury occupies an hour in running through a small aperture into the lower.

HOUR WHEEL. The wheel which turns on the cannon pinion and carries the hour hand.

IDLER. An idle wheel. A wheel for transmitting motion from one wheel to another either by contact or by means of belts as the wheel on a countershaft, or overhead fixture. An intermediate wheel used for reversing motion.

IMPULSE PIN. The ruby pin of the lever escapement which entering the notch of the lever, unlocks the escape wheel and then receives impulse from the lever and passes out at the opposite side.

INDEPENDENT SECONDS. A movement having a seconds hand that is driven by a separate train.

INDEX. The small curved plate with divisions upon its face, over which the regulator arm passes. The circular plate at the back of a lathe head, having holes drilled around its margin for the reception of a pin, for dividing a wheel or other object placed in a chuck. Sometimes called a dividing plate.

INERTIA. That property of matter by which it tends when in rest to remain so, or when set in motion to continue so.

INVOLUTE. The curve traced by the end of a string wound upon a roller, or unwound from it.—*Webster*. This was a favorite shape for wheel teeth at one time, but was abandoned because it was found that the pressure on the pivot was increased by it, and it is now entirely superceded by the epicycloidal.

ISOCHRONAL. Uniform in time; moving in equal time. When the long and short arcs of a balance are caused to be performed in the same time by means of a hair spring, that spring is said to be an isochronal one or isochronous. When the vibrations of a pendulum are all of the same duration, no matter through what extent of arc the pendulum moves, the vibrations are isochronal.

JACOT PIVOT LATHE. A Tool used but little in this country, the American lathe and its attchments having superceded it. It is used for reburnishing and dressing up pivots.

JEWELING. The act of fitting in jewels for pivots to run in to diminish wear of the acting parts. Sapphires and rubies are used in the better class of work while in cheaper watches

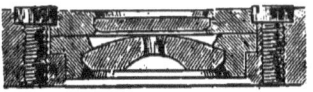

FIG. 126.   FIG. 127.

garnets are substituted. In escapement holes, where endstones are used, as in Fig. 127, the jewel in a loose setting is fitted into a recessed hole, and upon it the end-stone, also set in metal, is laid, and the whole secured by two small screws. In cheaper movements the jewel is rubbed in as shown in Fig. 126.*

---

* For full directions in regard to making and setting jewels the reader is referred to Watch and Chronometer Jeweling, published by Geo. K. Hazlitt & Co., Chicago, price 35 cts.

JEWELING AND STAKING TOOL. Hopkins patent jeweling and staking tool, shown in Fig. 128 is an ingenious device, and one that will be found very useful to the watch repairer. As the spindle, or handle, to which the cutters and burnishers P. P. P. are attached is sustained, in upright position, when in use by the long bearings through which it passes in the upright F, independently of the lower center, the hole to be cut may be centered either from below or above as preferred; and the depth to which it is desired a cutter shall work is regulated by adjustment of the sliding collar E, and this being a correct uprighting, as well as jeweling tool, with it a pivot hole, or a jewel setting the correct centre (upright) of which has been lost, may readily be corrected, or its true center again found, and, what in some cases would be a very desirable consideration, by a careful manipulation with the cutter, which is under perfect control of the operator, the position of jewel settings may be so changed so as to alter the depth of locking of the wheels to any desired extent. To regulate the depth to which it is desired a cutter shall work below the surface of a plate, lower the spindle D till, when moved out sufficiently far, the end of the cutter will rest down on the top of the plate to be operated upon, and fasten it there by lightly tightening the screw K; this done, adjust and fasten the collar E on the spindle D to the same height above the top of the upright F as it is desired the cutter shall work below the surface of the plate on which it now rests. This, when the spindle D has been again set free by loosening the screw K, will of course allow the cutter to sink into the hole to be operated upon to the exact distance the collar E had been set above the top of F. In adjusting the collar E the graduated wedge, No. 4, or the jewel to be set, as preferred, may be used as a guage. The burnishers, No. 9, both for opening and closing settings, the same burnisher, having chosen the one of proper size, is used for both purposes; the side being used for opening the setting, and the bevelled and rounded end for burnishing it down again over the jewel. The pieces 13 and 14 are made to fit in the lower end of the spindle D, (the cutter P having been removed,)

JEWELING TOOL.

same as in an ordinary drill stock, and are used for burnishing the edges of a jewel setting down flat over the jewel countersinking screw heads, giving end shake to wheels, etc.; and being easily made, any one owning the tool can make these for himself, of forms and sizes to suit the particular work in

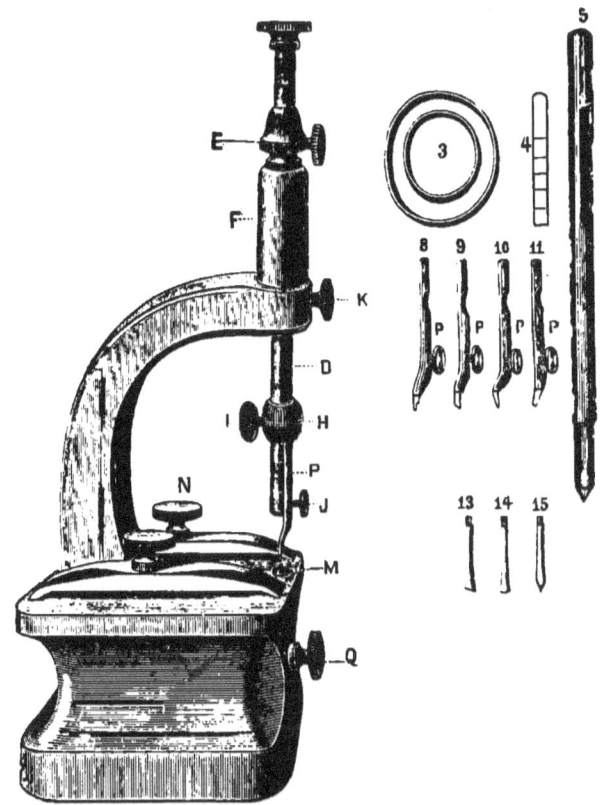

FIG. 128.

hand. For uprighting purposes, withdraw the spindle D and substitute No. 5, the rings No. 3 being intended for laying the work on, on the tool bed. For upright drilling through watch plates, mark the place to be drilled, (prick punch it slightly) with the cone point of No. 5; which done, turn the spindle No. 5 upside down and rest the upper end of the drill in the counter sink in its end, the drill being operated with a fiddle bow acting on a collet placed on its shank for the purpose. For cutting off bushings, level with a watch plate, either a cutter of the No. 13 or 14 class, or one of the P cutters can be used. For staking or riveting wheels upright on their pinions, lay the stake No. 7, level on the tool bed, (the center M having been fastened down out of the way), and with No. 5 center accurately the hole to be used in the stake, and fasten it there by means of the clamps N: then remove the cone end of No. 5, and place a punch with hole in its end of the required size, on the part m, and proceed as in an ordinary upright staking tool.

JEWEL PIN SETTER. Fig. 129 illustrates the Logan patent. It is an excellent tool and will save the workman considerable time and much annoyance by its use.

FIG. 129.

Every watchmaker is aware what a difficult and tedious matter it is to set a jewel pin correctly. With this tool the job is accomplished quickly and accurately.

JEWELING CALIPER REST. This tool will be found very useful for setting jewels in plates or settings, in counter-sinking for screw heads, opening wheels for pinions or bushings, turning barrel heads, etc. The sliding jaws of the calipers should be so adjusted that when the swinging part is brought back snugly against them, the front cutting edge of the cutter in the sliding spindle will exactly line with the center of the lathe spindle. Then if the calipers are at the right height, when a jewel or jewel setting is placed in the jaws of the caliper it will move the edge of the cutter outward from the lathe center just half the diameter of the jewel then in the caliper, and the cutting made at that distance from the center will exactly coincide with the size of the jewel to be set. If however, when set and worked as above, it is found that the hole cut is too large for the jewel, it will indicate that the calipers are too low down, and should be raised, provision for which is made in the construction of the tool. If on the other hand, the cutting is found too small to fit, it will indicate that the calipers should be lowered. The final cutting for the jewel seat should be made by running the center straight inward from the face of the plate; the adjustable screw stop on the back end of the slicing spindle, serving to gauge the depth of the cutting.

FIG. 130.

JEWEL PIN. To set a jewel pin in the table roller, (of American watches), correctly, is a difficult task. Where the jewel pin is broken off you will often save much valuable time by examining the broken part with your glass and noting the exact location of the pin before disturbing it. In some movements the jewel pin will be set as shown in Fig. 131, occupying about two-thirds of the hole in other movement the pin will not occupy much over one half the space, as shown in Fig. 132. By using care in selecting a jewel pin of precisely the same size as the old one and in inserting it in the same

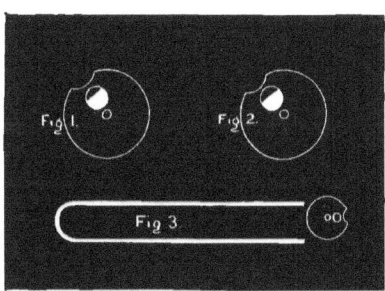

FIG. 131.   FIG. 132.
FIG. 133.

place, nine out of every ten movements will be found mechanically perfect and the balance have a good motion if the escapement is perfect. Most watchmakers remove the table roller from the balance staff, in case the jewel pin is loose. This you will find unnecessary if you will make the following described tool and use as directed. Take a piece of copper wire about half the thickness of a common pin tongue and bend it as shown in Fig. 133, so it will be about one and one-eighth inch long. Cut or saw a groove in the inside of the ends, sufficiently deep to hold on to the table roller, say one-fourth inch from the end. This can be easily bent to accommodate all sizes of tables. If you wish to soften the cement, to tighten, or replace a new jewel pin, it is only necessary to slip on the copper wire, and hold the extreme outer end in the flame of a small alcohol lamp, a few moments and sufficient heat will follow the copper wire to soften the cement. Care must be exercised to keep the pin in the proper position, and when sufficently heated, remove the wire quickly and allow the table to cool. By use of this little tool there is no need of removing the table roller, and absolutely no danger of injuring the finest expansion balance, as the tool need not, and must not touch the balance. The end of this tool is held in the flame by a pair of soldering tweezers. Always use shellac for cementing the jewel pin in the table roller.

JOINT PUSHER. A small piece of tempered steel wire mounted in a wooden handle and used for inserting and removing joint pins.

LACQUER. The ordinary lacquer of commerce is composed of spirits of wine and clear shellac in the proportion of 1 oz. of shellac to a pint of spirit. Heat should not be applied but the ingredeints placed in a glass stoppered bottle and shaken from time to time until the shellac is thoroughly dissolved or combined with the spirit. Various tints may be given lacquer by adding small quanties of aniline colors, previously well mixed with water and free from lumps.

LANTERN PINION. A pinion formed of two circular brass or other metal plates and connected by means of short steel wires.

LAP. A disc used in conjunction with a lathe for polishing or cutting. Laps are made of steel, copper, ivory etc., and are charged with the cutting or polishing compounds. See *Diamond Laps*.

LATHE. A mechanical device used for shaping articles by causing them to revolve while being brought into contact with cutting tools. Those who contemplate buying a lathe will do well to avoid the cheap imitations of the American pattern which are made by irresponsible makers in foreign countries, and fostered upon an unsuspecting public and

FIG. 134.

guaranteed true and "as good as the American." They are usually nicely finished, but inferior both in material and workmanship, their greatest failure being their untruth. If an untrue American lathe by any possibility is allowed to escape the inspector and finds its way upon the market, the manufacturer is only too glad to exchange it for a perfect article, for his reputation is at stake, but who are you going back on in the event of one of these cheap imitations proving untrue? There are American made lathes upon the market that are as inferior in many respects as the imitations, and the watchmaker will do well to do without a lathe until such time as he can afford to purchase one of known reputation. Among the first class American lathes upon the market may be mentioned the Hopkins, manufactured by the Waltham Watch Tool Company, of Springfield, Mass., shown in

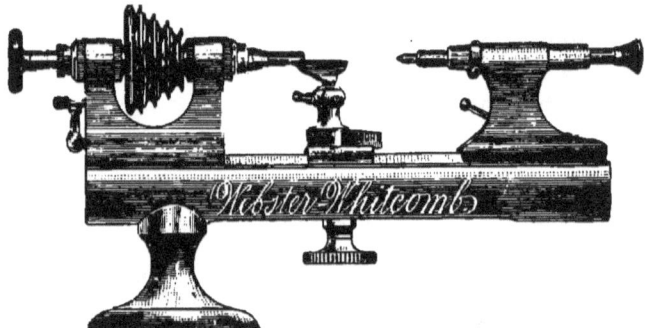

FIG. 135.

Fig. 134, the Webster-Whitcomb, manufactured by the American Watch Tool Company, Waltham, Mass., shown in Fig. 135, the Rivett, manufactured by the Faneuil Watch Tool Company, Faneuil, Mass., and the Moseley, manufactured by Moseley & Company, Elgin, Ill. An excellent lathe for the heavier work of watchmakers and jewelers, such as cannot be performed with satisfaction on the watchmaker's lathe, is manufactured by W. F. & John Barnes Company, Rockford, Ill., and is known as their No. 4 lathe. Space forbids a full description of the American lathe and directions for performing the many operations for which it is intended, as a volume the size of this could be fully utilized if the subject were treated comprehensively; suffice it therefore, to say, that the quality of the work and the satisfaction which the lathe gives to its owner depends greatly upon the care which he bestows upon it. The lathe itself and its various attachments should be kept scrupulously clean, well oiled and as little exposed as needs be to dust. When not in use it should be kept under a glass shade, or covered with a cloth or chamois skin. Lathe attachments are described under their respective heads.

LEVER ESCAPEMENT.* George Graham, the English horologist, invented the anchor deadbeat escapement used in clocks, and from it the lever, the favorite watch escapement of to-day is derived. In order to apply this latter escapement, (which only allows of very small arcs of vibration), to the watch, it was necessary, says Saunier, not only to alter its form but also to make the balance independent of the motive force, except during the actual period of lift. Thomas Mudge satisfied these requirements, by producing an escapement in which the two lifts were equal and an impulse was given at each vibration of the balance.

Saunier and other authorities declare that when the modern lever escapement is well made in conformity with the principles of mechanics, and the pallets and pivot holes are provided with jewels, it may be considered to be the best adapted for ordinary use.

Britten declares that, " although inferior for time keeping to the chronometer, when made with ordinary care it is so certain in its action that it is generally preferred for pocket watches. Its weak point is the necessity of applying oil to the pallets. However close the rate of the watch at first, the thickening of the oil in the course of time will inevitably affect its going."

The form of escapement presented in Fig. 138, is known as a *right angle* escapement. The *straight line* escapement, which is quite a favorite with Swiss and American watchmakers, is so called because the three centers of the wheel, the pallets and the balance are in a straight line. It is claimed that there is less friction and shake on the pivots in the straight line than in the right angle form, owing to the

---

*The student will do well to read: The Detached Lever Escapement by Moritz Grossmann; Modern Horology in Theory and Practice, by Claudius Saunier; Watch and Clock Making, by David Glasgow; The Watch and Clockmakers' Hand Book, by F. J. Britten.

direction of the pressures neutralizing each other to some extent.*

In America, Switzerland and France, the "clubbed" tooth is preferred for escape wheels, that is to say, a tooth similar to that shown in Fig. 136, made with the tip of the wheel formed into an inclined plane, thus dividing the impulse between the face of the pallets and the wheel teeth. Saunier in comparing the two forms of teeth says: "An escapement with pointed or ratchet teeth has the following objections and advantages: Both the pitch with the locking face and the drop are very nearly doubled; there is therefore an appreciable increase in the resistance opposed to unlocking, especially when the oil is at all thick. Out of the 10° through which the pallet moves, a greater proportion is expended in the unlocking. Lastly the fine pointed tooth must be made of brass, it is liable to wear and distortion, and is ill-adapted for retaining oil, which must be applied in very small quantities. On the other hand its advantages consist in: 1. The pallets having double width, so that a greater quantity of oil is retained on them; 2. The escapement will go for a considerable time after the oil has become bad or thickened. Some watchmakers indeed do not put any oil on either the teeth or pallets when the wheel is made of a particular kind of brass, but the point of the tooth wears in time; 3. The escapement is more easy of construction. When this form is adopted, the escapement can be made with sufficient accuracy by ordinary workmen; for if the planes are inclined to the requisite extent there will be no time lost in the lift.

As compared with the ratchet toothed wheel, the wheel with clubbed teeth possess the following qualities: It retains the oil better; the friction accurs at two points of contact instead of one; the impulse commences with a shorter lever and is therefore, more efficient; no wear or distortion or

---

* Saunier does not commit himself on this point; Glasgow and Britten both declare that there is no advantage in the straight line, though the former admits that it may be more handsome to look at, and the latter that it allows of the poising of the lever and pallets with less redundant metal. The principle reason why it is not made in England is that with the fuzee movements it is difficult to find room for it.

variation of the acting surfaces need be feared when the wheel is carefully made and of good material; it is possible, within certain limits, to reduce the pitch with the locking faces if necessary, and thus, while diminishing the effect of viscosity on these surfaces, to increase the *real lift* that corresponds to a given apparent lift. Lastly, the drop can be reduced to almost nothing.

It is undoubtedly true that, as a set off against these advantages, it may be objected that this escapement is of a highly scientific character, so that its construction is a matter of some delicacy, and requires the skilled hand of a first-rate workman. In conclusion, Saunier says, that the advantage is on the side of the clubbed tooth.

Britten says that on the other hand, English watchmakers maintain that as at some time during each impulse the planes of the wheel and pallet nearly coincide, the increased surface then presented to the varying influence of the adhesion of the oil is a serious evil. Then with clubbed teeth, there is more difficulty in satisfactorily replacing a wheel than

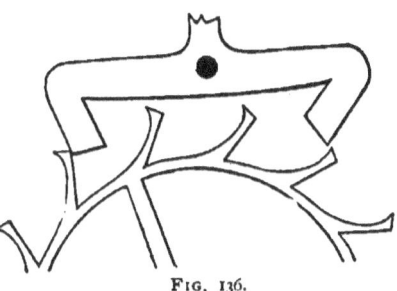

FIG. 136.

with ratchet teeth, for in the former case the planes must be of exactly the same angle and of the same length in the new wheel as in the old one. With brass wheels the impulse faces on the wheel get cut into ruts, but the Swiss avoid this by using steel wheels, and also much reduce the extra adhesion due to increased surface by thinning the impulse planes of the teeth. Swiss escapements are as a rule commendably light, but the levers are disproportionately long. The Germans make an escapement in which the whole of the impulse plane is on the wheel teeth, the pallets being small round pins, as in Fig 137. Britten thinks this a cheaper and simpler form, but Saunier says of a similar escapement, which was proposed by Perron in 1798, that the simplicity is more

LEVER ESCAPEMENT.   192

apparent than real, for it requires very great care in its construction, or otherwise its accuracy cannot be relied upon.

Britten gives the following very concise description of the action and proportion of the escapement:

ACTION OF THE ESCAPEMENT.

Fig. 138 shows the most usual form of the lever escapement, in which the pallets "scape" over three teeth of the wheel. A tooth of the escape wheel is at rest upon the locking face of the entering left-hand pallet. The impulse pin has just entered the notch of the lever, and is about to unlock the pallet. The action of the escapement is as follows: The balance, which is attached to the same staff as the roller, is traveling in the direction indicated by the arrow which is around the roller, with sufficient energy to cause the ruby pin to move the lever and pallets far enough to release the wheel tooth from the locking face, and allow it to enter on the impulse face of the pallet. Directly it is at liberty, the escape wheel, actuated by the mainspring of the watch, moves around the same way as the arrow and pushes the pallet out of its path. By the time the wheel tooth has got to the end of the impulse face of the pallet, its motion is arrested by the exit or right-hand pallet, the locking face of which has been brought into position to receive another tooth of the wheel. When the pallet was pushed aside by the wheel tooth it carried with it the lever, which in its turn communicated a sufficient blow to the ruby pin to send the balance with renewed energy on its vibration. So that the ruby pin has the double office of unlocking the pallets by giving a blow on one side of the notch of the lever, and of immediately receiving a blow from the opposite side of the notch. The balance proceeds on its excursion, winding up as it goes the balance spring, until its energy is expended. After it is

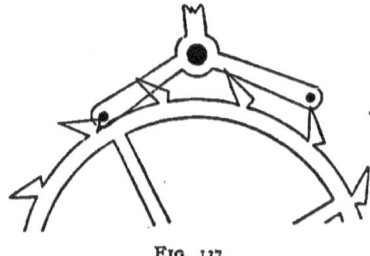

FIG. 137.

brought to a state of rest its motion is reversed by the uncoiling of the balance spring, the ruby pin again enters the notch of the lever, but from the opposite direction, and the operation already described is repeated. The object of the safety pin is to prevent the wheel from being unlocked except when the ruby pin is in the notch of the lever. The banking pins keep the motion of the lever within the desired limits. They should be placed as shown, where any blow from the ruby pin on to the outside of the lever is received direct. They are sometimes placed at the tail of the lever, but in that position the banking pins receive the blow through the pallet staff pivots, which are liable to be broken in consequence.

PROPORTION OF THE ESCAPEMENT.

The escape wheel has fifteen teeth, and the distance apart of the pallets, from centre to centre, is equal to $60°$ of the circumference of the wheel. The pallets are planted as close as possible to the wheel, so that the teeth of the wheel in passing just clear the belly of the pallets. When the tooth is pressing on the locking, the line of pressure should pass through the centre of the pallet staff. But as the locking faces of the two pallets are not equidistant from the centre of motion, a tangent drawn from the locking corner of one pallet would be wrong for the other, and, as a matter of fact, if a diagram is made it will be found that even when the pallets are planted as close as possible they are hardly as close as they should be for the right-hand pallet. To plant as close as possible is, therefore, a very good rule, and is the one adopted by the best pallet makers; though in setting out the escapement a chord of the width of the pallet is produced to find the centre of the staff, as shown in Fig. 140. The width of each pallet is made as nearly as possible half the distance between one tooth of the escape wheel and the next. As the teeth of the wheel must be of an appreciable thickness, and the various pivots must have shake, it is not found practicable to get the pallets of greater width than $10°$ of the circumference of the wheel instead of $12°$, which would be half the distance between one tooth and the next. This difference between the theoretical and actual width of the pallet is called the drop. The lever is pinned to the pallets, and has the same centre of motion. The distance between the centre of the lever and the centre of the roller is not absolute. The distance generally preferred is a chord of 96° of a circle representing the path of the tips of the escape wheel teeth, that is, the distance from the tip of one tooth to the tip of the fourth succeeding tooth. The proportion, as it is called, of the lever and roller is usually from 3 to 1 to 3½ to 1. In the former case the length of the lever (measured from the centre of pallet staff to centre of the mouth of the notch,) is three times the distance of the centre of the impulse pin from the centre of the roller, and in the latter case 3½ times. The portion of the lever to the left of the pallet staff hole acts as a counterpoise, and should really have the metal in it disposed at as nearly as possible the same distance from the centre as that in the other end of the lever, though this is rarely the case.

In this form of the lever escapement the pallets have not less than 10° of motion. Of this amount, 2° are used for locking, and the remainder for impulse. The amount of locking is to some extent dependent on the size of the escapement. With a large escapement less than 1½° would suffice, while a small one would require rather more than 2° The quality of the work, too, is an element in deciding the amount of locking. The lighter the locking the better, but it must receive every tooth of the wheel safely, and where all the parts are made with care the escapement can be made with a very light locking.

Presuming that the staff hole is correctly drilled with relation to the planes, a rough rule used for testing 10° pallets is that a straight edge laid on the plane of the entering pallet should point to the locking corner of the exit pallet, as indicated by the dotted line in Fig. 139. But this is clearly only an approximation, for any variation in the amount allowed for locking alters the direction of the planes.

When from setting the hands of a watch back, or from a sudden jerk, there is a tendency for the pallets to unlock, the

ENGLISH LEVER ESCAPEMENT.

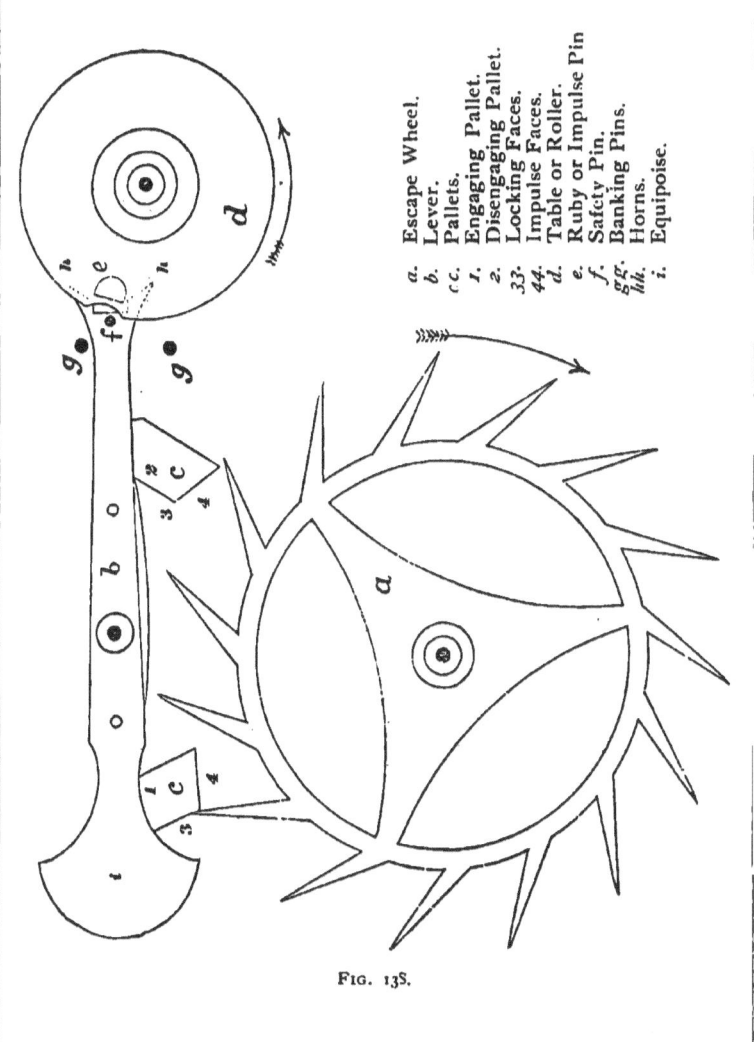

a. Escape Wheel.
b. Lever.
cc. Pallets.
1. Engaging Pallet.
2. Disengaging Pallet.
33. Locking Faces.
44. Impulse Faces.
d. Table or Roller.
e. Ruby or Impulse Pin
f. Safety Pin.
gg. Banking Pins.
hh. Horns.
i. Equipoise.

FIG. 138.

safety pin butts against the edge of the roller. It will be observed that when the ruby pin unlocks the pallets, the safety pin is allowed to pass the roller by means of the crescent which is cut out of the roller opposite the ruby pin. The teeth of the escape wheel make a considerable angle with a radial line (24°), so that their tips only touch the locking faces of the pallets. The locking faces of the pallets, instead of being curves struck from the centre of motion of the pallets, as would be otherwise the case, are cut back at an angle so as to interlock with the wheel teeth. The locking face forms an angle of 6° or 8° with a tangent to a circle representing the path of the locking corner. This is done so that the safety pin shall not drag on the edge of the roller, but be drawn back till the lever touches the banking pin. When the operation of setting the hands back is finished, or the other cause of disturbance removed, the pressure of the wheel tooth on the locking face of the pallet draws the pallet into the wheel as far as the banking pin will allow. The amount of this "run" should not be more than sufficient to give proper clearance between the safety pin and the roller, for the more the run, the greater is the resistance to unlocking. This rule is sometimes sadly transgressed, and occasionally the locking is found to be, from excessive run, almost equal in extent to the impulse. It will generally be found that in these cases the escapement is so badly proportioned that the extra run has had to be given to secure a sound safety action. In common watches the safety action is a frequent source of trouble. The more the path of the safety pin intersects the edge of the roller, the sounder is the safety action, and if the intersection is small the safety pin is likely to jamb against the edge of the roller, or even to pass it altogether. With an ordinary single roller escapement a sound safety action cannot be obtained with a less balance arc than 33°; 10° pallets with one degree of movement added for run, and with a lever and roller of 3 to 1, give a

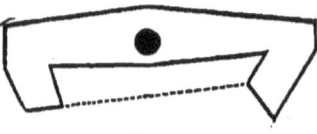

FIG. 139.

LEVER ESCAPEMENT.

balance arc of 33°—that is to say, the balance in its vibration is freed from the escapement except during 33°, when the impulse pin is in contact with the lever. Even with a balance arc of 33° the roller must be kept small in the following way to ensure soundness of the safety action. The hole for the ruby pin must not be left round. After it is drilled, a punch of the same shape as the ruby pin—that is, with one-third of its diameter flattened off—should be inserted, and the edge of the roller, where the crescent is to be formed, beaten in. By this means the roller can be turned down small enough to get a sufficient intersection for the safety pin.

It is useful in estimating the balance arc of a watch, to remember if it has a three-armed balance that 30° is one-fourth of the distance between two arms. With a compensation balance a third of the distance between two of the quarter screws is 30°.

A round ruby pin, although it is sometimes used in common watches, gives a bad action and necessitates a very large balance arc.

Fig. 140 is appended as a guide to students in setting out the escapement. A circle representing the extreme diameter of the escape wheel is taken as a basis, and on the left of the centre line is set off, by means of a protractor, the middle of one pallet (30°) and its width (10°). The chord of this arc of 10° is then produced till it cuts the centre line, and this intersection is taken as the centre of the pallet staff. From the pallet-staff centre curves, A and B, (representing the paths of the pallet corners,) are drawn. The amount of locking C (say 2°) and impulse D (say 9°) are set off from the chord of the left-hand pallet. The impulse plane is traced through the intersection of the angular lines with the curves A and B, and the line of the plane produced toward the centre of the staff as shown. From the centre of the staff is described a circle just touching the line so produced. The impulse plane of the other pallet forms a tangent to this circle. In this position of the pallets, a line drawn from the locking corner of the left-hand pallet to form an angle of 12° with the radial line from the centre of the wheel, will be required

LEVER ESCAPEMENT. 198

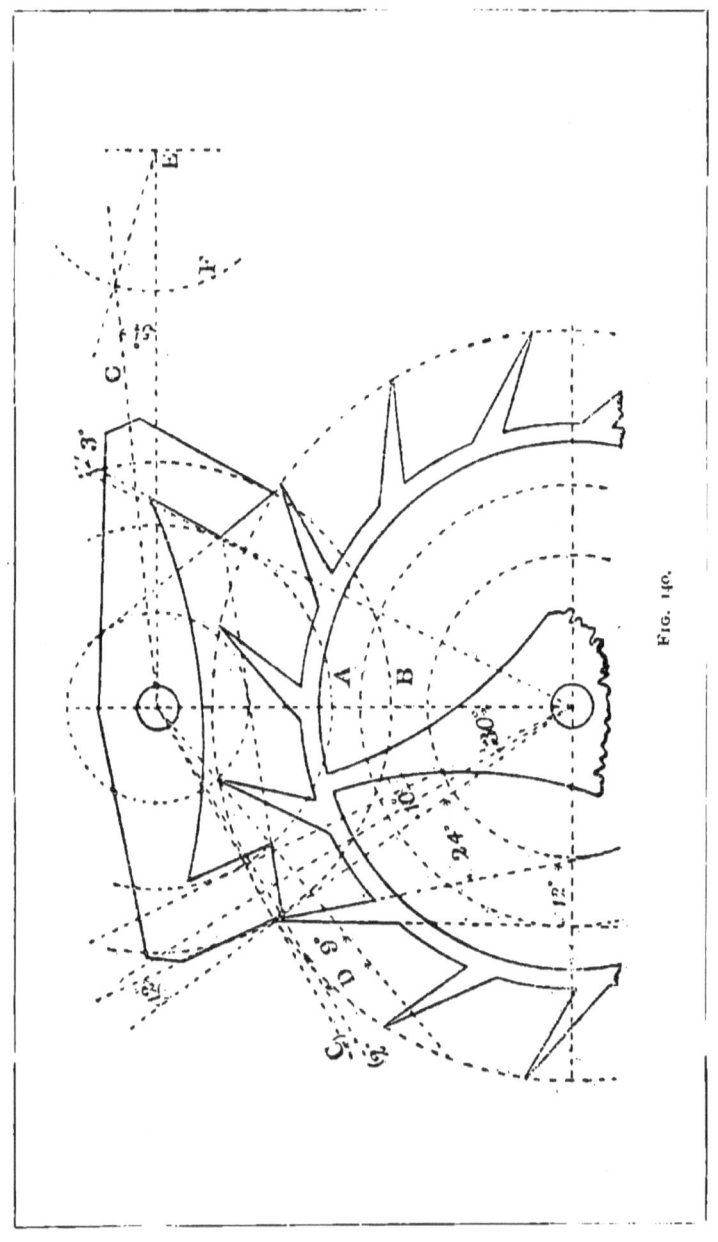

FIG. 140.

to show the locking face of the pallet, and a similar line forming 3° will answer for the locking face of the right-hand pallet. Mark off the centre of the roller (E), and take, say, one-fourth of the distance between this centre and the centre of the pallet staff for the position of the centre of the impulse pin, and describe the arc F to represent its path. The line G, forming with the centre line running through the roller an angle equal to half the total angle of the motion of the pallets, or 5½,° will represent the centre of the lever. The wheel teeth are set back about 24° from a radial line, so as to bear on their points only, and the rim of the wheel extends to about three-fourths of the whole radius. The remaining parts may be readily filled in from the foregoing remarks on the proportion of the escapement, and a study of Fig. 138.

DOUBLE ROLLER ESCAPEMENT.—THE HORN OF THE LEVER.

Low-angled pallets, says Britten, (i. e. pallets having but little motion), and small balance arcs are preferred for fine watches; the low-angle pallets as being less affected by changes in the condition of the oil which is used to lubricate the faces of the pallets than when the motion is greater, and the small balance arc because it allows the balance to be more perfectly detached from the escapement. With a double roller escapement, pallets with from 8° to 9° of motion are generally used, with a lever and roller to give a balance arc of from 28° to 32°. With low-angled pallets, and less than 30° of balance arc, a different arrangement than the usual upright pin in the lever must be made for the safety action. A second roller, not much more than one-half the diameter of the one in which the impulse pin is fixed, is mounted on the balance staff for the purpose, and a small gold finger, projecting far enough to reach the edge of the smaller roller, is screwed to the lever. The safety roller should not be less than half the diameter of the impulse roller, for the smaller the safety roller, the farther the safety finger enters the crescent before the ruby pin enters the notch of the lever; and, as directly the safety finger enters the crescent, the impulse pin must be within the horn of the lever, the smaller the safety roller, the longer must be the horn. Then, if the horns are excessively long, the extent of the free vibration of the balance is curtailed, because the ruby pin touches the *outside* of the lever sooner. It will be seen that in the single roller escapement (Fig. 141) the safety pin does not enter the crescent before the ruby pin enters the notch, and, therefore, in the single roller escapement the lever really requires but the smallest possible amount of horn. Fig. 141 shows the double roller arrangement. Here it will be seen that the safety finger enters the crescent some time before the ruby pin gets to the notch. During this interval, should the hands of the watch be set back, the pallets could not trip, for the horn of the lever would be caught on the ruby pin. I have tried to explain this fully, because double roller escapements occasionally fail to give satisfaction owing to the lever having insufficient horn. On the other hand, the levers of single roller escapements, where scarcely any horn is required, are often made with very long ones.

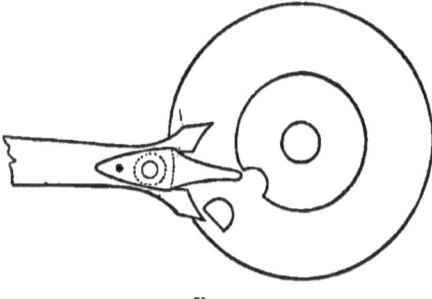

FIG. 141.

Besides getting a sound safety action with small balance arc, the double roller has three other advantages. (1) The impulse is given more nearly on the line of centres, and consequently with less engaging friction. (2) The safety roller being of a lesser diameter, the safety finger when in contact with it offers less resistance to the motion of the balance; and (3) the requisite amount of shake between the safety roller and banking pins is obtained with less run on the pallets. Double roller escapements are sometimes seen with pallets having 10° of motion, and even more, and with the safety roller nearly as large as the impulse one. An escapement made in this way really appears to lose most of the advantages of the extra roller. On the other hand, low-angle pallets are sometimes used with a long lever to get increased balance arc. This also is objectionable, for the pallets must have more draw to pull the longer lever up to the banking, and more draw means harder unlocking. It is really only to watches of a high character throughout that double roller escapements with low angle pallets and small balance arcs should be applied. For the ordinary run of work, the single roller escapement with 11° pallets and a balance arc of from 36° to 40° is well suited.

SIZE OF THE LEVER ESCAPEMENT.

Lever escapements are classed by the trade, says Britten, into the following sizes:

No. 0 in which the escape wheel is .185 of an inch in diameter.
1	"	"	"	"	.205	"	"	"
2	"	"	"	"	.225	"	"	"
4	"	"	"	"	.245	"	"	"
6	"	"	"	"	.265	"	"	"
8	"	"	"	"	.285	"	"	"
10	"	"	"	"	.295	"	"	"
12	"	"	"	"	.305	"	"	"

No. 1 is the smallest and No. 10 the largest size used in the ordinary run of work. The practice of J. F. Cole was to have the escape wheel three-sevenths of the diameter of the balance, but there is no strict rule for the size of an escapement to a watch, though there has been a disposition of late years to use smaller escapements than formerly, as they are found to yield better results. In course of time a ridge is formed at the beginning of the impulse planes of the pallets, where the wheel teeth fall. This ridge is more marked and farther along the impulse plane when there is much drop and the escape wheel is large and heavy, because the inertia of the wheel, which increases in proportion to its weight and the square of its diameter, is so great that the balance after unlocking the pallets carries them farther before the wheel acquires sufficient velocity to overtake them. Undue shake of the ruby pin in the notch will also cause this ridge to be accentuated. The practice of some of the best London makers is, for 6 and 8 sized movements, No. 2 escapement;

for 10 and 12 sized movements, No. 4 escapement; for 14 and 16 sized movements, No. 6 escapement; and for 18 and 20 sized movements, No. 8 escapement. Many manufacturers confine themselves to two sizes, "two's" for repeaters and ladies, and "sixes" for gentlemen's watches. A Coventry watch will be found usually to have a larger escapement than a London watch of the same size.

The escape wheel is of hard, well-hammered brass; the pallets are of steel (the practice of rolling the pallet steel to harden it is not a good one, as there is danger of magnetizing it in the operation), wider than the wheel, with the acting parts of ruby in the best, and garnet in the commoner escapements. The pallets are slit longitudinally, and the stones fixed in with shellac. The Swiss generally insert the stones across the pallets, so that they are visible. The impulse planes are curved so as to present a smaller surface to the wheel. The ruby, pin is fixed in the roller with shellac; the safety pin of gold, and the banking pins of brass. Non-magnetizable watches have the lever and pallets of some other metal than steel, generally aluminium bronze.

In a good lever escapement all the moving parts are extremely light.

In making a new lever it is well to start with it full long, because a deep notch is much easier to polish than a shallow one. When the notch is finished the horns can be filed off as required.

TWO PIN ESCAPEMENT.

As Britten has pointed out in the action of the escapement, the ruby pin performs the double office of unlocking the pallets by giving a blow on one side of the notch of the lever, and of immediately receiving a blow from the opposite side of the notch. George Savage, of London, saw there was a loss of power consequent on this double duty, and also in the unlocking action taking place before the line of centers of the lever and roller, and with a view to avoid this, introduced the escapement shown in Fig. 142. He reversed the order of things by cutting a small notch in the roller, and placing a pin in the lever, in lieu of the ruby

203   LEVER ESCAPEMENT

pin in the roller, which also answered the purpose of the guard pin. To effect the unlocking, he placed two small pins in the roller in such positions that one of them begins to unlock just before crossing the line of centers. By the time

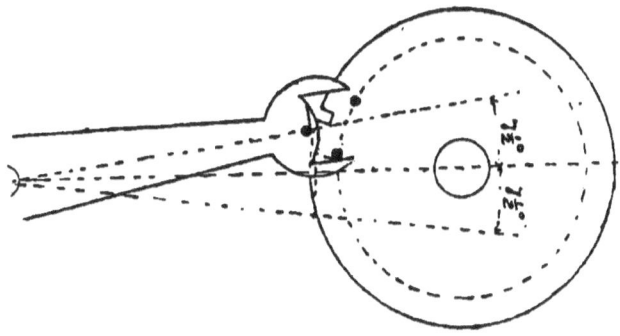

FIG. 142.

the unlocking is finished, the pin in the lever is drawn into the notch and gives the first portion of the impulse. It then leaves the notch, and the impulse is completed by the horns of the lever striking the second small pin in the roller, which has nearly or quite reached the line of centers by this time.

In order to get the safety pin well into the notch, says Britten, this escapement requires pallets having 12° to 15° of motion, which is objectionable, and the lever and roller action is besides a very delicate job, and fails if not thoroughly done; so that, although the idea is taking, this form of the escapement has never come much into use, and when it is made one wide stone is generally substituted for the two pins in the roller.

The unlocking nearer the line of centers is also accomplished in what is called the anchor or dovetail escapement, in which the ruby pin is wider than usual, and of a dovetail form. It is open to the objection that, on account of the increased width of the impulse stone and of the lever, banking will occur with a smaller vibration of the balance than with the usual form.

RESILIENT ESCAPEMENTS.

A watch balance in general use, says Britten, rarely vibrates more than a turn and a half, that is, three-quarters of a turn each way; yet occasionally, from pressing on the key after the watch is wound in going-barrel work, sudden movements of the wearer, or other cause of disturbance, the balance will swing round till the impulse pin knocks the *outside* of the lever. If this banking is violent, the timekeeping of the watch is deranged, and a broken pivot may also result if the pivots are small. To obviate the evil of such banking, various plans have been tried. The most usual is to make the banking pins yield to undue pressure, and allow the ruby pin to pass the lever, the wings of which are omitted. Mr. J. F. Cole devised a resilient escapement without any banking pins, in which the teeth of the escape wheel were so formed as to resist the entrance of the pallet into the wheel more than was required for ordinary locking. In the event of overbanking, the pallet compelled the escape wheel to recoil, so that the mainspring was really utilized as a spring banking. But in the use of any of these resilient arrangements there is a danger of " setting." When the banking is so violent that the ruby pin drives the lever before it, all is well, but it is sure to happen sometimes that just as the ruby pin is passing the lever its motion is exhausted, and it jambs against the point of the lever and stops the watch. In a recent arrangement Mr. Schoof claims to have overcome this tendency to set by using *very weak* spring bankings. Another objection to spring bankings is that in their recoil they are likely to drive the safety pin against the edge of the roller.

PALLETS WITH EQUIDISTANT LOCKINGS.

The drawing Fig. 138, shows the pallets at an equal distance from their centre of motion, and they are generally made so. But then, although the impulse planes are equal, the locking faces are not the same distance from the centre, and the locking resistance is therefore unequal. Pallets are occasionally made having the lockings equidistant. Although advocated by Grossman and other authorities, they are but seldom used. The action of the wheel tooth on the impulse plane of the entering pallet before the line of centres is an engaging action, and on the exit pallet after the line of centres a disengaging action. The friction is therefore greater on the entering pallet, and when an escapement sets on one impulse face, it is in nine cases out of ten the impulse face, of the entering pallet. From this it is argued by some that if either pallet should be placed further from the centre of motion it should not be the exit, but the entering pallet, so as to give it a more favorable leverage wherewith to encounter the greater friction which undoubtedly exists. But there is really no advantage in the longer arm, for it has to be pushed through a greater distance by the wheel tooth than the shorter one. Arrange the length of the pallet arms how you will, you get but the force of the wheel passing through half the distance between two teeth. As far as the relative adhesion of the oil goes, the advantage is with the shorter arm. But the chief objection to the equidistant lockings is that with them the leaving corner of the exit pallet dips further into the wheel than with circular pallets, thereby requiring more drop to give the requisite freedom. Britten gives the following hints on the

EXAMINATION OF THE LEVER ESCAPEMENT.

See that the balance staff is perfectly upright. See that the wheel is perfectly true on edge and on face, and that the teeth are equally divided and smooth; also by gently turning the wheel backwards, see that the pallets free the backs of the teeth. If the wheel is out of truth, it must be set up in the lathe and re-bored. It can be fixed either with shellac or in a brass sink bored out the exact size to receive it. If the divisions are unequal, or the wheel has some thick teeth, it should be discarded. It is useless to attempt to make the wheel right, and to reduce the corners of the pallet to free the wheel is simply to spoil the escapement for the sake of the wheel. At the same time, it must be left to the operator to judge whether the amount of the inaccuracy is serious. The whole affair is so minute that no rule can be given.

Is the wheel the right size? If the lockings are too light, and the greater part of the shake INSIDE, the wheel is too small, and should be replaced by one larger. Before removing the wheel, gently draw the balance around until the point of the tooth is exactly on the locking corner, and see if there is sufficient shake. If not, it will be prudent to have the new wheel with the teeth a little straighter than the old ones. If the lockings are too deep and most of the drop OUTSIDE, the wheel is too large and should be topped.*

The wheel is so fragile that care is required in topping, which is done by revolving it in the turns against a diamond or sapphire file. A brass collet is broached to fit friction-tight on one of the runners of a depth tool; one side of this collet is then filed away, leaving sufficient substance to avoid bursting into the hole. On this flat a small piece of sapphire file is attached with shellac, taking care that the *face of the file is parallel to the centre of the runner*. The escape wheel on its pinion with a ferrule attached is placed in the centres of the depth tool *further from the adjusting screw*, and the collet and file on one of the opposite centres, and that centre fixed firmly by its clamping screw. A very light hair bow is used to rotate the pinion, and the depth tool laid on its side on the work board—the tool being closed by its screw until the teeth of the wheel *nearly* touch the surface of the file; now if a slight pressure is made by the fingers on the uppermost limb of the tool, at the same time rotating the wheel by the bow, the *spring* of the tool will allow the teeth to be brought into contact very slightly and without fear of bending the teeth; the wheel can be reduced as much as is necessary.

If the wheel is the right size and there is no shake (which try as before directed), the discharging corner of the pallets may be rounded off by means of a diamond file if they are of garnets. If they are of ruby, they may be held against an ivory mill charged with diamond powder. If the lockings are too light and there is but little shake, they may be made safe

---

* In planting the wheel and pallets it is always best to err, if at all, by making them too deep rather than too light. If they are a shade deep, topping the wheel soon puts matters right.

LEVER ESCAPEMENT.

by polishing away the locking face a sufficient quantity. If one locking is right and one is too light, the one that is too light may be made safe by polishing away the locking face as before, or the pallet may be warmed and the stone brought out a bit. The locking faces of the pallets should be sufficiently undercut to draw the lever to the banking pins without hesitation. If they require alteration in this respect, polish away the upper part of the locking faces so as to give more draw, leaving the locking CORNER quite untouched. But proceed with great care, lest in curing this fault the watch sets on the locking, as small watches with light balances are very liable to do. If a watch sets on the lockings, or on one of them, the locking face or faces may be polished away so as to give less draw—i. e. have most taken off the CORNER of the locking. If the watch sets on the the impulse, the impulse face may be polished to a less angle if the locking is sufficiently deep to allow of it. For it must be remembered that in reducing the impulse the locking of the opposite pallet will also be reduced. In fact, the greatest caution should be exercised in making any alteration in the pallets.

Sometimes in new escapements, the oil at the escape wheel teeth will be found to thicken rapidly through the pallet cutting the wheel, showing that one or both corners of the pallet are too sharp. If ruby, the corner may be polished off with a peg cut to the shape of a pivot polisher, and a little of the finest diamond powder in oil; if garnet, diamantine on a peg will do it very well. Great care should be taken to remove every trace of the polishing material, or the wheel may become charged with it.

See that the pivots are well polished, of proper length to come through the holes, and neither bull-headed or taper. A conical pivot should be conical only as far as the shoulder; the part that runs in the hole must be perfectly cylindrical. They must have perceptible and equal side shake, or if any difference be made the pallet pivots should fit the closest. Both balance staff pivots should be of exactly the same size. The end shakes should all be equal. Bad pivots, bad uprighting, excessive and unequal shake in the pivots are responsible for much of the trouble experienced in position timing. With unequal end shakes the pallet depth is liable to be altered owing to the curved form of the pallet faces. The action of the escapement will also be affected if the end shakes are not equal, by a banking pin slightly bent, a slight inaccuracy in uprighting, and other minute faults. The infinitesimal quantity necessary to derange the wheel and pallet action may be gathered from the fact that a difference of .002 of an inch is quite enough to make a tripping pallet depth safe or correct depth quite unsound.

When the wheel and pallets are right, see that the impulse pin is in a line with an arm of the balance, and proceed to try if the lever is fixed in the correct position with relation to the pallets. Gently move the balance around until the tooth drops off the pallet. Observe the position of the balance arm, and see if it comes the same distance on the other side of the pallet hole when the other pallet falls off. If not the pins connecting pallet and lever are generally light enough to allow of the lever being twisted. When the lever is right with relation to the pallets, see that the pallets are quite firmly fixed to the lever, and that the lever and pallets are perfectly in poise. This latter is an essential point in a fine watch to be timed in positions, but it is often neglected.

See that the escapement is in beat. When the balance spring is at rest, the impulse pin should be on the line of centres, that is in the middle of its motion. If this is not so, the spring should be drawn through or let out from the stud if the position of the index allows; if it does not, the roller may be twisted around on the staff in the direction required.

Is the roller depth right? If the safety pin has insufficient freedom while there is enough run, the roller is probably planted too deep. On the other hand, if it is found that while the safety pin has plenty of freedom there is no shake between the bankings, the roller depth is probably too shallow. When the impulse pin is led around there should be an equal clearance all around the inside of the horn, and the pin must fall safely into the notch. If it binds in the horn and bottoms in the notch it is too deep, and, on the other hand, if with excessive clearance in the horn the pin when it falls does not pass well into the notch, it is too shallow. The readiest method of altering is to warm the roller, remove the impulse pin, and using a to-and-fro motion with a wire and oilstone dust, draw the hole in the required direction. If the pin is deep in the notch and too tight in the roller to give a little, it should be removed and flattened off a trifle more. If too shallow, a triangular pin, or one of some other shape with the point of contact more forward, can generally be substituted by polishing out the hole towards the crescent. If not, the staff hole in the lever may be drawn to allow of shifting the lever sufficiently; or the recesses for the jewel settings of the balance staff pivots may be scraped away on one side and rubbed over on the other to suit. See as it passes around that the impulse pin is free when in the notch.

Just as the safety pin is about to enter the crescent, the impulse pin must be well inside of the horn. In the single roller escapement a very little horn is required, unless the crescent has been made of an unnecessary width. In very common work one occasionally sees a flat filed on the edge of the roller instead of a crescent. There is no excuse for such a piece of bungling.

A fault occasionally met with is that the impulse pin after leaving the notch just touches on some part of the inside of the horn in passing out. If a wedge of cork is placed under the lever, so that the lever moves stiffly, it can be readily seen whether or not the impulse pin is free to leave the notch and is free all round the horn when the wheel tooth drops on the locking.

See to the safety action. When the tooth drops on to the locking, the safety pin should be just clear of the roller. If it is not clear, the edge of the roller should be polished down until it is right. If there is more than clearance, the safety pin must be brought closer to the roller. See upon pressing the safety pin against the roller that the tooth does not leave the locking, and that the impulse pin is free to enter the notch without butting on the horn of the lever; also that the safety action is sound, so that the pin is in no danger of passing the roller. If the action is not sound, the diameter of the roller should be reduced and the safety pin brought towards it sufficiently to get a sound action if it can be done, but if the escapement has been so badly proportioned as not to allow of a sound action being obtained in this way, the pin must be shifted forward and the bankings opened to allow more run.

See if the banking pins are so placed as to allow of an equal run on each side. If not they should not be bent, for with bent banking pins a difference in the end shakes of the pivots will cause a difference in the run. The banking pin allowing of the most run should be removed, and the hole broached out to receive a larger pin.

LOCKING. That portion of the pallet on which the escape wheel teeth drop.

MAGNETISM. The agent or force in nature which gives rise to the phenomena of attraction, polarity, etc., exhibited by the loadstone, magnet, etc. A watch will become magnetized by too close proximity to a powerful magnetic field, such as is developed in a dynamo electro machine for producing electric light, or by coming in contact with an ordinary magnet, as well as other sources of magnetic or electro-magnetic influences, and by these means all its steel parts become permanent magnets. Each piece of steel has then assumed definite polarity, so that if it is balanced on a point like a compass, it will, like the latter, indicate the direction of the earth's magnetic poles. The influence of these separate magnets, one on the other, and the influence of the earth's magnetism on the different parts, become very potent disturbers of time keeping. Hairsprings, balances, and other small steel parts often become magnetized through being handled with magnetized tweezers or being placed near or in contact with other steel tools that have been magnetized.

Mr. B. Frese exemplifies the influence of the separate magnets produced in a watch by its parts becoming magnetized as follows: if we take two compasses and place them side by side, so that the two bearing points of the needles will form a right angle to their direction, neither of them will show any variation from their natural position or the position they are compelled to take by the influence of the earth's magnetism; but by moving one a little to the North or South of this position, we notice a deflection in both, which is caused by the poles of unequal names having been brought near to each other. Besides this main disturbing influence upon accurate time keeping, we must also consider the disturbance caused by direct attraction, which takes place by two magnetized parts when their equal, as well as their unequal, polarities come close together, but when two extremities of equal polarity come close together or in contact, the stronger magnetized piece will cause the weaker to assume its own polarity, so that when the South polarity of a strongly magnetized piece is brought in contact with the South polarity of a weaker, the South of the latter will be changed to North, and the North to South when the two North polarities have been in contact. The largest steel parts in a watch are the mainspring and the case springs, and these are, therefore, the most potent to cause a disturbance in a steel or compensation balance, aside from the earth's magnetism; the balance being the medium by which nearly all the disturbance is caused, as during its vibrations it takes different positions to the polarities of the other steel parts, as well as the earth's polarities, which is the greatest disturber, aside from the mainspring, the polarities of which change in relation to the balance as the watch runs down. The force one magnetized piece exerts on the other multiplies with decreased distance. The fork, pallets and 'scape wheel are too small in bulk to cause much disturbance, either by direct attraction or directive force, unless they are charged to saturation, which very seldom occurs. If a magnetized balance is placed on a poising tool, with the staff in North and South direction, it will appear out of poise, caused by the earth's magnetism, and will maintain its North polarity uppermost. If it is placed in an East direction, it will no longer allow the North polarity to remain uppermost, but will cause the same to move toward the North and indicate the magnetic dip, the amount of which varies in the different latitudes of the globe. If we place the balance in a horizontal position, its North and South polarities will coincide with those of a compass, showing that if the balance were the only part magnetized in a watch, that magnetism causes more complicated variations than a balance out of poise to the same extent. That trying to poise a magnetized balance would be useless, is self-evident, for the reason, that in a horizontal and North and South positions no equilibrium can be obtained. The influence of magnetized parts that do change position in the watch, is a constant one, as long as the size of vibration is maintained, and is therefore not the cause of serious disturbance. The substituting of new case springs will, therefore, be of little or no benefit.

To detect magnetism, place a pocket compass upon a table or show case and place the watch to be operated upon on the table close to the compass and to the East and West of it. Before starting the test, stop the watch and keep it from running by inserting a wedge made from a thin slip of paper beneath the balance. Turn the compass box around until the needle points to zero before approaching the watch to it. Having placed the watch to the East or West of the compass, proceed to turn the movement, presenting first one figure of the dial and then another to the compass and at the same time noting the deflection of the compass needle. Note whether the deflection is towards the East or West, i. e. whether it repels or attracts the needle. If the movement is not magnetized the compass needle will remain stationary. If it is magnetized the needle will be deflected and by noting the spot you can very readily detect the magnetized part. Magnetism may be removed from small steel parts by placing them in the lathe and revolving them rapidly and at the same time approaching them with a horseshoe magnet and then gradually withdrawing the magnet. It is not good policy however to place any magnetized piece in your lathe as you are liable to magnetize chucks and they will cause you no end of trouble in the future. Demagnetizers are now to be purchased so cheaply that it will starcely pay you to experiment with home made substitutes. See *Demagnetizer*.

To Demagnetize Watches. As watches only become magnetized by being brought into too close contact with magnets, dynamos and the like, it is an utter waste of time to try and demagnetize them by applying heat or cold or rubbing on decoctions of various kinds. Magnetic influence is the only remedy for the evil. The application of the remedy is effected in various ways. If we suspect that a watch is magnetized, the first thing to do is to prove it. It is well to try all watches for magnetism before starting on repairs, and this can be done in the presence of the customer. Place a fair sized pocket compass on, or gummed to the under side of your show case glass in such a position that when at rest the needle will point to O. Place the watch a little to the east or west of the compass and revolve it slowly, watching the needle of the compass to see if the needle is deflected. Be careful to keep the centers of the watch and compass at a given distance apart. If magnetized the needle of the compass will deflect to the right and left as the watch is revolved. Note the deflection at a given point and then proceed to revolve. In this way you can closely approximate the location of the affected part. By taking the movement apart you can in the same manner readily determine the affected part or parts and they can be demagnetized without much difficulty. All of the steel parts of a watch except the balance and spring can be readily demagnetized in the following manner: Place a bar magnet upon a piece of white paper, previously marked with lines say one-eighth of an inch apart. Lift the affected part with a pair of brass or non-magnetic tweezers and approach one end of it within one-eighth of an inch of the magnet, then reverse and approach the opposite end to within one-fourth of an inch, reverse and approach first end to within three-eights of an inch and so on until you reach a distance where the magnet exerts no influence. Test your piece, as previously described, with a compass, and if the cure is not effected repeat the operation. The circular form of the balance renders it somewhat more difficult to treat successfully, and it is best demagnetized as follows: Fasten the balance on a large cork, say from one and a half to two inches in diameter, by means of small brass pins bent at right angles, and mount the cork in your lathe and revolve. Take a ten inch compound magnet and approach it as closely to the balance as possible and then gradually withdraw the magnet, keeping the balance revolving meanwhile, thus presenting every portion of it to the influence of the magnetic force. In some cases it will be found impossible to demagnetize the balance although the operation may be repeated many times. A close examination and test of the balance by means of a compass will show that each arc of the balance has a positive and negative end, and the cross bar will be found in the same condition. Under such circumstances it is absolutely necessary to thoroughly magnetize the balance by applying it to the magnet. You can then demagnetize it, as previously described, without difficulty. It is advisable not to use your regular lathe in this operation but rather to use some old lathe, or a polishing lathe will be found very desirable. See *Demagnetizer*.

MAINSPRING. The ribbon of steel which serves to produce the motive power for a watch, chronometer, or clock. It is said to be the invention of Peter Hele, a clockmaker of Nuremberg, about the year 1500.

The motive force due to the tension of a spring is more or less variable. The causes of this want of uniformity, says Saunier, are as follows: The elastic reaction of a spring becomes greater as the spring is further wound up. A metallic blade is very rarely homogeneous, and worked with sufficient care to avoid different parts being of variable strength. Its energy alters with time dependent on the duration and intensity of the flexure, and this change nearly always occurs irregularly throughout its length. Its elastic force diminishes slightly on elevating the temperature, and lastly a spring rubs against the bottom and lid of the barrel in uncoiling. The successive coils also adhere and rub together, either permanently or occasionally. All these resistances are from the nature of the case variable.

Various forms of mainsprings have been adopted from time to time. The cylindrical spring was one in which the central coils were made thicker with a view to diminish the differences in the pull of the spring when wound up to varying degrees and to increase its energy when nearly run down. The spring when fully wound up rubbed together in the central coils, so that the motive force when it was fully wound was neutralized by the friction. These springs are very rarely seen now, as they were expensive to manufacture and the advantages they possessed were more apparent than real. The taper spring was another form, which is rarely seen now. The thickness of the metal in these springs, gradually diminished throughout its entire length, the effect being to make the coils, when fully wound up, separate, and on this account the spring developed freely. This form was abandoned on account of the cost of manufacture. The third form is the ordinary spring in use to-day, the thickness of whose coils are the same throughout. The development is less uniform than with the tapered spring, as is also the separation of the coils, but it is cheaper of construction, and the variations do not exceed the limits that ordinary escapements can neutralize.

M. M. Roze, in a work on the mainspring, lays down and demonstrates the following theorems:

1. A mainspring in the act of uncoiling in its barrel, always gives a number of turns equal to the difference between the number of coils in the up and down positions.

For example, if 17 is the number of coils when the spring is run down, and 25 is the number when against the arbor, the difference between 17 and 25 or 8, will represent the number of turns in the uncoiling.

2. With a given barrel, spring and arbor, in order that the number of turns may be a maximum, it is necessary that the length of the spring be such that the occupied part of the barrel, (exclusive of that filled by the arbor,) be equal to the unoccupied part; in other words, the surface covered by the spring when up or down must be equal to the uncovered surface of the barrel bottom.

The diameter of the arbor is not an arbitrary quantity, as it depends on the duration of flexure and thickness of the spring, and this depends greatly on the quality of the metal;

if it is too small it is liable to rupture the spring and deprive it of part of its elastic reaction, and if too large, part of this reaction will be wasted. M. Roze demonstrated that the thickness of the spring should be to the diameter of the arbor as 1:26 or 34, according as the rotation of the barrel takes place more or less rapidly. For example, 1:26 is best suited to watches; 1:30 for chronometers, and 1:34 for clocks or time pieces that are expected to go for longer periods.*

Cleaning Mainsprings. Workmen have often been seen cleaning a mainspring by seizing it with a rag and then drawing it out pitilessly and unmercifully. No other consequence can follow such treatment than the breakage of the spring on the earliest possible occasion. Cleaning is best done in the following manner: Lay the spring in benzine. As soon as the adhering oil is dissolved, take it out and seize it with a soft linen rag which imbibes the greater part of the adhering benzine. Cover the palm of the left hand with a corner of the rag, put the spring flat upon it and with the index finger of the right hand, around which another part of the rag is wound, press gently upon it, and let it assume a conical shape; by suitable motions of the finger while wiping, the spring will turn, and every part of its blade may easily and thoroughly be cleansed of all impurities. A spring treated in this manner will be freed of all matter, while at the same time its molecular arrangement is not violently interfered with, in a way calculated to injure its elasticity.

MAINSPRING PUNCH. A punch used by watchmakers for perforating mainsprings. Fig. 143 is Bullock's and is a very handy style. It is inserted in a vise when used. These punches are also made in the form of tongs or plyers.

MAINSPRING WINDER. A good mainspring winder is a necessary adjunct to every watchmaker's bench.

---

*If the reader is desirious of studying the subject at length, he is referred to Saunier's Modern Horology, pp. 661 to 673 inclusive, and a Simple and Mechanically Perfect Watch, by Moritz Grossman. Geo. K. Hazlitt & Co., Chicago.

MAINSPRING WINDER.

The Stark patent winder, shown in Fig. 144, is a very superior tool, is simple and durable, and should last for a life time. The winder is fastened in the vise, the adjustable nut is then turned until the barrel will fit loosely over the jaws, the barrel is then removed and the spring wound on the arbor inside the jaws. Now let the handle turn backward until the arbor is free from the center, pull the arbor back and turn it half round, place the barrel back again over the jaws and spring, and hold it up tightly against the face of the winder with the left hand, at the same time push the arbor forward with the right hand until the barrel and spring are free from the jaws, and the spring will be found in its proper place without further operation. There are two sizes of winding arbors, one for small and the other for large barrels. The arbors are easily changed by turning the thumb screw up until it is free, then changing the arbors and screwing the thumb screw down again.

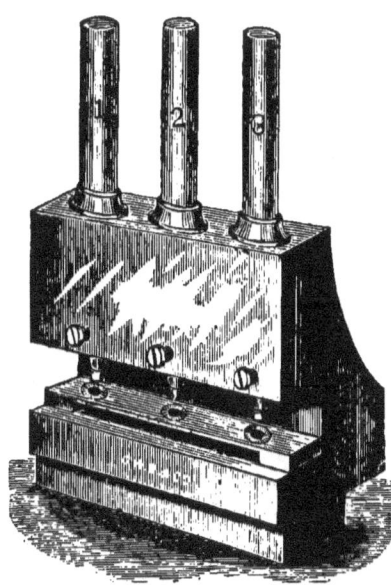

FIG. 143.

The Vaughan patent mainspring winder, shown in the illustration, is intended for removing and replacing springs in clock barrels. Fig. 145 shows the machine ready for use; Fig. 146 shows the arms adjusted to the

FIG. 144.

MAINSPRING WINDER. 218

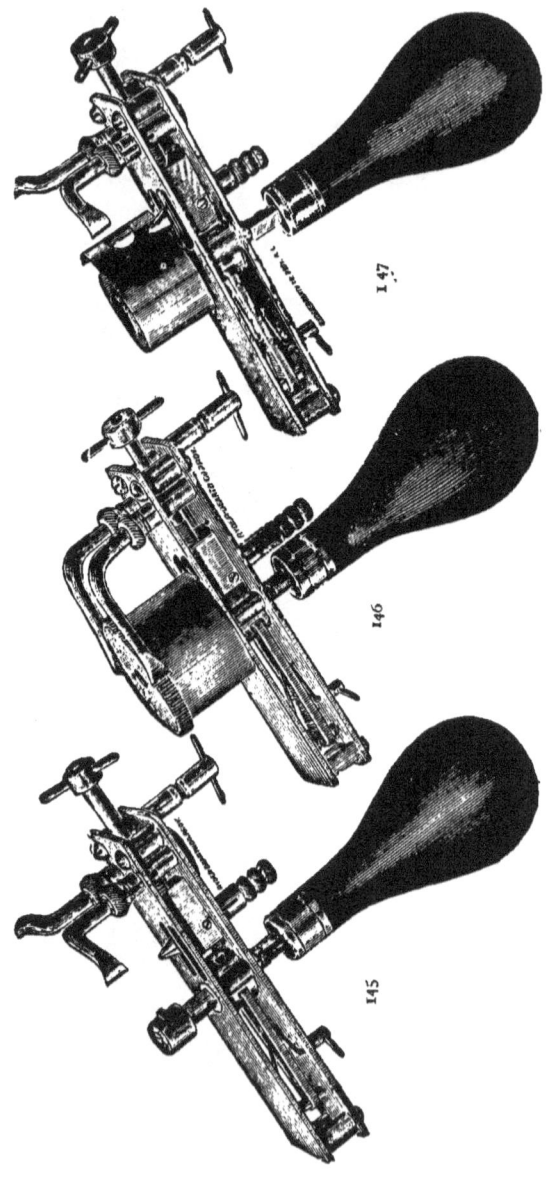

teeth of barrel, for holding barrel while spring is being wound. Fig. 147 shows the winder holding the spring after the barrel has been removed and also as wound, ready to place in the barrel.

The claims made for this device are: It winds either way, as the case may require. Every part is adjustable so that it will handle any spring, and hold any size barrel. Through the whole operation of removing the spring from the barrel and replacing it, the spring is kept in its natural position. After spring and barrel have been cleaned and barrel polished they need not be touched with the hands if the operator chooses to handle them with paper. The spring can be oiled when wound, as in Fig. 147, which carries the oil to bottom of the barrel and prevents any excess of oil getting on the outside. It does not require a vise, but can be used in one place as well as another. There is no strain on the hands more than winding the spring after it is in the clock. The plates and all the working parts are made of steel, and though light and neat in appearance, is strong and durable.

To take the spring out of the barrel, adjust the arms used to hold the barrel, to the right height to meet the teeth of the barrel and swing them wide open, securing them by the thumb screw on the back of the winder. Place the barrel containing the spring over the winding arbor of the machine and catch the hook on the arbor to the spring. Swing the pawl lever to allow you to wind the way you desire, and turn the handle, allowing the barrel to turn with it, until the hook in the barrel, to which the outer end of the spring fastens, comes to within about one-half inch of the jaws which hold the outer edge of the spring on the machine. Free the arms and swing them into the teeth of the barrel, and with the barrel in the center of the machine, again secure them firmly by the thumb screw. Take the machine in the left hand, which will allow you to hold the arms tightly to the barrel and the barrel down to the winder without any danger of their springing away. Wind the spring nearly up, which will free the outer coil from the barrel and enable you to adjust the jaws to the spring. Crowd the jaws on to the spring as far as possible and fasten them firmly to the spring by means of the thumb screw at the upper end of the winder. The spring is now transferred from the barrel to the winder, and the arms can be released and the barrel removed. Reverse the pawl lever, turn the handle up a trifle when the pawl will change sides, allowing the spring to let down.

To replace the spring in the barrel, wind the spring on the machine, as shown in Fig. 3. Place the barrel over it with the hook opposite the hole in the spring. Reverse the pawl lever and let the spring down. Release the jaws from the spring and the work is done. The arms for holding the barrel are only used in taking the spring out.

MAINTAINING POWER. A mechanism for driving a watch or clock while being wound.

MALTESE CROSS. A wheel in the shape of a maltese cross, used in stop works.

MANDRIL. A cheap form of lathe, but little used in this country, being superceded by the American lathe. It is known also as Swiss Universal Lathe. The mandril is worked by means of a handle, and is usually made with wheel

FIG. 148.

and pinion, although a round belt or gut is sometimes used. It has a face plate, pump center, tail stock and slide rest. This tool is superfluous where the workman has an American lathe with slide rest and universal head; for on a lathe with these attachments, a greater variety of work can be performed in less time and in a better manner.

MASS. The amount of matter a body contains. It must not be confounded with weight, for the mass of a body remains the same no matter in what part of the world it may be, but its weight would vary in different latitudes.

MATERIAL CUP. This cup will be found very useful to those who keep small material in bottles. The material being placed in the cup spreads out over the bottom, and the piece wanted is easily selected. The remainder can then be returned to the bottle through the spout with no danger of losing a piece.

MATTING. The grained or frosted surface given to work before gilding or silvering. See *Electro-Plating*.

MERIDIAN DIAL. An instrument for determining when the sun is on the meridian.

MICROMETER. An instrument used for measuring very minute distances with extreme exactness. See *Gauge*.

MILLIMETER. A lineal Measure based on the thousandth part of a meter, or about one-twenty-fifth of an inch. It is used principally by French watchmakers.

MILLING FIXTURE. This attachment is fitted to the slide rest and holds the wire chuck vertically under the center of the lathe, so that articles held in the chucks can be fed under mills or saws held in the saw arbor.

FIG. 149.

MOMENTUM. The amount of motion in a body which is obtained by multiplying its mass by its velocity.

MOTION WORK. The wheels of a watch or clock which cause the hour hand to travel one-twelfth as fast as the minute hand.

MOVEMENT. A term usually applied to the mechanism of a watch or clock independent of a case.

FIG. 150.

MOVEMENT BOX. A metal box with glass sides for holding watch movements while timing, etc. before casing. In the Rockford box shown in Fig. 150 stem wind movements can be wound without fingering or exposure to dust.

MOVEMENT COVER. A glass shade to protect a movement or portions of a movement from dust and from being lost while undergoing repairs. Fig. 151, illustrates an improved cover with wooden base divided into compartments for the reception of the various parts so they may be kept separate and readily picked out.

FIG. 151.

MOVEMENT HOLDER. A metal frame as shown in Fig. 152, having three adjustable arms for holding the movement by clamping on to the plate. It is useful in putting a watch together, as it rests upon the bench and leaves both hands free to work with and the plates are kept free from finger marks.

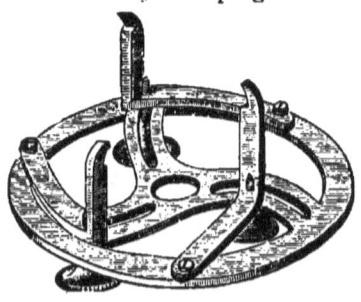

FIG. 152.

MOVEMENT REST A wooden, bone or rubber shell, similar to eye-glass frames, for holding movements while undergoing repairs, oiling, etc.

NON-MAGNETIC WATCH. A watch whose parts cannot be polarized in a magnetic field; a watch whose quick moving parts are made of some other metals than steel or iron. Paillard who has studied non-magnetic metals with great care, makes his balance springs of palladium, and his balances of palladium alloyed with copper, silver and other metals. In some instances, says Britten, he appears to have used a palladium alloy for the inner part, and brass for the outer part of the rim, and in others to have formed both laminae of different alloys of palladium. Aluminum bronze, (*See Alloys*), which combines strength with lightness, is particularly suited for the lever and pallets. The American Waltham Watch Company have obtained remarkable results in non-magnetic watches, with an alloy of platinum. Steel in its hardened and tempered form, has long been used for the balance springs of watches, but from the fact that it owed its elasticity to the process of fire hardening, it has always been uncertain in its action, and often two springs from the same piece of steel would give very different results when put to the same tests. This, it is claimed, is not true of the alloy used by the Waltham Company. The non-magnetic spring, they claim, is a natural spring; it requires no rolling or hammering to harden or make it elastic. Its elasticity is a property of the alloy, and from nothing mechanical done to it, that it cannot be annealed or robbed of its elasticity can be shown by heating it to a red heat of nearly 1100 degrees Fahr., with no change of elasticity. At this degree of heat, steel is annealed, or becomes soft, and of no use as a spring.

FIG. 154.

In the expansion balance of ordinary construction, intended to compensate for temperature, steel is used as the metal of lowest expansion ratio, but in this case never in its hardened and tempered form. Such a balance would be too irregular in its action. No two balances would work alike, and anyone manufacturing such, would find a difference of temper or degree of elasticity in each arm and inside steel laminae. The greatest controlling factor in the expansion balance, is the brass outside laminae, and unless it is hammered or rolled it is of no practical use. A good expansion balance of the usual make depends more on the brass than the steel for its action, and it is a well known fact that brass is one of the most uncertain alloys known, and will often, when not in use, deteriorate to such an extent as to have no value for its original purpose. The Waltham non-magnetic balance is said to stand a change of temperature of 400 degrees Fahr., and return to its original form as shown by gauges. (See description of gauge and illustration at Fig. 8) under head of *Balances*. The non-magnetic balance metals while having the expansive ratio required, also have a greater natural degree of elasticity than the brass and steel construction, thus making a balance that when in use in the watch, retains its shape, and will not get out of poise.

OIL. One of the most essential things to the good performance and durability of a watch or clock is good oil. A little thought given to the subject of oil will show how very essential it is that only the very best attainable be used. The mechanism of a fine watch, and particularly one of a complicated nature, is expected to perform regularly and with little or no variation, although after a thorough cleaning and oiling that mechanism may not fall into the hands of the repairer oftener than once a year, and in the majority of cases it is a longer interval of time. There are few mechanical contrivances from which so much is expected as a fine watch or chronometer, and yet there are none that receive in proportion to their mechanism, so little care and attention. The engineer carefully wipes and oils his engine at least once a day; the machinist does the same with his lathes and the machines under his care, but the watch, a mechanism far more complicated and from which much more is expected, in regard to correct performance, does not receive this care oftener, on an average, than once a year. How essential is it then that the lubricant be of the finest possible quality.

The essential requisites of an oil that will insure correct performance of a watch during this time are:
1. It must remain liquid when exposed to severe cold.
2. It must evaporate slowly under intense heat.
3. It must not corrode on metal.
4. It must not become gummy.

What oils best withstand these tests? For many years European watchmakers gave the preference to pure olive oil, but experiment has proven that this oil is wholly unfit for watches and the same may be said of all vegetable oils, for they invariably become gummy and turn green when placed in contact with brass. Neat's foot oils were found to possess similar unfitting qualities, and mineral oils are found to evaporate too quickly.

Nothing then remains but fish oils and those made from a species of porpoise known as the black fish, are considered the very best. Fine watch and chronometer oils of this class are prepared from the head and jaw only, which parts yield a limited quantity of very pure oil, known as "jaw and melon oil." This oil is carefully extracted without allowing any flesh or blood to come in contact with it, and after trying is filtered and retained in its native purity as nearly as possible, no bleaching, either by sun, acids or alkalies being employed. There is a popular fallacy existing in the trade that oils should be used when fresh, and even the acknowledged authority, Saunier, says, "do not buy from motives of economy, bottles that have laid for years in the shop." This may be true, and probably is, in regard to vegetable and animal oils, which are likely to become rancid if kept for a long time, but Wm. F. Nye, one of the largest and most celebrated manufacturers of fine watch and chronometer oils in the world, declares that black fish oils are improved by age, and his oils are seldom placed upon the market in the same year as obtained. We are indebted to the same authority for the statement that oils of this kind are clearer and more brilliant after some years than fresh oils. The Nye oils are tried at New Bedford, Mass., and in the following winter are sent to St. Albans, Vt., where it is chilled down and filtered at an average temperature of 25° below zero, and in some instances, even as low as 37° below zero. In this manner the specific gravity and density of the oil is increased, a finer grain and texture are secured, giving increased resistance to the effects of both heat and cold. The two prominent manufacturers of black fish oils in this country, and we might say in the world, are Wm. F. Nye and Ezra Kelley, both of New Bedford, Mass. The watchmaker should be very careful what oils he uses, as many on the market are of foreign manufacture and are made from the olive, or are combinations of animal and vegetable oils.

OILER. A fine steel wire, mounted in a wooden or bone handle and used for applying oil to the mechanism of a watch

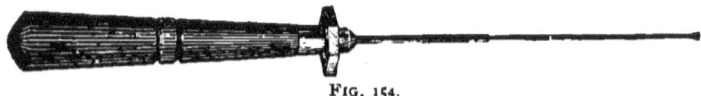

FIG. 154.

or clock. Fig. 154 is a Bullock oiler, made with 14k. gold tip, and has a collet which keeps the point from touching the bench and also prevents oiler from rolling.

OIL SINK. The cavity turned in watch and clock plates and jewels, around the pivot holes. Experience, says Britten, has shown that when the oil sink in chronometers and clocks where the plates are not gilt is thoroughly well polished, not only is the oil drawn to the pivot more freely, but it is less decomposed by contact with the metal than when the sinks are rougher. Oil sinks should be deep and small in diameter rather than shallow and wide. Saunier says that care should be taken that the internal faces of the holes in which the shoulders of the axis rest, as well as the external faces, when these holes are provided with end-stones, are hollowed in *tallow drop* form, with a very slight interval between the bottom of the hole and the end-stone. When these precautions are taken, the oil, if not present in too great a quantity, will neither spread nor run down the axis, but will remain partly in the oil sink and partly attached to the shoulders of the axis, and in the case of pivot holes with end-stones, as the oil is exhausted, that spread over the end-stone will be drawn into the pivot hole through capillarity.

OILSTONES. A mixture of one part alcohol and two parts glycerine will be found a much better lubricant for the oilstone, where small tools such as watchmakers use, are sharpened, than will the ordinary oils used. Oilstones often become so saturated with oil as to be almost useless and are often abandoned on this account. Such a stone if soaked in benzine for a few days will come out as good as new.

Circular Oilstones. Circular stones will be found much superior to the ordinary flat oilstones commonly used, for sharpening drills, gravers and other cutting tools where it is desirable to have an exact angle. An Arkansas or Turkey stone dressed down to circular form, and say $1\frac{1}{2}$ inches in diameter when mounted on a lathe chuck will be found to be far superior to the common flat stone. Apply a small quantity of watch oil, or what is better, a mixture composed of one-half alcohol and one-half glycerine, and hold your graver or drill at the exact angle you want the cutting edges and turn at a moderate speed. Truer angles and better work can be obtained in this manner than by any other. Emery and corundum wheels mounted in a similar manner will be found very handy accessories to the watchmakers' bench.

OILSTONE DUST. A preparation of powdered oilstone, used for smoothing pivots and other steel parts.

OVERBANKING. When the balance vibrates excessively and causes the ruby pin to push past the lever it is known as overbanking.

OVERCOIL. The last coil of a Breguet hairspring where it is bent over the body of the spring towards the center is called the overcoil.

PALLET. That portion of an escapement by means of which the escape wheel gives impulse to the balance.

PALLET STAFF. The staff or axis of the pallets.

PALLET STONES. The stones which form the rubbing surfaces of a pallet.

PALLET STONE ADJUSTER. Fig. 155 is a Bullock pallet stone adjuster, which will be found very useful in holding pallets and protecting them from heat while heating cement in order to adjust stones.

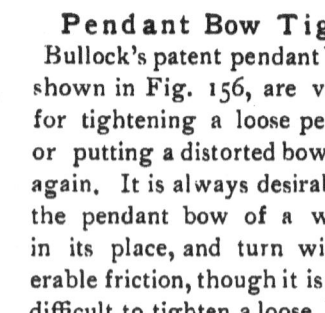

FIG. 155.

PEG WOOD. Small round sticks of wood used for cleaning out pivot holes, etc.

PENDANT. The portion of a watch case to which the bow is attached and the portion connecting it with the case.

Pendant Bow. The ring of metal to which the chain is attached to the case.

Pendant Bow Tightener. Bullock's patent pendant bow pliers, shown in Fig. 156, are very handy for tightening a loose pendant bow or putting a distorted bow into shape again. It is always desirable to have the pendant bow of a watch tight in its place, and turn with considerable friction, though it is sometimes difficult to tighten a loose bow when the seat is worn deep.

FIG. 156.

PENDULUM. The mass of metal or other substances whose vibrations regulate the train of a clock. The theoreti-

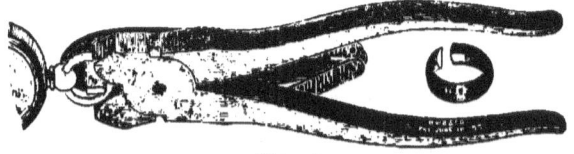

FIG. 157.

cal length of a pendulum to beat seconds or other time depends upon the location of the clock, for the force that gravity exerts upon a body depends on the distance of the body from the center of the earth. The length of a seconds pendulum at

The Equator is	-	39 inches.
Rio de Janeiro,	-	39.01.
Madras,	- -	39.02.
New York	- -	39.10.
Paris,	- - -	39.13.
London,	- - -	39.14.
Edinburgh,	-	39.15.
Greenland,	- -	39.20.
North or South Pole,		39.206.

PENDULUM SPRING. The ribbon or ribbons of steel used in suspending the pendulum.

PILLAR. Posts of brass used to keep the plates of a watch in position.

PILLAR PLATE. The plate of a watch to which the pillars are attached.

PINION. The smaller of two toothed wheels which are geared into one another. The tooth of a pinion is called a pinion leaf.

Pinion Grinder and Polisher. The ends of the leaves of pinions, when ground flat and polished, add very much to the beauty of a job when completed. Proceed to turn down your pinion in the lathe and fit it in the usual manner, ready for finishing. Now select a suitable chuck to hold the pinion in the lathe and take a few copper cartridge shells, used in 22 or 32 calibre revolvers, and drill four holes in the end to fit the staff of the pinion you wish to polish. Fit a piece of wood about three inches long in the open end of the cartridge shells to use as a handle; do not allow the handle to enter the shell over one-fourth of an inch, so that it will not strike against the pivot of the pinion while polishing. Now file flat the closed end of the cartridge and your grinding and polishing tool is complete. Insert the pinion in one of the holes of the shell so that the flat surface of the shell will come up squarely against the face of the leaves of the pinion. Apply a paste made of emery flour and sweet oil and run the lathe at a high speed, pressing slightly against the pinion leaves. Transfer from one hole to another to insure flatness. Clean off the pinion with benzine and examine to see that the marks of the turning tool are all out. If not, proceed as before. Take another shell prepared in like manner, and use crocus and oil instead of emery, and grind out the scratches of the emery. After removing these, wash thoroughly in benzine and with another copper shell proceed to polish, using a paste of diamantine and oil or alcohol. A good polish will soon appear. Care must be exercised to see that the work is thoroughly cleaned after each process. The shells can then be laid away in separate boxes for future use. During leisure moments you can prepare a number of these shells to fit almost any job and you will find them very handy for many purposes.

PIN PALLET ESCAPEMENT. An escapement used mostly in French clocks, in which it is often placed in front of the dial. The pallets are formed of semi-circular stones, generally cornelian.

This excellent escapement, says Britten, (invented by M. Brocot), rarely seen except in small French clocks, appears to be worthy of more extended use. The fronts of the teeth of the escape wheel are sometimes made radial, as shown in Fig. 158; sometimes cut back so as to bear on the point only, like the " Graham;" and sometimes set forward so as to give recoil to to the wheel during the motion of the pendulum beyond the escaping arc. The pallets, generally of cornelian, are of semi-circular form. The diameter of each is a trifle less than the distance between the two teeth of the escape wheel. The angle of impulse in this escapement bears direct reference to the number of teeth embraced by the pallets. Ten is the usual number, as shown in the drawing. The distance between the escape wheel and pallet staff centers should not be less than the radius of the wheel $\times 1.7$. This gives about $4°$ of impulse measured from the pallet staff center.

English clockmakers rather object to this escapement on account of the difficulty of keeping oil to the pallets, which is aggravated if there is much space between the root of the

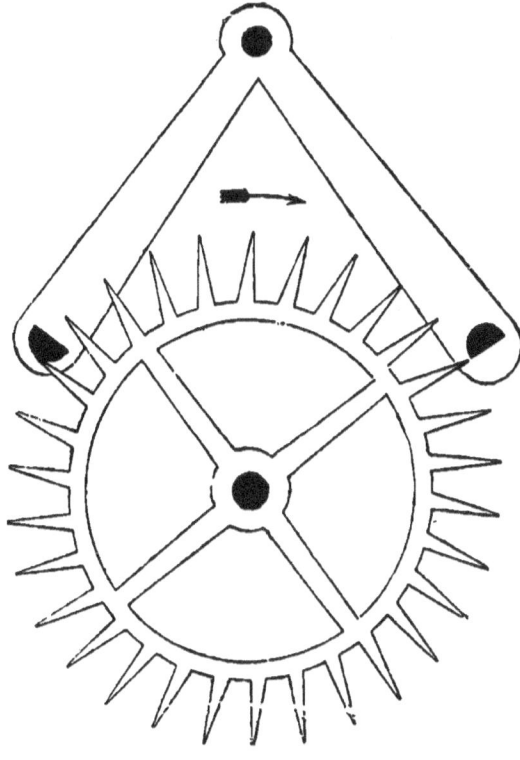

FIG. 158.

pallet stone and the face of the wheel. The effect of the want of oil is much more marked if the pallets are made of steel instead of jewel. Any tendency of this escapement to set is generally met by flattening the curved impulse faces of the pallets.

PIN VISE. An improved form of pin vise is that shown in Fig. 159, manufactured by Mr. Logan. It is hollow throughout its entire length and closes together, the same as a chuck on the American lathe. It will hold a small drill or wire perfectly true and will be found very useful for many purposes.

Fig. 159.

PIN WHEEL ESCAPEMENT.

The pin wheel escapement was invented by Lepaute about 1753. A clock escapement analogus in its action to the "Graham." The impulse is given by nearly half-round pins standing out from the face of the escape wheel. The one advantage over the Graham is that the pressure on the pallets is always downwards, so that excessive shake in the pallet staff hole, which may be looked for in course of time, especially in large clocks, would not affect the amount of impulse.

This escapement is used principally in turret clocks. The chief objection to it practically, says Britten, is the difficulty of keeping the pins lubricated, the oil being drawn away to the face of the wheel. To prevent this a nick is sometimes cut around the pins, close to the wheel, but this weakens the pins very much. The best plan is to keep the pallets as close as they can be to the face of the wheel without touching.

Lepaute made the pins semi-circular, and placed alternately on each side of the wheel so as to get the pallets of the same length. This requires double the number of pins, and there is no real disadvantage in having one pallet a little longer than the other, provided the short one is put outside, as shown in the drawing. Sir Edmund Beckett introduced the practice of cutting a piece off the bottoms of the pins, which is a distinct improvement, for if the pallet has to travel past the center of the pin with a given arc of vibration before the pin can rest, the pallets must be very long unless very small pins are used.

The escaping arc is generally 20, and the diameter of the pins is then 40 measured from the pallet staff hole.

Then with a given diameter of pin, to find the mean length of pallets, divide the given diameter by .069.

Or if the mean length of pallets is given, the diameter of pins may be found by multiplying the given length by .069.

The opening between the extreme points of the pallets =2°, that is, half the diameter of the pins.

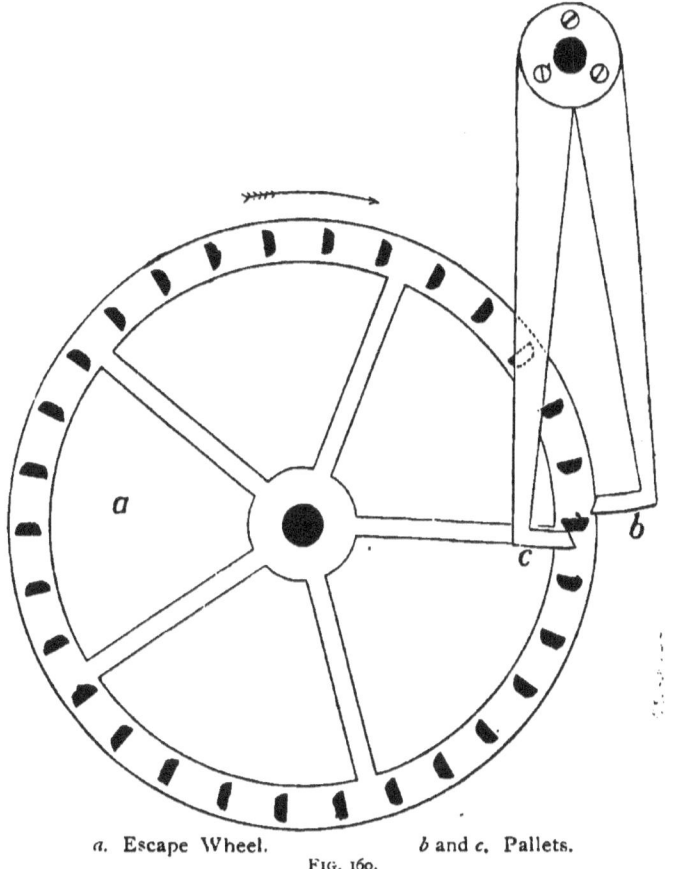

a. Escape Wheel.　　b and c, Pallets.
FIG. 160.

With an escaping arc of 3° the mean length of the pallet arms is ten times the diameter of the pins.

The angle of impulse is divided between the pins and the pallets, and care must be taken that the pallets are not cut back too much. When a pin escapes from one pallet, the bottom of the succeeding pin must fall safely on the rest of the other pallet. It is best before finishing the impulse planes to place the pallets in position, and mark them off with reference to the pins. The thickness of the two pallets and one pin contained between them equals, less drop which is very small, the space between two pins from center to center. The pallets are of steel, hardened at the acting parts, and screwed to a collar on the pallet staff. The rests are slightly rounded so as to present less surface to the pins, and the curves struck from a little below the pallet staff hole so as to be hardly "dead." The pins should be of gun-metal or very hard brass, or aluminium bronze, round when screwed into the wheel, and cut to shape in an engine afterwards.

PIVOT. The end of an arbor or shaft that rests in a support or bearing.

Length of Balance Pivots. Saunier recommends the removal of the endstone to see that the pivot projects enough beyond the pivot hole when the plate is inverted. Remove the cock and detach it from the balance. Take off the balance spring with its collet from this latter and place it on the cock inverted, so as to see whether the collet is central when the outer coil is midway between the curb pins. Remove the cock endstone and endstone cap, place the top balance pivot in its hole and see that it projects a little beyond the pivot hole. Place the balance in the calipers to test its truth and at the same time to see that it is in poise. It must be remembered, however, that the balance is sometimes put out of poise intentionally. See *Poising the Balance*.

The Play of Pivots. Saunier gives the following rules for the play of escapement pivots: In the cylinder escapement about one-sixth the diameter of the pivot. In the duplex escapement about one-tenth the diameter of the pivot. In the lever escapement about one-eighth the diameter of the pivot A large hole causes the pitching of the depths to vary with position, and a deficient play renders the escapement more sensitive to thickening of the oil. There is less inconvenience when the play is somewhat in excess than when it is deficient.

In determining the play of train wheel pivots proceed as follows: Allow the train to run down and if it does so noisily or by jerks it may be assumed that some of the depths are bad, in consequence either of the teeth being badly formed, or the holes too large, etc. To test the latter point, cause the wheels to revolve alternately in opposite directions by applying a finger to the barrel or center wheel teeth, at the same time noting the movement of each pivot in turn, in its hole. A little practice will soon enable the workman to judge whether the play is correct. The running down of the train will also indicate whether any pivots are bent. It is important that the center pivots project beyond the holes in the plate and bridge.

To Straighten Pivots. Saunier recommends that a number of straight holes be drilled in a plate at exactly right angles to its surface. Introduce the pivot into a hole that it fits with very little play, and redress it by causing the staff to rotate, at the same time holding the plate in the hand. Caution is necessary, since there is some risk of bending the pivot too far.

The Friction of Train Pivots. It is very important to reduce the friction of the wheel pivots to a minimum quantity, and to make it constant so that the motive power be transmitted with the greatest possible uniformity to the balance or pendulum, which is necessary to enable the latter to maintain its arc of oscillation of the same magnitude. The friction of the pivots is due to the pressure of the motive power and the weight of the wheels. The wheel work nearest the motive power must have strong pivots so that they possess sufficient resistance, neither wear the pivot holes to one side nor enlarge them, by which the friction would be increased and at the same time alter the true point of engagement. In tenor with the distance of the wheels from the motive power, the thickness of their pivots must decrease because these latter sustain less pressure, and are subject to a greater velocity than the first parts.

Pivoting Cylinders. It often happens that cylinders are broken while turning down pivots. To avoid this proceed as follows: Select a piece of silver or German-silver joint wire, the opening of which is slightly larger than the diameter of the cylinder, (lower end); cut off a piece the length of the cylinder proper, leaving the pivot projecting through. Fill the cylinder with lathe wax and slip on the little piece of joint wire while the cement is quite warm. Proceed to true up by the pivot in the usual way and when the wax is quite cold, turn down and polish the pivot before removing from the lathe. If care is used in cutting the joint wire the proper length, it will answer as a gauge for the length of the cylinder. If the joint wire is properly cemented on the cylinder, it is almost impossible to break it. The lower part of the cylinder can be left in this condition and the upper part can be turned down to fit the balance, hair-spring, collet and pivot. After this is done remove from the lathe and dissolve the cement in alcohol in a bottle.

Shape of Pivots. Pivots must be hard, round and well polished; their shoulders are to be flat, not too large, with ends well rounded off so that they do not wear the cap jewel. The jewel holes must be round, smooth and not larger than is requisite for the free motion of the pivot which is surrounded with oil. Their sides must be parallel to those of the pivots, so that they sustain the pressure of the pivot equally at all points of their length. The holes, if of brass or gold, must have been hammered sufficiently hard, so that the pores of the metal are closed to prevent too rapid a wear. It is well if the oil sinks are of a size that will accommodate a sufficient quantity of oil, which, if too little, would soon dry out or become thickened with the worn off particles of the metal. The under turnings of the pinion leaves are conical, but in such a way that the thicker part be nearest to the pivot, because by this disposition the oil is retained at the pivot by attraction, and does not seek to spread into the pinion leaves, as is often the case, especially with flat watches in which this provision is frequently slighted.

PIVOT GAUGE. A steel plate with tapered slit for measuring the diameter of pivots. See *Gauge, (Dennison's)*.

PIVOT POLISHER. The pivot polisher is used for grinding and polishing conical and straight pivots and shoulders. It is also useful for drilling, polishing or snailing steel wheels,

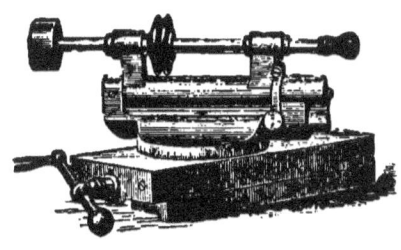

FIG. 161.

milling out odd places in plate or bridge where only a part of a circle is to be removed, etc. The circular base being graduated to degrees it can be set at any angle. The spindle has a taper hole for drill chucks, which makes the fixture very useful for drilling either in the center or eccentric, and by using the graduations on the pulley of the headstock an accurately spaced circle of holes may be drilled. Fig. 161 is the American Watch Tool Company's polisher; Fig. 162, the Mosely, and Fig. 163, the Rivett pattern.

FIG. 162.

The polisher is used as follows: After the pivot is turned to proper shape, put on your polisher (spindle parallel with lathe bed), with lap back of pivot. Use cast iron lap first. (Square corners for square shoulders, and round corners for conical.) Lap for conical shoulder can be readily cornered with a fine file, and cross-grind with fine oil stone to remove any lines made by graver. Lines on end can be removed same way, or in fingers rubbed on piece of ground glass which has on it a paste of oil stone and oil well mixed.

This will rapidly bring them up to a sharp corner nicer than by the graver. On the iron laps use No. 1 crocus or very fine oil stone powder, well ground down in oil to a paste. When roughed out to your liking, wipe off the crocus, and with a little oil touch the pivot gently, repeat the second time. Then change lap for one of box-wood, and use crocus No. 4, very fine and well ground down to paste. Proceed as with first lap, being careful at all times to keep the lap properly oiled and not pressed too hard against the work, particularly in the last operation. Also be sparing of your grinding or polishing material. About three specks of polish with point of a small knife is sufficient. Bring the lap up carefully against the work until spread all the way around, then proceed, bearing in mind that grinding is not polishing, and that to polish nicely the work and lap must be very nearly the right shape. To thoroughly clean the laps, dip in benzine.

FIG. 163.

POISING TOOL. A tool used for poising or ascertaining if the metal in a balance is evenly disposed around the axis. See *Balance*.

POLISHING. See *Cleansing, Pickling and Polishing*. For polishing of steel, pivots, etc. See *Steel, Pivots, etc.*

POTENCE. A bracket used for supporting the lower end of the balance staff in full-plate watches.

PUMP CENTER. The small, pointed steel shaft in the center of a universal head, which is used for centering the work.

PUSH PIECE. The movable part of a pendant used for opening the case. The small movable projection on the side of a case which is pushed in when setting the hands.

QUARTER SCREWS. The four timing screws in a compensation balance.

RACK LEVER. A watch escapement, said to have been invented by Abbe Hautefeuille in 1734. The lever terminated in a rack, which worked into a pinion on the balance staff.

RATCHET. A wheel having pointed teeth and fixed to an arbor to prevent it turning backward. A click or pawl falls in between the teeth of the wheel and prevents it turning backward. See *Click.*

RECOIL ESCAPEMENT. An escapement in which the teeth are pressed backward or recoiled by the pallets after coming to rest, as in the Anchor Escapement.

RED STUFF. Sesquioxide of iron, used for polishing brass and steel by mixing with oil. Crocus, rouge and clinker are various grades of red stuff.

REGULATOR. The small steel hand or lever to the shorter end of which the curb pins are attached, and which by moving from side to side practically shortens the hair spring. See *Curb Pins.*

REPAIR CLAMPS. The Magic repair clamps shown

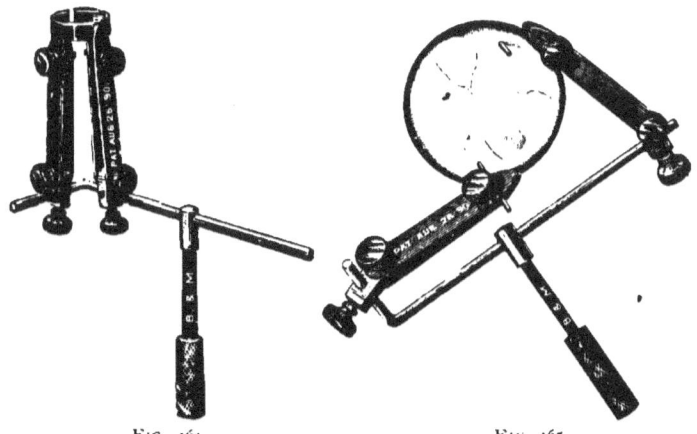

FIG. 164.   FIG. 165.

in Figs. 164 to 166 are used for holding various kinds of work in position, while repairing, soldering, etc. In addition to the uses shown in the illustrations, it is also applicable for dozens of operations that will suggest themselves to the possessor.

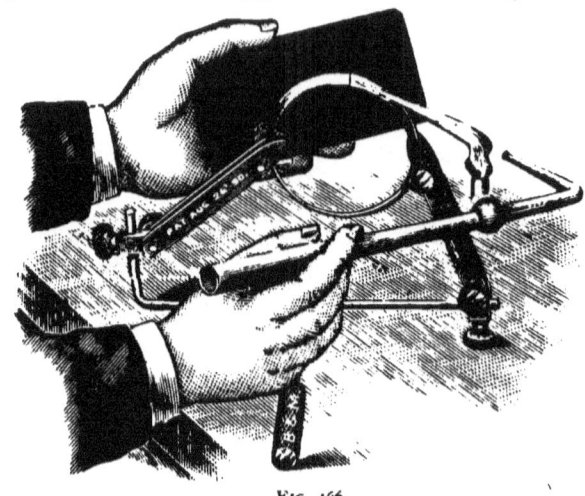

Fig. 166.

It is so arranged that the end screws can be used as feet and the handles as a support (as shown in the illustration), so that the tool with the work in it will stand up, leaving the operator free to use charcoal or asbestos block in one hand and blow pipe in the other. It is especially valuable for holding dials, when soldering on feet.

REPEATER. A watch which indicates the time by repeating it by means of gongs or bells. There are hour, quarter, half-quarter, five-minute, and minute repeaters. They were first made about 1686, and are said to be the invention of Daniel Quare.

To Bend Gong Wires. The bending of a gong wire in a repeating watch, in order to free it from any point it touches, often results in diminishing the sound considerably. In such a case Immisch advises as follows: If the spring touches on the outside and must consequently be bent inward, it should be laid upon a convex piece of brass corresponding in shape with the inner side of the spring at the place where it is to be bent; then if the outside be slightly hammered with the sharp edge of a hammer, the small indentations produced will cause the outside to lengthen a little and the inside to contract in proportion. The change of form will be very gradual and the granular disturbance, being spread over a large area, will not be great enough to effect the tone in the least. The more a spring is bent to and fro in any direction the more it will lose its elastic force. In soft springs especial care should be taken to make any change very gradual, repeating the operation oftener rather than to bend too much at one time, and thereby necessitate the bending back of the spring. If a perfectly adjusted and very soft spring should be bent and brought back again to exactly its former position, the vibrabrations would be no longer isochronous, and by repeating the experiment the elastic force or the spring curve will become so small compared with that possessed by the body of the spring, that instead of exercising a control over the latter, its motion becomes subservient to it. A harder spring will bear a much greater amount of manipulation, and a Breguet spring, the form of which in itself necessitates a certain amount of bending, must always have a greater degree of hardness than that necessary for helical springs, in order that the advantage possessed by this form should be of the greatest possible use. It is also necessary that a certain time should elapse before ascertaining the result of the change affected. Metallic bodies possessing any degree of elasticity, if forced into a different shape, do not retain the newly acquired shape exactly, but have a tendency to return in some degree toward that shape from which they have been forced. The reactionary force becomes gradually less active, until after a time it ceases altogether. The time required for the shape to become permanent differs greatly with the degree of elasticity. It is sometimes desirable to bend a spring, but the repairer being afraid of breaking it abandons the idea. Suppose it is desirable to bend a side click spring of a Swiss bridge watch, which by the way, is generally made of poor steel. Take hold of the end in which the screw goes with a pair of brass-nosed sliding tongues, holding it in the left hand; then press a piece of brass against the click, bending it in the direction desired, and at the same time holding it over the flame of a spirit lamp until the center or spring part becomes a straw or dark red color. The fact that spring-tempered steel is brought to a dark red-blue twenty times over, will not reduce it below its former temper; on the contrary, it will tend to equalize and improve the temper and render it less liable to break. Suppose a cylinder pivot, or any pivot of any of the escapement parts are bent and you wish to straighten it by this process; take a small brass ring, fit it to the pivot and hold over the flame of the lamp, bending it at the same time in the desired direction.

RESILIENT ESCAPEMENT. A form of the lever escapement in which the lever yields, when pressed upon on the outside by the impulse pin, and allows the pin to pass. See *Lever Escapement*.

RING GAUGE. A gauge used by jewelers for meas-

uring the internal dimensions of finger rings.

RIVETING STAKE. A steel block pierced with a number of different sized holes. See *Staking Tool*.

ROLLER REMOVER. There are numerous designs in the way of roller removers upon the market, but lack of space prevents description and illustrations of them. Fig 168

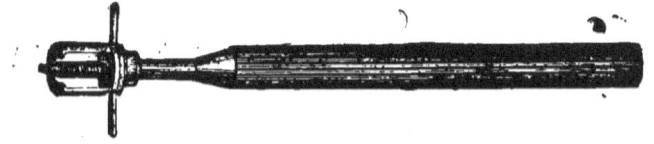

illustrates the Bush remover while Fig. 169, illustrates that made by Mr. Logan. They are both excellent tools and do the work in a satisfactory manner. These tools are so thoroughly understood by watchmakers that a detailed description of their modus operandi seems superfluous.

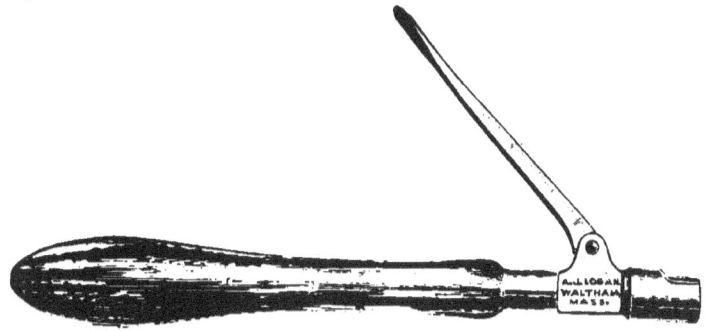

FIG. 169.

ROSE CUTTER. A hollow cutter, as shown in Fig. 170, used for reducing the size of wire, as in forming heads when making screws.

ROUGE. See *Red Stuff*.

FIG. 170.

ROUNDING UP TOOL ATTACHMENT. The Webster rounding up tool attachment, shown in Fig. 171, is a

FIG. 171.

very useful adjunct to the lathe. It is attached to the top of the slide-rest. To operate, a pointed taper in the taper chuck is put in the lathe spindle. The wheel to be rounded up is put into the fixture and the wheel adjusted vertically so that the point of the lathe center will be at the center of the thickness of the wheel, after which the lower spindle of the fixture should not be moved. Now remove the wheel, also the taper chuck, and put the saw arbor, with the rounding-up cutter, in the lathe spindle, and adjust the longitudinal slide of the slide-rest so that the rounding-up cutter will be back of and in line with the center of the rounding-up fixture, after which the longitudinal slide of the slide-rest should not be moved. Now put the wheel and supporting collet in place, and proceed with the rounding-up.

RUBY PIN. The impulse pin in the lever escapement.

RUBY ROLLER. The roller in the duplex escapement which locks the escape wheel teeth.

SAFETY PIN. In the lever escapement, a pin that when the hands are turned backward, prevents the pallets leaving the escape wheel.

SAFETY PINION. - A center pinion which allows the barrel to recoil when the mainspring breaks.

SAPPHIRE FILE. A piece of flat brass to which a piece of sapphire, previously flattened is attached by means of shellac. It is used for working upon garnet pallets and other soft stones. The sapphire is ground upon a diamond mill and its surface rendered coarse or fine according to the mill used. A strip of copper and diamantine is sometimes used instead of sapphire files.

SAW ARBOR. The saw arbor or chuck, as shown in Fig. 172, is made with a projection turned to receive a saw, diamond or emery lap, etc. They are manufactured by the various lathe manufacturers, though the patterns vary somewhat from the illustration here shown.

Fig. 172.

SCREWS. Odd sized screws, not to be had from the material dealers may be readily made by means of the screw plate and rose cutter. The rose cutter is quite a valuable adjunct to the lathe, and is fixed to the spindle in the same manner as the chuck, and will be found exceedingly useful for quickly reducing pieces of wire for screws, etc., to a gauge. For screws, the wire should be of a proper size for the screw heads, and a cutter selected with a hole the size of the finished screw. The point of the wire is rounded to enter the hole of the cutter, against which it is forced by the back center of the lathe, the serrated face of the cutter rapidly cutting the superfluous metal, the part intended for the screw passing into the hole in the cutter. Some care is required in rounding the point of the wire, for if not done equally all around, the screw will not be true to the head.

To Remove Broken Screws. It sometimes happens that a screw gets broken off in a watch plate in such a manner that it is impossible to remove it with tools without marring the plate. In such an event proceed as follows: put enough rain water in a glass tumbler to thoroughly cover the plate and add sulphuric acid until the water tastes a sharp sour. Place the plate in the solution and allow it to remain a few hours, when the screw will partially dissolve and drop out. Remove from the solution, wash thoroughly in clean water, then in alcohol and dry in saw dust. The solution will not injure the brass plate or gilding in the slightest, but care must be taken to remove all other screws or cement jewels, previous to immersion.

Any one having an American lathe can, with small expense of time and labor, make a small attachment which will easily and quickly remove a broken screw from the the plate or pillar of any watch.

Take two common steel watch keys having hardened and tempered pipes—size, four or five—having care that the squares in each are of the same size and of good depth. Cut off the pipes about half an inch from the end; file up one of these for about half its length, on three equal sides, to fit one of the large split chucks of the lathe. Drill a hole in one of the brass centers of the lathe of sufficient size and depth, into which insert the other key-pipe, and fasten with a little solder. Soften a piece of Stubs' wire, to work easily in the lathe, and turn down for an eighth of an inch from the end to a size a little smaller than the broken screw in the plate; finish with a conical shoulder, for greater strength, and cross-file the end with a fine slot or knife-edge file, that the tool may not slip on the end of the broken screw; cut off the wire a half inch from the end, and file down to a square that will fit closely into one of the key-pipes. Make a second point like the first one and fit to the other key-pipe; harden in oil polish, and temper to a dark straw color. Fit the brass center into the tail stock. To use, put the tools in the place in the lathe, place the broken end of the screw against the end of the point in the lathe head; slide up the back center and fasten the point firmly against the other end of the screw, that it may not slip or turn; revolve the plate slowly, and the broken screw, being held fast between the two points, will be quickly removed. To remove a broken pillar screw: Place the broken screw against the point in the lathe-head, holding the plate firmly with the right hand, the pillar on a line with the lathe center; turn the lathe-head slowly' backward with the left hand, and the screw will be removed. Should the tool slip on the broken screw, and fail to draw it out, drill a hole in the pillar from the lower or dial side, down to the screw point, (if the size of the pillar in the plate will admit of so doing), and with the second point in the back center, remove the screw in the same manner as the plate screw in the first process. Five or six sizes of these points will be found sufficient for the majority of these breakages that may occur. See *Screw Extractor.*

To Blue Screws. See *Bluing Pan.*

Left-Handed Screws. A screw plate for left-handed screws can easily be made by screwing a good piece of steel of the desired size into a right-handed screw plate, removing, filing down on two sides to leave only a knife edge and hardening. Drill hole in steel plate and cut with the screw described by turning with reverse or left-handed motion. Left-handed screws can be made very successfully with this plate.

SCREW EXTRACTOR.

Screw Driver. A well made and light screw driver is an important tool to the watchmaker. The point should be well polished and of a width nearly equal to the diameter of the screw head. One of the best forms on the market is the

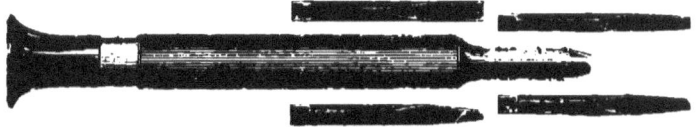

FIG. 173.

Waltham, shown in Fig. 173. It has four different sizes of blades which are readily adjusted to position. Screw drivers are sometimes made in sets, the various width of blades being readily detected while on the bench, as the color of the handle of each width is different.

SCREW EXTRACTOR. The Bullock Screw Extractor, shown in Fig. 174, is a simple yet very valuable accessory to the watchmaker, who finds he has a plate in which a screw

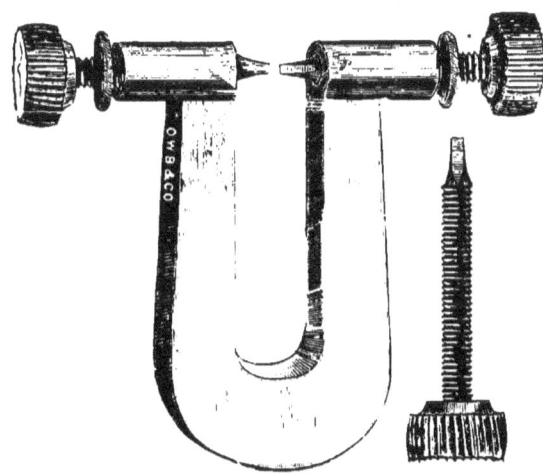

FIG. 174.

has been broken off. To use this tool, first fasten it in your vise, then bring one end of broken or rusted-in screws against screw center and the broken screw head against the tool screw driver; turn the washers so as to hold the broken screw firmly in place; turn the plate gently, and the broken screw will follow the screw driver point out of the place. It may be necessary in some instances to turn the screw driver point against the broken head with a good deal of force in order to start the screw. A little benzine or kerosene applied to the screw will help to loosen it.

SCREW HEAD SINK CUTTER. This tool is not kept by material dealers, although a tool which somewhat resembles it, known as the countersinker, is. The countersinker does not have the central pivot for centering up by. We sometimes have American watches brought to us with the end-stone (cap jewel), broken, and a new one must be put in. The jewel being set in brass is held in place by two screws on opposite sides, the screw heads being let in or sunk even with the surface, half of the screw head projecting over on the end-stone. The end-stones furnished by the watch companies are not sunk for these screw heads but are round and of the proper diameter. These cutters will cut away from the jewel the space to be occupied by the screw head in a very few moments, and as perfectly as as you like.

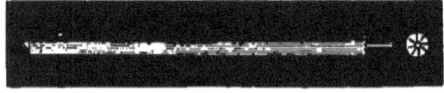

FIG. 175.

All the American companies do not use the same diameter of screw head in the cock and potance, consequently you will be compelled to make a separate tool for the Waltham, Elgin, Hampden, Illinois and other makes of watches where the sizes are different. With a set of six of these cutters you can fit any American Watch. They are easily made and will repay you for the trouble.

Cut off a piece of wire of the required diameter, about one inch long and place it a chuck that fits it snugly, and turn one end to a center about forty degrees. Now reverse the wire in the chuck, and be sure it is true; select a drill that will pass through the screw hole in the cock or potance freely and proceed to drill a hole in the center of the end of the wire about one-sixteenth of an inch deep. Remove from the lathe and with a sharp file and graver proceed to cut a series of teeth as equal and even as possible. Use a good strong glass while working and be sure you have every tooth sharp and perfect, as upon this depends the quick and nice work you expect from the tool. When this is well done, proceed to temper fairly hard, and polish up the outside to make it look workmanlike. Now select a piece of steel pivot wire of a size that will almost fit in the hole drilled in the end of the tool, and polish down to the proper size to drive in the hole tightly. Allow this wire to project about one-sixteenth of an inch, taper the point and polish. The tool being completed you are ready for work.

Select an end-stone of a diameter to fit tightly in the cock or potance, as may be required; place the hole jewel in place and then the end-stone pressed down tightly against the hole jewel. Place your cutter in a split chuck that fits true; select a small or medium sized drill rest and place in the tail-stock spindle. Hold the cock or potance, with the jewels in place, against the drill rest, level, and proceeding to run the lathe at a fair speed; slowly feed the cock or potance to the cutter, the projecting pivot in the end of the cutter passing through the screw hole and acting as a guide to keep the cutter in the center of the hole. Caution must be exercised or you will cut the recess for the screw heads too deep, as these little cutters are very deceiving and cut much faster than you would suppose. In fitting an end-stone, select one that is more than flush when the jewel hole and end-stone are in the proper position, and after sinking the screw head as described turn off on the lathe almost flush or level. Make a small dot on one side of the end-stone, as a mark or guide in replacing it. Remove the end-stone and proceed to polish the top of the setting on a plate glass polisher.

SCREW PLATE. A plate of hard steel in which are threaded holes of various sizes for making screw threads.

SCREW TAP. A tool for producing screw threads in holes.

SECOND HAND REMOVER AND HOLDER.

The minuteness of the second-hand makes it very difficult to manipulate. The little tool shown in Fig. 176 will be found very useful in handling these hands. To use it, raise the

FIG. 176.

spring with the thumb, and push the tool along the dial astride the arbor; then let go the spring and raise the tool. The spring will hold the second hand firmly untill replaced. For broaching, hold the tool, spring side down, firmly on bench or vise.

SHELLAC. A resinous substance used extensively by watchmakers and jewelers for holding work. Shellac is a corruption of Shell-lac. *Lac* is the original name of the resinous product which is exuded from an insect which feeds upon the banyan tree. In its natural state it incrusts small twigs and is known as *slick-lac*. It is then broken from the wood and boiled in alkaline water and the product, from its shape, is called *seed-lac*. It is then melted and reduced to thin flakes, known in commerce as *shell-lac* or *shellac*.

SIDEREAL CLOCK. A clock adjusted to measure sidereal time. It usually numbers the hours from 0 to 24. See *Time*.

SIDEREAL DAY. The interval of time between two successive transits over the same meridian of the vernal equinox, or first point of Aries. It is the true period of the earth's rotation. See *Time*.

SILVER. A soft, white, precious metal, very malleable and ductile and capable of taking a high polish. For Silver Plating, see *Electro-Plating*.

Separating Silver. The silver-holding alloy or metal is dissolved in the least possible quantity of crude nitric acid. The solution is mixed with a strong excess of ammonia and filtered into a high cylinder, provided with a stopper. A bright strip of copper, long enough to project beyond the liquid, is next introduced, which quickly causes separation of pure metallic silver. The reduction is completed in a short time, and the reduced silver washed first with some ammoniacal solution and then with distilled water. The more ammoniacal and concentrated the solution, the more rapid the reduction. The strip of copper should not be too thin, as it is considerably attacked, and any little particles which might separate from a thin sheet would contaminate the silver. The operation is so simple that it seems preferable to all others for such operations as the preparation of nitrate of silver from old coins, etc. Any accompanying gold remains behind during the treatment of the metal or alloy with nitrate acid. Chloride of silver, produced by the impurities in the nitric acid is taken up by the ammoniacal solution like the copper, and is also reduced to the metallic state; and whatever other metal is not left behind, oxidized by the nitrate acid, is separated as hydrate, (lead bismuth), on treating with ammonia. Any arseniate which may have passed into the ammoniacal solution, is not decomposed by the copper.

To Distinguish Genuine Silver. File or scrape the surface of the articles to be tested, rub the exposed portion on a touchstone and apply a test water consisting of 32 parts of distilled water and 16 parts of chromic acid. Rinse the stone in water and if the article is genuine silver a red spot will be left upon the stone, but if it is an imitation the mark will be unaffected. The finer the quality of the silver the more intense will be the red spot.

Silver Assay with Testing Tube. Place in the tube enough of the pulverized mineral to fill one inch of the space, and on this pour nitric acid in quantity to occupy two inches more, and hold the mixture over the flame until the acid boils. The acid will dissolve whatever silver may be present, and must be passed through filtering paper to remove extraneous matter, and returned to the tube. Next add a few drops of water saturated with salt; any silver or lead that may be present will be precipitated in a cloudy form to the bottom. Drain off the acid, place the precipitate in the sunlight, and in a few minutes, if it contains silver, it will turn to a purple color, and may be again liquified by the addition of spirits of ammonia. The testing tube is formed of thin glass, about five inches long, and less than one inch diameter; bottom and sides of equal thickness. Where the tube is lacking, a cup may be used instead.

Silver Assay by Smelting. If no lead is present, mix 600 grs. of the pulverized ore with 300 grs. carbonate of soda, 600 grs. of litharge, and 12 grs. charcoal in a crucible; add a slight coal of borax over all, put on the furnace, melt, take off, give it a few taps to settle the metal, let it cool, and remove the button.

To Clean Silver Plate. The tarnish can be removed by dipping the article from one to fifteen minutes—in a pickle of the following composition; rain water, 2 gallons, and potassa cyanuret ½ pound; dissolve together, and fill into a stone jug or jar, and close tightly. The article after having been immersed, must be taken out and thoroughly rinsed in several waters, then dried with fine, clean sawdust. Tarnished jewelry can speedily be restored by this process; but be careful to thoroughly remove the alkali, otherwise it will corrode the goods.

Cleaning Silverware. Hyposulphate of soda the simplest and most effective cleansing material for silverware; it operates quickly and is cheap. A rag or a brush moistened with the saturated solution of the salt cleanses, without the use of cleaning powder, strongly oxidixed silver surfaces within a few seconds.

Cleaning Silver Tarnished in Soldering. Expose to a uniform heat, allow it to cool, and then boil in strong alum water; or, immerse for a considerable length of time in a liquid made of one-half ounce of cyanuret of potassa to one pint of rain water, and then brush off with prepared chalk.

Cleaning Silver Filigree. Anneal your work over a Bunsen flame or with a blowpipe, then let grow cold (and this is the secret of success), and then put in a pickle of sulphuric acid and water, not more than five drops to one ounce of water, and let your work remain in it for one hour. If not to satisfaction, repeat the process.

To Frost Silver. To produce a frosted surface upon polished silver use cynide of potassium with a brush; the silver should not be handled during the process, but held between pieces of boxwood or lancewood. The proportion should be, 1 ounce of cynide potassium in 1 pint of water.

To Frost Silver. Silver goods may be frosted and whitened by preparing a pickle of sulphuric acid 1 dram, water 4 ounces; heat it and immerse the silver articles until frosted as desired; then wash off clean, and dry with a soft linen cloth, or in fine clean sawdust. For whitening only, a small quantity of acid may be employed.

To Frost Silver. The article has to be carefully annealed either in a charcoal fire, or with a blowpipe before a gas flame, which will oxidize the alloy on the surface, and also destroy all dirt and greasy substances adhering to it, and then boiled in a copper pan containing a solution of dilute sulphuric acid—of 1 part of acid to about 30 parts of water. The article is then placed in a vessel of clean water, and scratched-brushed or scoured with fine sand; after which the annealing and boiling-out is repeated, which will in most all cases be sufficient to produce the desired result. If a very delicate dead surface such as watch dials, etc., is required, the article is, before the second annealing, covered with a pasty solution of potash and water, and immediately after the annealing plunged in clean water, and then boiled out in either sulphuric acid solution, or a solution of 1 part cream tartar and 2 parts common salt to about 30 parts of water. If the article is of a low quality of silver, it is well to add some silver solution, such as is used for silvering, to the second boiling-out solution.

If the article is very inferior silver, the finishing will have to be given by immersing it in contact with a strip of zinc in a silver solution.

SLIDE REST. The slide rest is a tool holder to be used on a lathe; it is so universally used by all modern watchmakers that a full description is superfluous. Fig. 177 is a Moseley, and is a fair example of a modern slide rest for watchmakers' use. The tool holder varies with the different makers but the rests proper are all made on the same general principle, that of two sliding beds working at right angles to one another and carrying a tool holder, capable of being raised or lowered or set at any desired angle.

FIG. 177.

SNAIL. A cam resembling in form a snail, used in the striking attachment to clocks.

SNAILING. The ornamentation of the surface of metals by means of circles or bars, sometimes erroneously called damaskeening.

SNAP. A small catch or fastening, as in a bracelet. The fastening of one piece of metal to another by springing of the edges, as in the bezel of a watch case.

SNARL. To emboss or raise figures upon metal work by driving the metal up from the back with a die or snarling iron, as in metal vases.

SNARLING IRON. An ⌒ shaped steel tool which is used in snarling or embossing metal vases, etc. One end of the snarling iron is placed in the vise and the shank being struck with a hammer, the repercussion of the other end drives out the metal. The snarling iron is only used on vases, pitchers, and like hollow ware.

SOLDERING. The act of joining two metallic surfaces by means of a more fusible metal or metallic cement. Solders are commonly divided into two groups known as hard solders and soft solders; the former fuse only at a red heat, while the latter fuse at low degrees of heat. In hard soldering it is frequently necessary to bind the parts to be soldered together with what is known as binding wire, which is made of soft iron, the repair clamps shown in Fig. 165 or soldering forceps shown in Fig. 178. The blow pipe is used most extensively for soldering, although small soldering irons are used on the larger kinds of work. It is of the utmost importance that the meeting edges of all articles to be soldered be scraped or chemically cleaned. While soldering, articles are usually placed upon a piece of charcoal, though asbestos or pumice stone is better for the purpose. Charcoal emits gases from the coal while under the blowpipe which enter into the alloy of gold or silver and render it brittle. To prove this, reduce a small piece of 10k gold to a liquid form on a piece of charcoal, and treat a piece similarly on a piece of asbestos or pumice stone, and after allowing each to cool, subject both to a heavy pressure and note the difference in their malleability and ductility.

Hard Solders. Under this name very different alloys are used, depending upon the metals to be united. The following table shows the composition of various hard solders which have stood a practical test for various purposes:

	Part Brass.	Parts Zinc.	Parts Tin.
Refractory	4.00	1.00	
Readily Fusible,	5.00	4.00	
Half White,	12.00	5.00	1.00
White,	40.00	2.00	8.00
Very Ductile,	78.25	17.25	

Gold Solders. Gold Solders should approach the articles to be soldered in both color and fusibility as nearly as possible. The following gold solders are in general use:

	Parts Gold.	Parts Silver	Parts Copper.	Parts Zinc.
Hard solder for 750 fine	9.0	2.0	1.0	
Soft solder for 750 "	12.0	7.0	3.0	
Solder for 583 "	3.0	2.0	1.0	
Solder for less than 583 "	2.0	2.0		
Readily Fusible Solder	11.94	54.74	28.17	5.01
Solder for Yellow Gold	10.0	5.0		1.0

Silver Solders. The following hard silver solders have been thoroughly tested:

	Parts Fine Silver.	Parts Copper.	Parts Brass	Parts Zinc.
First - -	4		3	
Second -	2		1	
Third - -	19	1	10	5
Fourth -	57	28.6		14.3

Soft Solder. The soft solder most frequently used consists of 2 parts of tin and 1 of lead. The following table gives the composition of various soft solders with the respective melting points·

Number.	Parts Tin	Parts Lead.	Melts at Degrees F.	Number.	Parts Tin	Parts Lead.	Melts at Deg. F.
1 - - -	1	25	558°	7 - -	1½	1	334°
2 - - -	1	10	541	8 - -	2	1	340
3 - - -	1	5	511	9 - -	3	1	356
4 - - -	1	3	482	10 - -	4	1	365
5 - - -	1	2	441	11 - -	5	1	378
6 - - -	1	1	37	12 - -	6	1	380

Aluminium Solder. The following alloys are recommended for the purpose; 1. Melt twenty parts of aluminum in a suitable crucible, and when in fushion add 80 parts zinc. When the mixture is melted, cover the surface with tallow, and maintain in quiet fusion for some time, stirring occasionally with an iron rod; then pour into molds. 2. Take 15 parts of aluminum and 85 parts zinc, or 12 parts of the former and 88 parts of the latter, or 8 parts of the former and 92 parts of the latter; prepare all of them as specified for No. 1. The flux recommended consists of three parts balsam copaiba, one of Venetian turpentine, and a few drops of lemon juice. The soldering iron is dipped into this mixture.

Soldering Fluxes. For hard solder use borax rubbed to a paste with water on a slate. For soft soldering dissolve a small piece of zinc in pure hydrochloric acid until effervescence ceases. Take out the undissolved zinc after twenty-four hours, filter the solution, add $\frac{1}{3}$ its volume of spirits of sal-ammoniac and dilute with rain water. This fluid is non-corrosive.

Soft Solder for Smooth Surfaces. Where two smooth surfaces are to be soldered one upon the other, you may make an excellent job by moistening them with the fluid, and then, having placed a sheet of tin foil between them hold them pressed firmly together over your lamp until the foil melts. If the surface is fitted nicely, a joint may be made in this way so close as to be almost imperceptible. The bright looking lead, which comes as a lining for tea boxes, is better than tin foil.

To Dissolve Soft Solder. Nitric acid may be used safely for gold not lower than 12k and is very effective. The following is suitable for all grades of gold and silver: Green copperas 2 oz., saltpeter 1oz., reduced to a powder and boiled in 10 oz. of water. It will become crystalized on cooling. Dissolve these crystals by the addition of 8 parts of spirits of salts to each part of crystals, using an earthenware vessel. Add 4 parts of boiling water, keep the mixture hot, and immerse the article to be operated upon, and the solder will be entirely removed without injuring the work.

Soldering Stone Set Rings. There are various ways for doing this, but the following will be found as good as any: Take tissue paper and tear it into strips about three inches wide, twist them into ropes, and then make them very wet and wrap the stone with them, passing around the stone and through the ring until the center of the ring is a little more than half full of paper, always winding very close, and then fasten upon charcoal, allowing the stone to project over the edge of the charcoal, and solder very quickly. The paper will prevent oxidation upon the part of the ring it covers, as well as protecting the stone.

SOLDERING FORCEPS. By the use of this ingenious device any article to be repaired can be adjusted in any desired position in a much shorter time, and with more accu-

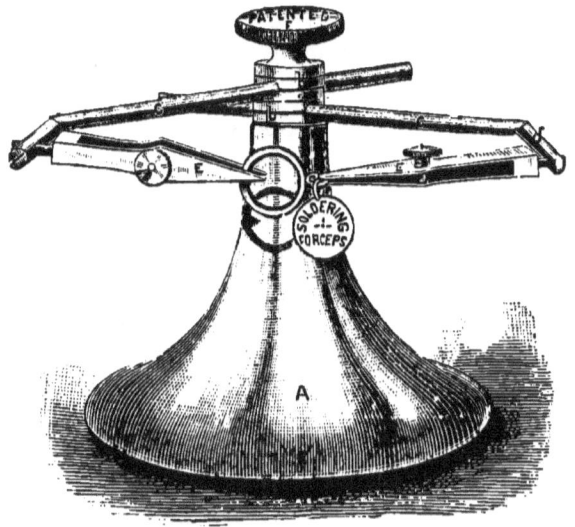

FIG. 178.

racy than by the ordinary process of binding with wire to a piece of charcoal. The Crane Patent Soldering Forceps are so constructed that any two pieces can be as readily brought together as can be done with the fingers, no matter at what angle or position you may desire them. Each part works independent of the other, and the whole is held securely in place by means of a nut, as shown in Fig. 178, at F, and both hands being free, charcoal can be held behind the article, thereby concentrating the heat, the same as when held directly upon it. In soft soldering it can be used to great advantage. The forceps EE, revolve in parts dd, which are fastened to arms CC, by means of a hinge joint. The arms CC run through the collars bb, so that they can be lengthened or shortened, and the forceps raised or lowered as desired. The collars bb turn independently of each other on base A, and being split the whole is held firmly in position by nut F. See also *Tweezers*.

SPECIFIC GRAVITIES. The following table shows the specific gravities of numerous metals employed in the arts, together with their melting points, malleability, ductility, and tenacity.

Metals.	Specific Gravity	Melting points.		Order of Malleability.	Order of Ductility.	Tenacity.*
		Fahrenheit	Centig'de			
Platinum	21.40 to 21.50	infusible except by the Oxyhydrogen blow-pipe		6	3	274
Gold	19.25 to 19.50	2016°	1102°	1	1	150½
Mercury	13.56 to 13.59					
Lead	11.40 to 11.45	612	322	7	9	27½
Silver	10.47 to 10.50	1873	1023	2	2	187
Bismuth	9.82 to 9.90	497	258			
Copper	8.89 to 8.96	1994	1090	3	5	302
Nickel	8.50 to 8.60	2700	1482	10	10	
Iron	7.77 to 7.80	2786	1530	9	4	549
Tin	7.25 to 7.30	442	228	5	8	34½
Zinc	6.80 to 7.20	773	412	8	7	109½
Antimony	6.75 to 6.80	a little below red heat				
Arsenic	5.70 to 5.90	volatilizes before fusing				
Aluminum	2.56 to 2.60	1300	705	4	6	300

SPECTACLE TOOL. Nearly every watchmaker knows what a troublesome thing it is to repair spectacle frames. When soldered, the solder will run through and fill the groove for the glass, and it is no easy matter to cut the solder out of the groove with a graver. The graver will slip, scratch and mar the frames in spite of the greatest care.

---

*Number of lbs. sustained by 0.787 of a line in diameter in wires of the various metals.

This spectacle tool will cut out the groove in gold, silver, steel or any other spectacle frames in a moments time, smoothly and perfectly. This tool is not for sale by material dealers, but can be made by any ingenious watchmaker. Take a piece of Stubs' polished steel wire, say number forty, by steel wire gauge, and one and a fourth inches long. Insert the wire in a chuck in your lathe, allowing the end to project about one-fourth inch; proceed to turn both ends to a center, as shown in Fig. 179. Select two female centers of the proper size; place one in the taper chuck of your lathe and the other in the tail stock spindle; fasten a dog on the piece of wire, and proceed to turn the wire even and straight throughout its entire length. Remove from the lathe, select a split chuck that will fit snugly, place the wire in the chuck, allowing

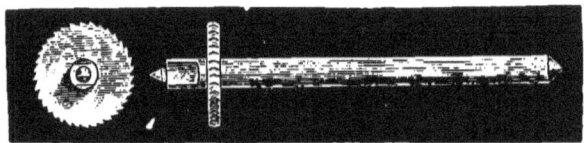

FIG. 179.

about three-eighths of an inch to project; remove the T rest of your lathe, and insert in its stead a filing fixture. By the aid of the index on the lathe pulley and the filing fixture, proceed to square the end of the wire, (about one-fourth inch), of a size to fit in an American ratchet wheel Now select two ratchets of the same thickness and size and place them on the square cut on the wire. Proceed to round up the balance of the square not occupied by the ratchets, and with the screw plate cut a nice full thread on the end up to the square. Now cut off a small piece of steel wire, the same in diameter as the body of the tool, true it in your lathe chuck and drill a hole in the centre about one-eighth inch deep. With a screw tap, of the proper size to fit the screw on the end of the shaft, which is now a small spindle, tap a good thread in the hole. This short piece is intended for a nut. With a graver cut it off to the desired length, replace the two ratchets and screw on the nut; replace the spindle in your lathe and turn up the nut round and true. While in the lathe, square half the length of the nut on two sides only. This is intended for a grab or hold for your pliers in removing the nut from the little spindle. You can vary the width of the cut by using two or three ratchets as is desired. In order to make the groove rounding, the shape of the spectacle glass, hold an oil stone to the edge of the ratchets while revolving, which will round them very slightly. American ratchet wheels make good cutters and any width of groove can be cut. When the teeth get dull they can easily be sharpened or new wheels can be substituted. With this tool you can cut the solder out of spectacle frames in a very few minutes. It will also prove useful in enlarging spectacle frames, in fitting new lenses.

SPLIT SECONDS. A variety of double chronograph in which there are two center-seconds hands.

SPRUNG OVER. A watch in which the hairspring is attached to the staff above the balance.

STAFF. An axis or arbor.

STAKE. An anvil. To fasten by means of a stake.

FIG. 180.

STAKING TOOL. A tool needed by every watchmaker, consisting of a shifting table or stake, around which holes of various sizes are arranged in a circle, so that any desired hole may be brought under a suitable punch moving in a vertical holder. Usually twenty-four tempered steel punches and four stumps are provided, which will be found sufficient to cover all the operations in the ordinary run of watch repairs, and the ingenious workman can from time to time add to these by making punches in his spare moments, if he finds from experience that he is in need of punches of a different shape. Fig. 180 is a fair example of this tool.

STAKING TOOL ANVIL AND SCREW HOLDER. Smith's patent staking tool anvil and screw holder, shown in Fig. 181, will be found a very handy tool for removing and putting on rollers, for putting hairspring collet on balance staff, or for riveting in bushings. The plain staking block or anvil is usually made of a solid piece of polished steel, in the form of a cube, or circular as in Fig. 182. The example shown has a reversible center hub which makes it valuable for putting on hands, etc.

FIG. 181.

STAR WHEELS. The wheel of the stop work which is pivoted to the barrel and also known as the Maltese cross.

STEADY PINS. Pins used to secure two pieces of metal in relative positions, as a bridge and plate.

STEEL. Iron when combined with a small portion of carbon. The varities of steel are very great. Puddled steel is made from pig iron by a modification of the puddling process. Cast steel is made from wrought iron or blister steel by mixing it with powdered charcoal, after which it is melted in a crucible, cast into ingots and rolled or hammered into plates or bars. Blister Steel is made from wrought iron by interlaying it with charcoal and keeping it at a high temperature for a number of days. Bessemer steel is made from the liquid cast iron as it comes from the smelting furnace by blowing air into it, thus burning out a portion of the carbon.

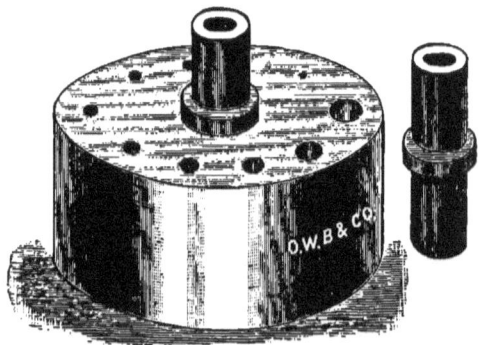
FIG. 182.

To Anneal Steel. There are nearly as many methods of annealing as there are workmen. The commonest methods are as follows: Heat to a dull red, bury in warm iron filings or ashes, and allowing the article to cool very gradually. Another method is to heat the piece as slowly as possible, and when at a low red heat put it between two pieces of dry board and screw them up tightly in a vise. The steel burns its way into the wood, and on coming together around it they form a practically air-tight charcoal bed. Brannt gives the following method which he says will make steel so soft that it can be worked like copper: Pulverize beef bones, mix them with equal parts of loam and calves' hair and stir the mixture into a thick paste with water. Apply a coat of this to the steel and place it in a crucible, cover this with another, fasten the two together with wire and close the joint hermetically with clay. Then put the crucible in the fire and heat slowly. When taken from the fire let it cool by placing it in ashes. On opening the crucible the steel will be found so soft that it can be engraved like copper.

To Anneal Small Steel Pieces. Place the articles from which you desire to draw the temper into a common iron clock key. Fill around it with brass or iron filings, and then plug up the open end with a steel, iron or brass plug, made to fit closely. Take the handle of the key with your plyers and hold its pipe into the blaze of a lamp till red hot, then let it cool gradually. When sufficiently cold to handle, remove the plug, and you will find the article with its temper fully drawn, but in all other respects just as it was before. The reason for having the article thus plugged up while passing it through the heating and cooling process is, that springing always results from the action of changeable currents of atmosphere. The temper may be drawn from cylinders, staffs, pinions, or any other delicate pieces by this mode with perfect safety.

Harding and Tempering Steel. The process of heating steel to a red heat and immediately chilling it is the same among all workmen, but the agents employed for chilling are very numerous. The receipts here given are from various sources, and the reader must adopt the one which he finds on trial, is the best adapted to his wants.

In all cases the object should be heated to a red heat before plunging. If an object to be hardened is long and slender, it should invariably be inserted in the hardening compound endwise, otherwise it will come out warped and distorted. The same rule applies to thin or flat objects. A preparation is used in hardening, consisting of one teaspoonful of wheat flour, two of salt and four of water. The steel to be hardened, is to be heated sufficiently, dipped into the mixture, to be coated therewith, then raised to a red glow, and dropped into cold soft water. Another method is to raise the object to the required heat and then drop it into a mixture of ten parts mutton suet, two parts salammoniac, five parts resin and thirty-five parts olive oil. Oil, tallow, beeswax, and resin are also employed for hardening. If an intense brittle hardness is desirable drop the object into mercury or nitric acid. In heating very small or thin objects, they should be placed between two thin pieces of charcoal and the whole brought to the required heat. In this way you avoid uneven heating and hence it will be uniformly tempered. When it is desirable to harden an article without discoloring its surface, it should be placed in a metal tube or bowl of a clay pipe, and surrounded with charcoal that has been previously heated to expel all moisture, and when raised to the proper heat the whole should be immersed in the hardening liquid.

Mat for Steel. The article to be treated must first be ground flat and free from scratches in the usual manner. When this is accomplished take oilstone powder, mix it with oil and then add a little bluestone powder. Grinding is performed best upon a composition or iron plate, or a file of the same material; glass is not as well suited for the purpose. A large quantity of grinding powder and oil should be used. Very hard articles take a good mat grinding with difficulty, and whenever possible it is advisable to anneal them blue.

Do not press too hard in grinding; the small grains of oilstone should assume a rolling motion whereby they will to a certain extent, wear hollows with their sharp edges in the surface of the steel, all of which together will impart the handsome, mat, appearance. If too much pressure is brought to bear, and the grinding material is too dry, it will cake on the steel and produce the disagreeable scratched surface so often seen.

The quantity of bluestone necessary for grinding can be scraped off from a large piece, after which the scrapings must be thoroughly crushed. The oilstone powder must not be too fine and should be of uniform grain. The proportions are 1 part of bluestone to 4 of oilstone powder.

Tempering. Before tempering, the surface of the object must be thoroughly cleaned and freed from grease by the application of oilstone dust, emery, or some like scouring agent. The object should not be handled with the fingers after cleaning, or it will be difficult to obtain the requisite tint. The following table by Stodart will be valuable to the student:

1.—	430° F.	Very Pale Straw Yellow,	220° C
2.—	450 F.	A Shade Darker Yellow,	235° C
3.—	470° F.	Darker Straw Yellow	245° C
4.—	490° F.	Still Darker Straw Yellow,	255° C
5.—	500° F.	Brown Yellow,	260° C
6.—	520° F.	Yellow tinged with Purple,	270° C
7.—	530° F.	Light Purple,	275° C
8.—	550° F.	Dark Purple,	290° C
9.—	570° F.	Dark Blue,	300° C
10.—	590° F.	Paler Blue,	310° C
11.—	610° F.	Still Paler Blue,	320° C
12.—	630° F.	Light Bluish Green,	335° C

After letting an object down to the required color it should be allowed to cool gradually, and no artificial means employed to hasten the cooling. A piece of steel may be let down to the same color several times without in any way injuring it or altering its properties. Tempering of small articles is performed satisfactorily by means of the bluing pan. (See

Fig. 34). Small articles are also tempered by placing them in a vessel, say a large spoon, covering them with oil and heating them to the requisite degree. This is a favored method of tempering balance staffs and similar articles. The temper is usually judged by the color of the smoke; Saunier gives the following rule: When smoke is first seen to rise the temper is dark yellow, (or No. 2). Smoke more abundant and darker, (No. 5). Black smoke still thicker, (No 7). Oil takes fire when lighted paper is presented to it at No. 9. After this the oil takes fire of itself and continues to burn. If the whole of the oil is allowed to burn away No. 12 is reached.

The Color of Steel at various degrees of temperature. The following table gives the temperature corresponding to the various colors of steel when heated.

1.	980° F.	Incipient Red.	525° C.
2.	1290 F.	Dull Red.	700 C.
3.	1470 F.	Incipient Cherry Red.	800 C.
4.	1650 F.	Cherry Red.	900 C.
5.	1830 F.	Clear Cherry Red.	1000 C.
6.	2010 F.	Deep Orange.	1100 C.
7.	2190 F.	Clear Orange.	1200 C.
8.	2370 F.	White.	1300 C.
9.	2550 F.	Bright White.	1400 C.

Combined Hardening and Tempering. M. Caron, with a view to combining the two operations of hardening and tempering, suggested that the temperature of the water used for hardening, be heated to a pre-determined degree. Thus the requisite temper may be given to gun-lock springs by heating the water in which they are hardened to 55° C., or 130° F.

To Work Hard Steel. If steel is rather hard under the hammer, when heated to the proper cherry red, it may be covered with salt and hammered to about the shape desired. More softness can then be obtained, if required to give a further finish to the shape, by sprinkling it with a mixture of salt, blue vitriol, sal-ammoniac, saltpeter and alum; make cherry red again, sprinkle with this mixture, and hammer into shape. This process may be repeated until entirely finished. When ready, the steel is hardened in a solution of the same mixture. This method is recommended by prominent workers.

To Remove Rust. Kerosene oil, (refined petroleum), or benzine are the best agents for the removal of rust, where the object is not pitted. When pitted, however, it can only be removed by mechanical means such as scouring with emery powder and oil.

To Prevent Rust. Rub the article with a mixture of lime and oil, or a mixture of equal parts of carbolic acid and olive oil, or with plumbago.

Anti-rust Varnish for Steel. The rusting of steel and iron tools and instruments is very perfectly prevented by coating them with a varnish made by dissolving 1 part of white wax in 15 parts benzine, and applying with a brush. The very thin layer of wax forms a perfect covering for bright tools and when desired is very easily removed.

Browning or Bronzing for Steel. Aqua fortis and sweet spirits nitre, each half an ounce, sulphate copper 2 ounces, water 30 ounces, tincture muriate of iron 1 ounce. Mix.

To Protect Steel From Rust. Immerse in a solution of carbonate of potash for a few minutes and it will not rust for years, not even when exposed to damp atmosphere.

To Temper Small Steel Articles. The tempering of small drills, for drilling holes in arbors, staffs, etc., which we find are very hard and difficult to perforate, may be effected in the following manner. After having filed the drill to its proper size (being careful not to flatten the cutting face), you then warm it moderately, not allowing it to become red, and run it into borax. The drill is thus coated over with a crust of borax and secluded from the air. Now it may be hardened by heating it only cherry red; after this it is inserted into a piece of borax, or what in better still, plunged it into mercury; taking care not to breathe the mercury fumes. Drills prepared in this way, without being brittle, will become exceedingly hard and the watchmaker will be enabled to drill articles which could not otherwise be perforated with a drill. Do not use broken broaches to make your drills as the steel in them is often burned, rendering the metal unfit for use in small tools. In order to make the quality of your drill a certainty, always take a new piece of round steel for the purpose.

To Harden Steel in Petroleum. According to B. Morgossy, the articles to be hardened are first heated in a charcoal fire, and, after thoroughly rubbing with ordinary washing soap, heated to a cherry red. In this condition they are plunged into petroleum; ignition of the petroleum need not be feared if no flame is near at hand. Articles hardened by this method show no cracks, do not warp if plunged endwise, and after hardening remain nearly white, so they can be blued without further preparation.

Hardening Liquids. If water is used for hardening, 32° F. will be found about right for the sized articles hardened by watchmakers and if the article is very small, ice may be added to the water. A solution composed of 1 quart of water, 1¼ lbs. of sal-ammoniac, 10 oz. of refined borax, 1¼ ozs. of red wine, is used extensively for fine cutlery. A mixture of 1 lb. of resin, 3 ozs. of lard, ½ lb. train oil and ½ oz. of assafoetida is said to be excellent for fine steel work.

Directions for Plunging When Hardening. Thin articles, as steel plates or articles of small diameter, such as drills, should always be plunged into the hardening compound, end or edge foremost to avoid warping. If an article is thicker on one side than the other, as a knife blade, the thick side should enter the compound first. Heat the article only as far as you wish to harden it and immerse it as far as it has been made red hot.

Tempering by Electricity. Watch springs have of late years been successfully tempered with the aid of electricity. The steel ribbon is passed through a bath of oil and an electric current of sufficient strength to keep it at the proper heat is passed through the ribbon. The heating is thus effected without contact with the atmosphere and the spring is not liable to blister as in ordinary methods. The temper is drawn in the same manner and the heat can be controlled to a nicety and is uniform throughout. The spring is then finished by means of rolls.

Glass Polisher for Steel. French plate glass ground on one side makes a good polisher for flat work. A piece four inches square, nicely finished on the edge, is about the right size.

Tempering Magnets. M. Ducoetet uses the following process for temperiug and magnetizing steel to be used as magnets. Two soft iron pole pieces are placed in the bottom of a water tight vessel and are connected with the poles of a powerful electro-magnet. The vessel is partially filled with water, and oil is poured into the vessel, which floats upon the surface of the water. The red hot bar is then passed through the liquids and comes in contact with the magnets. This softens the steel without depriving it of its power of being magnetized.

To Engrave Name on Steel Tools. Coat the tool or article, if made of iron or steel, with a thin layer of wax, draw the name, initials or design through the wax, exposing the metal, and place the tool in a mixture of 6 parts by weight of water and 1 part of sulphuric acid. In a few hours remove, and if etched sufficiently, wash in clean water and dissolve the wax by heat.

STOP WORK. The mechanism which prevents the overwinding of a timepiece.

STRAIGHT LINE LEVER. That form of lever escapement in which the escape wheel arbor, pallet and balance staff are all planted in a straight line, as in Fig, 183.

STUD. A small piece of metal which is slotted to receive the outer coil of the hair spring.

SWEEP SECONDS. A movement in which a long seconds hand moves from the center of the dial instead of at the bottom, as in chronographs and split seconds watches.

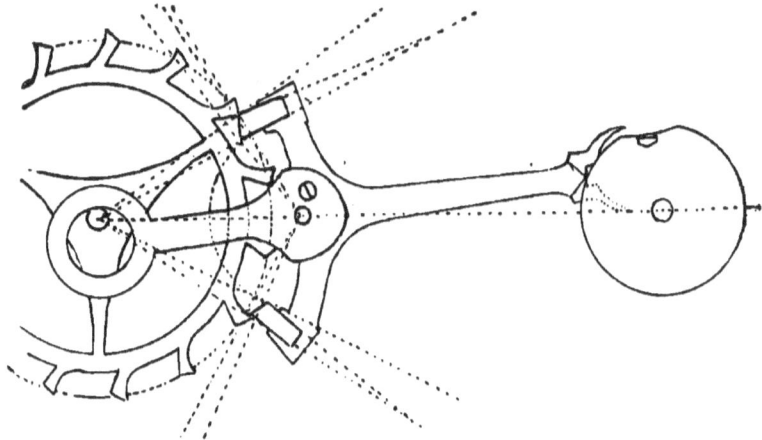

FIG. 183.

TABLE. The roller of a lever escapement that carries the impulse pin.

TAILSTOCK. The sliding block or support in a lathe that carries the tailscrew.

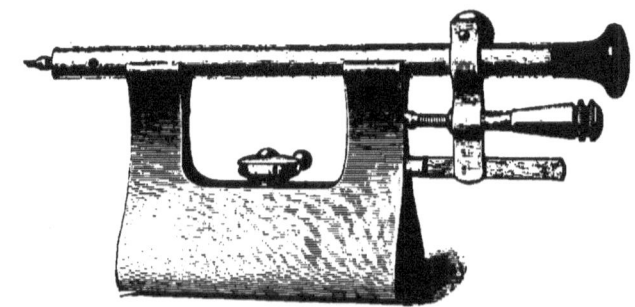

FIG. 184.

Half Open Tailstock. The half open tailstock shown Fig. 184, is cut away so that the spindles can be laid in, instead of being passed through the holes. This fixture will be found exceeding convenient when several spindles are to be used for drilling, counterboring and chamfering.

Fig. 185.

Screw Tailstock.

This attachment is very convenient for heavy drilling, the spindle being moved by a screw with hand wheel attached.

Traverse Spindle Tailstock. This attachment shown in Fig. 186, will be found very convenient for stright drilling. Where the watchmaker has a great deal of drilling to do he will find this attachment invaluable.

Fig. 186.

TESTING NEEDLES. Small strips of steel with gold points usually running from 4k. to 20k. inclusive, and used in conjunction with a touchstone for determining the quality of gold. The gold to be tested is first rubbed upon the touchstone, and the needle which most closely aproximates to it in quality, in the judgment of the operator is also rubbed upon the stone. The two marks are then treated with nitric acid and the difference in color indicates the difference in quality of the two marks. See *Touchstone*.

THIRD WHEEL. The wheel in the train of a watch which lies between the center and fourth wheels.

THREE-QUARTER PLATE. A watch in which enough of the upper plate is cut away to allow of the balance vibrating on a level with the plate.

TIME. The measure of duration. A particular period of duration. Time is measured by the interval between two successive transits of a celestial body over the same meridian; if measured by the sun it is called solar time, or if by a star sidereal time.

Absolute Time. Time irrespective of local standards or epochs; time reckoned for all places from some one common epoch; as, all spectators see a lunar eclipse at the same instant of absolute time.—*Webster*.

FIG. 187.

Apparent Time. Time as reckoned by the sun; the instant of the transit of the sun's center over the meridian constituting 12 o'clock.

Astronomical Time. Mean solar time reckoned by counting the hours continuously up to twenty-four from one noon up to the next.—*Webster*.

Civil Time. The reckoning of time for the common purposes of life. The division of time into years, months, days, hours and seconds.

Cidereal Time. Time regulated by the transit, over the meridian of a place of the first point of Aries, or vernal equinox, and chiefly used in astronomical observations.

The sidereal day is 3 m., 56 s. shorter than the mean solar day. The pendulum of a clock to show sidereal time must be a trifle shorter than that of one used to show mean time, both clocks having the same train. On or about the 15th of April the two clocks would agree, but from that time on there would be a divergence of 3 m., 56 s. per day. In the absence of a transit instrument and a table giving the right ascension of particular stars, Britten advises the selection of a window having a southern aspect, from which a chimney or a steeple or any other fixed point may be seen. To the side of the window attach a thin plate of brass having a small hole in it, in such a manner that by looking through the hole towards the edge of the elevated object, some of the fixed stars may be seen; the progress of one of these being watched, the

Days.	Stars Gain			Days.	Stars Gain		
	Hrs.	Min.	Sec.		Hrs.	Min.	Sec.
1	0	3	56	11	0	43	15
2	0	7	52	12	0	57	11
3	0	11	48	13	0	51	7
4	0	15	44	14	0	55	3
5	0	19	39	15	0	58	58
6	0	23	35	16	1	2	54
7	0	27	31	17	1	6	50
8	0	31	27	18	1	10	46
9	0	35	23	19	1	14	42
10	0	39	19	20	1	18	38

instant it vanishes behind the fixed point a signal is made to a person observing the clock, who then notes the exact time at which the star disappears, and on the following night the same star will vanish behind the same object 3 m., 56 s. sooner. If a clock mark 10 h. when the observation is made, when the star vanishes the following night it should indicate 3 m., 56 s. less than 10 h. If several cloudy nights have rendered it impossible to compare the clock with the star, it will then be necessary to multiply 3 m., 56 s. by the number of days that have elapsed since the observation, and the product deducted from the hour the clock then indicates gives the time the clock should show. The same star can only be observed during a few weeks, for as it gains nearly a half hour a week it will, in a short time, come to the meridian in broad daylight and become invisible; to continue the observation, another star must be selected. In making the observation, care must be taken that a planet is not observed instead of a star; Mars, Jupiter, and Saturn, are those most likely to occasion this error, more especially Saturn, which from being the most distant of the three resembles a star of the first magnitude. The planets may, however, be easily distinguished, for being comparatively near the earth, they appear larger than the stars; their light also is steady because reflected, while the fixed stars scintillate and have a twinkling light. A sure means of distinguishing between them is to watch a star attentively for a few nights; if it change its place with regard to the other stars it is a planet.

Solar Time. Sun time. Time marked by the diurnal revolution of the earth with regard to the sun. A mean solar day is the average length of all the solar days in the year. The difference between true and mean time is called the equation of time. There are only four days in the year when the apparent and mean time are the same, and the equation of time nothing. These are December 24th, April 15th, June 15th, and August 31st. Between December 24th and April 15th, and between June 15th and August 31st, the apparent is always before the mean time, whilst in the remaining intervals it is later.

TIMING. See *Adjustment*.

TIMING SCREWS. Quarter screws of a compensation balance.

TOUCHSTONE. A piece of black basaltic rock, obtained chiefly from Silesia and used for testing the quality of gold. The piece of gold or metal to be tested is drawn upon the surface of the touchstone and the streak left is treated with nitric acid. Nitric acid eats away the streak if it is brass or any similar alloy, while if gold the alloy in the gold only is attacked. Testing needles of known alloy are then rubbed on the surface of the touchstone and treated with the acid and a comparison made. See *Testing Needles*.

TRAIN. The toothed wheels in a watch or clock that connect the barrel or fusee with the escapement. In a going-barrel watch the teeth around the barrel drive the center pinion, to which is attached the center wheel; the center wheel drives the third wheel pinion, which carries the third wheel; the third wheel drives the fourth wheel pinion, on which the fourth wheel is mounted; the fourth wheel drives the escape pinion, to which the escape wheel is fixed. The number of teeth in the various wheels and pinions is determined by the following considerations: The center arbor to which the minute hand is fixed always turns once in an hour, the fourth wheel, to the arbor of which the seconds hand is fixed turns once in a minute, so that the product obtained by multiplying together the number of teeth in the center and third wheels must be 60 times the product obtained by multiplying together the numbers of third and fourth pinions. Two other points may be settled before deciding the rest of the train. 1st. The number of turns the barrel makes in 30 hours, which is the time allowed from winding to winding. Four turns would be a suitable number, and in that case the barrel would contain 7½ times the number of teeth in the center pinion. 2nd. The number of vibrations made by the balance in an hour. If 18,000 be decided on, then, assuming the escape wheel to have the usual number of 15 teeth, the escape pinion must make 10 rotations a minute, and the fourth wheel must have 10 times as many teeth as the escape pinion. The barrel teeth and center pinion, which have considerable pressure to bear, must be of adequate strength, but the pitch of the teeth and size of the wheels are gradually diminished as the train nears the escapement. In the last wheels of a train, small and light wheels are especially needed, so that they get quickly into motion directly the escapement is unlocked, and are stopped with but little shock when the escapement is locked again. The remarks on the train of a going-barrel watch apply equally to the going train of a clock. The considerations which guide in deciding the numbers for the striking train of a clock are the number of blows to be struck from winding to winding, the fall of the weight or turns of the barrel or fusee, as the case may be, and the number of pins in the pin wheel. English lever watches usually have either a 16,200 or an 18,000 train. American and Swiss watches, both lever and horizontal, have 18,000 trains as a rule.—*Britten.*

TRANSIT INSTRUMENT. A telescope mounted at right angles to a horizontal axis. Used in connection with a clock or watch for obtaining the time of transit of a heavenly body over the meridian of a place.

TRAVERSE SPINDLE GRINDER. This tool will be found very useful for grinding cutters, lathe centers, pump centers, reamers, counter sinks, squaring up barrel arbors after hardening, or any hardened steel tool. In the hand of an ingenious workman, it will be found exceedingly useful, as by its aid a great variety of work can be performed that cannot be accomplished without it. Fig. 188, is the Mosely pattern, and is designed to attach to the slide rest.

Fig. 188.

TURNS. A small dead-center lathe used but little in this country.

TWEEZERS. The watchmaker will do well to purchase tweezers that are made of non-magnetic material as

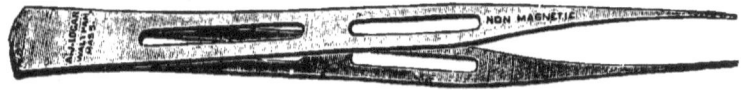

Fig. 189.

they are no more expensive than ordinary ones of good make. Steel tweezers often become magnetized and by their use you convey the magnetism to the delicate parts of a movement. There are several makes of non-magnetic tweezers

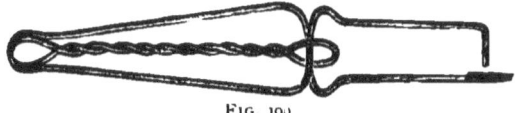

FIG. 190.

upon the market all of which possess points of excellence. Soldering tweezers are made similar to Fig. 190, with hawk bill, for holding work while hard or soft soldering. See also *Soldering Forceps.*

TWO PIN ESCAPEMENT. A variety of the lever escapement having one small gold pin in the lever and two in the table, and the unlocking and impulse actions are divided between them.

UNIVERSAL HEAD. The universal head, shown in Fig. 191, has entirely superseded the clumsy universal mandril

FIG. 191.

in this country. It is more accurate, less clumsy and complicated and will perform the same work. The face plate is 3½ inches in diameter, but by the use of two crescent-shaped slots, it will hold anything in size and shape of watchwork. The pump center is operated from the back by the rubber knob and can be used either with or without a spring. The jaws, which will pass the center, are held in position on face plate by springs, and are fastened from the back. Peep holes are provided in these heads in order that the workman may examine the back of the work at all times. In the Mosely head, shown in Fig. 191, these holes are of taper form. Fig. 192 shows a universal face plate to be used on chuck in lathe. It is smaller and less expensive than the universal head and answers very well for some work, but cannot be recommended very highly as it is not as accurate. The pump center is used to center from the back any object confined in the jaws, but it sometimes becomes necessary to mount the object by means of wax upon a plate and hold the plate in the jaws. In such a case the work must necessarily be centered from the front. This can be done accurately by means of a piece of pegwood, as ordinarily performed on the lathe, by placing the point in the central hole and the pegwood resting on the T rest, and observing if the free end of the pegwood remains stationary. See also *Centering Tool or Indicator*.

FIG. 192.

VERGE ESCAPEMENT. A recoil escapement in which the pallet axis is set at right angles to the axis of the escape wheel. The verge, the earliest probably of all the escapements, is shown in the engraving. It has no pretensions to accuracy, says Britten, in presence of such escapements as the lever and chronometer.

The balance in this escapement has no free arc, and its vibration is limited to about 110° each way. The escape wheel, or "crown wheel," as it is called, has either 11 or 13 teeth, and in the plan of the watch its arbor lies horizontally. The balance staff, or verge, is made as small as proper strength will allow, and planted close to the wheel so that the tips of the teeth just clear it. The pallets, which form part of the verge, are placed at an angle of 95 or 100° with each other. The latter angle is generally preferred.

VERGE ESCAPEMENT

The drawing is a plan of the escape wheel and verge as they lie in the watch. The width of the pallets apart, from center to center, is equal to the diameter of the wheel. A tooth of the escape wheel is just leaving the upper pallet (*c*); as it drops off, the under tooth will reach the root of the lower pallet (*d*), but the motion of the verge will not be at once reversed. The escape wheel will recoil until the impetus of the balance is exhausted. The teeth of the wheel are undercut to free the face of the pallet during the recoil.

Generally in French, and occasionally in English watches, the pallets are even more open. An increased vibration of the balance and less recoil can be obtained with a larger angle, but to get sufficient impulse the verge must be planted closer to the wheel. This necessitates cutting away a part of the body of the verge to free the wheel teeth. Then, as the

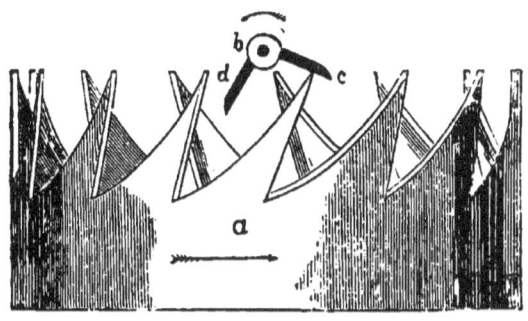

FIG. 193.

a. Escape Wheel. | *b*. Verge. | *c d*. Pallets.

wheel tooth impinges on the pallet almost close to the centre of the verge, there is more friction on the pivots, and the wheel tooth gets so small a leverage that the escapement often sets, unless the balance is very light. On the other hand, with the opening between the pallets only 90°, as it is in many English watches, the vibration of the balance is too small and the recoil too great. An opening of about 100° avoids the drawbacks incidental to the two extremes, and may therefore be adopted with advantage.

To ensure good performance the body or arbor of the verge should be upright, and when in the frames and viewed through the follower potance hole should be seen crossing the balance wheel hole of the dovetail. The position of the eye should be in a line with the arbor of the balance wheel pinion when in the follower; the drops of the pallets equal, and the balance wheel teeth true.

VERNIER CALIPER. See *Gauge*.

VERTICAL ESCAPEMENT. An escapement in which the escape wheel is at right angles to the balance staff or pallet axis.

VIENNA LIME. A pure anhydrous lime obtained from Vienna. It is extensively used for final polishing purposes, particularly in watch factories. The action of Vienna lime is different from most other polishing agents for the effect is not produced, as in the case of rouge, by simple abrasion, for unless the lime be used while it is slacking, the result will not be satisfactory. The material should therefore be kept in air-tight bottles, and only enough for immediate use taken out at one time. Take a small lump from the bottle, slightly moisten with water and break down with any clean tool. Spread the lime paste on a box-wood slip and apply to the article to be polished, using quick strokes.

WATCH. A small time-piece to be carried in the pocket.

Cleaning and Repairing. As the movement is taken down, note should be taken of any needed repairs or alterations, either in the watch or case. See that the movement is tight in the case and that the stem turns easily. Examine movement carefully with eye glass and if a Swiss bridge movement, examine the depths of the wheels, see if minute wheel pinion touches the dial, and if balance pivots have too much side shake. Try the side shake of a Swiss bridge with a pair of fine and light tweezers, see if the guard and bankings are correct. In a great many Swiss watches and also English watches, the jewel pin is too small for the fork, and often it does not enter properly. Memorize these little things as you go along, and repair them in this regular order. After examining the escapement, let the mainspring down; remove the hands first, after taking the movement out of case with a modern tool made for that purpose, that does not interfere with the dial.

Now remove dial, and notice if it fits right; if the hand arbors come in the center of the holes. Oftimes this can be corrected by bending the feet with a pair of flat pliers, so the edge of the dial will correspond with the movement, and the hand arbors. Sometimes in American watches, the screws do not reach the dial feet; alter this by turning the shoulders off in lathe, so they will go further in. If the pins, (when the dial is pinned on,) are too high above the plate, fill them with a little pin and soft solder, and drill or punch new holes in the proper place. When you put a new dial on a Swiss watch, where the feet do not correspond to the holes, cut off the feet of new dial and file or grind the enamel flat around the feet and grind the enamel away with an emery wheel, where the new feet are to go. Now take a piece of copper wire, long enough for both feet, and the proper thickness, put it in lathe and hollow out the ends with a graver, so it will hardsolder flat on an old piece of dial copper about three-sixteenths of an inch round. If too large put it in the lathe by the foot and turn it off. Now have feet prepared for new dial; take a little dissolved shellac and put it on the bottom of each of the dial feet and put the feet to their places in the movement plate.

Slightly moisten the places on the dial, where the new feet come, with dissolved shellac, and lay dial on these feet and see that second pivot comes properly through the dial, and that the edge of the dial corresponds with the edge of the movement plate. Now in this position let dial and movement lay over night, and in the morning the feet will be hard. Now lift your dial off carefully, turn it upside down, and bend up two brass clamps like a hair pin, but not so long, and clamp these feet on the flat part and lay this dial on a cork or piece of wood, feet up. Now put on your soft solder fluid, and blow a broad flame over it, and after the fluid has boiled you can put on your solder and blow again. Now dip it in a solution of cyanide of potassium, and wash off with soap and water, and brush dipped in clean water after the dirt is removed. Then dip it in alcohol, and dry in box-wood sawdust.

The balance of course is removed during this process of fitting the dial. Now examine further and we find our center pivot worn and the hole in the bridge or upper plate too large. We now turn the pivot smooth with a graver, and grind with a pivot polisher, or a hand oil stone file, or pencil made of iron wire. Now clean off with pith, and polish with rouge or crocus. Now take the bridge or upper plate, and with a round face-punch in staking tool, close the hole. Now use a round broach and open the hole to its proper size, so it will fit the pivot correctly. Run this broach through, with the bridge screwed to its place, letting the broach go through the opposite hole at the same time. Now in an English watch, we may need a new bush, as the hole may have been bushed to one side and the center wheel be out of upright; but the question is, how to make the best job, so it will be strong, neat and workman like.

If you are compelled to put in a bush, or upright a hole in the center of a Swiss, English or American watch, first broach out the hole about twice its size and tap it with a fine thread. Now put in a threaded bush to fit snug; now rivet it in the staking tool, center the opposite hole in the universal head, center with a graver point and drill the bush in the lathe with a drill a shade smaller than the pivot. Now broach out in the lathe to suit the pivot and turn the bush off nicely with your slide rest. After sharpening your cutter on an oil stone, run it over a fine emery stick to remove the burr on the cutting edge. Now with moderate high speed you can turn off this bush in good style. Should the endshake be too tight, lay your plate, (English or full American), on a movement cup or ring, and with a wooden punch, and hammer punch it outward. Treat a mainspring barrel in a similar manner when the endshake of the arbor is too tight, by laying it on a small silk spool, one end of the spool turned conically inward, so the outer edge only will touch the barrel. Strike the arbor with a horn, ivory, or wooden mallet.

We oftentimes find American and English center pinions badly worn, so that when they are trued and polished up, there will be no shoulder left for the cannon pinion. When they are so badly worn as that, take a piece of steel, sometimes an old English cannon pinion, (this will not have to be drilled), put it in lathe and turn a collar out of it, first preparing center pinion to receive this collar. Have this collar a little higher and a little thicker than the pivot is to be, and to go on loosely. Now soft solder it on to its place, wash clean and dry, and put the center wheel with its pinion back in the lathe and finish off with graver and oil stone, file and rouge as before mentioned. The collar can be hardened and tempered in first class style, by putting a piece of binding wire through it and holding over the lamp and dipping in water or oil. Now you can clean it off by running a pointed pegwood through it, then run over it with a fine emery stick, then lay on the bluing pan and turn to a dark chestnut color.

Take the mainspring out of the barrel, hold the arbor in the same way and revolve the barrel and you can see if it runs true. Now to true this barrel, either Swiss, English or American, close the top or bottom hole with a round-faced punch, in a staking tool. In a Swiss, close the bottom and in an English the top hole. An American seldom needs this treatment. Now put barrel together and center it in universal head, and with a narrow and short cutter in slide rest open the hole that you closed to fit the arbor. When fitted, take it out and revolve it as before and our barrel will be dead true. Now in our key winder Swiss, we find the ratchet worn, and it needs a new one. As the arbor and ratchet are one piece, we turn the ratchet about half off, edgewise. Now we turn it flatwise, and file or grind the square a little lower, so it will receive the new ratchet. This new ratchet must have a recess turned in it to fit over the part of the old ratchet. The square hole must fit the square snugly. Now if this new ratchet is not too hard and the teeth not too fine, it will last better than the original. Now in English watches the square is oftentimes badly worn or too small. In this case draw the temper of the old square, turn it down by holding it in a step chuck by the fuzee, taking off the great or fuzee wheel, and maintaining ratchet. After turning it down and squaring the pivot, cut a left-hand thread in a suitable piece of steel and on the old square, (which of course is turned down in the step chuck), and fit this piece of steel on the old arbor, down to the pivot shoulder, against the stop cam. Now turn it down with a graver, and square up the end in a lathe, and drill a very small hole through near the end of the square upper end. Now take and unscrew the new square and harden and temper it. Hold it over the lamp by a piece of binding wire and dip in oil when cherry red. Now hold it in a chuck and clean if off with an emery stick. Now turn to a dark brown, screw back on, and grind and polish up. No graver is needed on this job after it is hardened and tempered. The thread need not go all the way down; half way will do, but the new square must go against the shoulder tight up to the lower round part of the square. When all done put the little pin through, which keeps it from coming off when turned to the right.

On opening a barrel observe the condition of the mainspring, and the inside of the barrel head. Often in good watches the inside of the barrel head is not flat and the mainspring scrapes it. Turn this flat with a step chuck and slide rest, at high speed, and sharpen the cutter as before mentioned. Now examine the mainspring and see if it is the proper strength and width, and examine the hook or brace, and stop work, the teeth of the barrel, etc. Now, sometimes in American watches, the barrel touches the balance; alter this by countersinking the lower hole of the arbor in the movement plate and bending the bridge down a little in the center, with a wooden spool and wooden punch, as in end shaking the center hole in American watches and the barrel arbor.

Oftentimes we find the winding pinion too shallow for the bevel wheel; remedy this by either lowering the pinion deeper into the wheel or the wheel into the pinion. Oftentimes in Waltham watches, of the old series, the intermediate winding wheel is too deep in the ratchet wheel. This can be corrected by the banking screw, by putting in one with a larger head. Now very often the intermediate setting wheel is too shallow in the minute wheel. Correct this by stretching the lever where it touches the yoke, and taking off a little of the yoke where it banks for the hand setting. Remember that the yoke should be perfectly steady and firm, in turning the hands either way. The teeth of the minute wheel are often ruined when the cannon pinion is a little tight and the intermediate hand setting and minute wheels are too shallow. Never touch the arbor of the cannon pinion, but see that it is perfectly smooth and round. If the cannon pinion is too high from the plate turn a little off from the under side. Take pinion off with a pair of brass lined pliers. If the cannon pinion is too loose on the arbor, (if a stem-wind), punch it in the same place, with a punch in the staking tool, having a V shaped stump to lay the cannon pinion on, and holding it with a peg-wood or broach while punching it. Use a punch a little rounding. A cannon pinion should work smoothly all around. Now in a Swiss watch with a hallow center pinion, when its arbor is too loose, lay the arbor on a small flat anvil, or steel, or brass block, in front of you, not on vise, and hold a small square file across it and tap it with a small hammer, rolling it while you tap it. This raises a nice burr all around it. If a little too tight take it off with an oil stone slip. This can be done when the watch is clean and running.

Now examine the click, and see that it has a loose end shake, and that the point goes freely in and out of the teeth of the wheel. Sometimes the point is too blunt, and in many cases the click spring is too strong. Click springs should have a very low temper, and a nice slender shape, as the bending they perform is very little. They should not scrape on the plate, nor hold the click down too tight, if made like some Elgin clicks.

Now the end shake of the ratchet or ratchet wheel, should have some attention. You can easily manipulate this, if the ratchet is between the plates. End shake it with the winding arbor. Now we have the stem winding wheels, etc., in proper shape. The minute wheel pinion may rub on the dial. This remedy by grinding the dial away with an emery wheel, and oftentimes free the hour wheel the same way. If there is too much end shake, put on a spring washer, cut it square and turn the corners up. We can examine the train from the third wheel to the scape wheel; see if the holes are large, and end shake correct. In some cases in Swiss watches, where the third and center wheels are under the same bridge, you can sometimes turn the shoulder of the lower pivot back.

Sometimes we find pivots too loose in their holes, and in some cases, a new jewel can be put in to fit the pivot to a better advantage. In this case we must be guided by our practical experience, as in many other instances. True pinion or staff in a split chuck, flatten the old place, that you are to center with, on an oilstone slip, and center it with a graver. Nine out of ten Swiss or English, and a few American pinions, can be drilled without annealing. Use oil and a properly made drill. For a bow drill use a rounding point, and in an American lathe an obtuse angle point, to cut only one way. Drill pinion or staff, and if you are compelled to draw the temper, do it in the following way: Use a cap made of copper wire, holding the opposite end of staff or pinion in a pair of brass-lined flat plyers; set copper cap on and blow a sharp blaze on the cap to blue article to be drilled. Remove the color with a peg-wood and rouge; first with rouge and oil, and then with dry rouge. Never leave a pinion or staff discolored. Now, if article cannot be trued in a split chuck, cement it in, but you can true five out of every ten in a No. 1 Mosely lathe, without cement. For drilling it is not necessary that the article should run dead true; but it should be dead true, in turning the pivot on and finishing. Now, in pivoting after the hole is drilled and the plug is hammered in, turn your pivot to its proper shape with a graver and almost with the point. Turn pivot down to about three degrees thicker than pivot is to be. Now we have our pivot finished with a graver. Now use an iron wire, about two millimeters thick and about five inches long, flattened about one inch on one end with a file, filing crosswise, and now and then retouching with a fine file. This is done so the file lines or marks will retain the grinding powder to be used with oil. For a staff pivot, always file the corner off a little, so it will conform to the conical shoulder, and file or grind, holding the oil-stone charged file so the latter and the pivot will traverse at an acute angle. This is done to prevent the pivot from lining. Now, if down to the desired size and shape, use another such tool, made of brass or zinc and charged with rouge and oil, and polish pivot in the same manner that you grind it. At last touch it up with dry rouge and a peg-wood. Diamantine and oil or alcohol can also be used to good advantage before using the rouge.

After all repairs clean your work in the following manner: Use good benzine or gasoline and cyanide of potassium; a lump as large as a wallnut to a pint of water. Keep in a glass or china cup with a cover on it. Clean the lever in benzine only and dry in the sawdust. Have an alcohol cup, with cover, plenty of clean soft water (in cold weather use warm water), and a medium soft brush, like a paint brush, about a half inch thick for the benzine. A long, three or four row brush to use with good castile soap and water, and three, four or more pieces of brass wire made into loops or strings, by bending an eye on each wire like a fishing hook. The wire can be almost any length, from three to six inches, and from three-tenths to five-tenths mm. thick. This with about three pints of boxwood sawdust, put through a sieve to get out the coarse particles, and a soft camel's hair brush to use dry on the work after it has been cleaned, completes the outfit for cleaning. Put a wire through the top plate, hang in the benzine, and brush it carefully with the benzine brush, principally the pivot holes. After this has been done, pick up the stem wheels, wheels and small parts, unscrew the safety pinions and wash and clean with the wheels. Oil the thread sparingly when you put it back. String all of these small parts on a wire. Put the lower plate on with the barrel. Use a very thick wire for the balance (dip it separately), and move it about in the benzine; dry it in sawdust, dip in cyanide solution, in clear water, then in alcohol. Then move it about in the sawdust; this will clean the balance and hair spring and roller. After the plates and wheels have gone through the benzine or gasoline, dip them in the cyanide and wash with brush and water and castile soap. Dip in clean water, then in alcohol and then in sawdust. By this process, every speck of oil will be removed, and the gilding or nickle finish will not be injured, as with old fogy chalk, and a variety of powder. Sometimes the dirt in the pinion is thick and hard, and it must be removed with peg-wood; sometimes it has been oiled with linseed oil and left to dry; this can be boiled off in oil and cleaned as mentioned. To get dirt or hard gum out of the wheel teeth, make a kind of pad with stiff writing paper, draw the edge of these papers through the teeth; this will clean them nicely. When taking the cleaned parts from the sawdust, hold them with Dennison's watch papers, and brush off with a three or four row soft camel or fine goat hair brush. In setting the watch up, set the stem work up first and oil it properly. Right here, in oiling, is where it requires judgment. For the stem work use a heavier oil than for the train. Use refined clock oil for the stem wheels, as they necessarily require a heavier oil and it also has less tendency to spread. Use watch oil in oiling the center pivots, and they being large should have more oil than the third, fourth and scape wheels, etc. Put the proper amount of oil on the end-stone or cap jewel before putting the latter to its place, also the barrel arbor. Oil the pallet faces sparingly before putting the lever to its place. Now if your balance and hair spring are true and in poise, and the pivots have their proper freedom and end shake, and the roller its proper freedom, and everything is all right throughout, your watch will move off all right. To ascertain if exactly in beat, hold a peg-wood against the teeth of the fourth wheel, and move it slightly forward and observe the motion of the balance. If one pallet throws the balance further than the other, turn the hair spring by the collet slot, so that the lift will be equal on both pallets. When in beat examine the escapement again, see if the balance clears the stud, cock, center wheel, etc. See if all the screws are tight, and by all means have the hair spring so the second coil will not get into the curb pins. After this the train can be oiled. The barrel pivot next to the ratchet, or ratchet wheel should be oiled before the ratchet or wheel is put on. It is well to oil the balance jewel holes after it has been put in beat, on account of dragging in dust with the pivots if they should be oiled before. After this put on the dial wheels; do not oil the minute wheel posts; see that the hour wheel has its proper end shake. In cheap watches put on a thin washer to steady the hour hand and and wheel; put the dial on and see that the second and hour wheel sockets are in the center of the holes after the dial is properly fastened. If you have any steel hands to bend, it will pay you to bend them with a pair of hot tweezers, as this will avoid breaking them. Now set your second hand with your second pendulum regulator, and regulate pendant up. Meantime you can clean the case with water, ammonia and a soft cotton rag. An old tooth brush can be used in the corners. Stiff joints in front case can be loosened up with benzine. This will take the dirt out, and the joint will work free. Cases should be cleaned like all other repaired work. Often we find balance hole jewels entirely too thick, so they will take an unreasonably long pivot to reach through them. To remedy this, use an iron point charged with diamond powder that fits the concave of the jewel, and then polish in the same manner with a finer grade of diamond powder, diamantine and rotten stone. Keep the jewel wet with water in grinding and polishing, and use the highest speed you can produce. Care must be taken in this operation, as it requires a little experience. Like everything else, you will find a great deal of difference in grinding a garnet or a ruby or sapphire, also in polishing them. Zinc and lead points are used in polishing with diamantine and rotten stone and water. If the above process is understood it can be quickly done. The hole can also be polished, but in some cases it will pay better to put in a new and perfect jewel. F. C. R.

WATCH BOW PLIERS. Pliers of a peculiar shape as shown in Fig. 194, and used for manipulating watch bows.

WATCH CASE TOOL. The Hopkins' patent watch case tool is designed for the two-fold purpose of easing a case

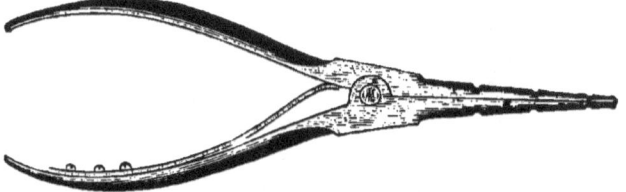

FIG. 194.

when it opens too hard, and for making one stay shut when it opens too easy. It is illustrated in Fig. 195. The part D is intended only for use when the spring catch of a hunting case has worn the case so it will not stay shut.

FIG. 195.

For making a back case stay shut when it opens too easily, use the cutting tooth B, in the following manner: rest the beveled edge of the tool from A to C, down level on the ledge against which the dome or back case closes, as represented in the illustration, taking care to keep the end A as well as the tooth B down level on the ledge, and inward against the part to be re-under cut, in which position with the end D, resting in the hollow of your right hand, back of the little finger, and with your thumb resting on the inner cap to steady your hand, hold the tool thus quite still, and with your left hand give a circular movement to the watch, crowding the part to be under cut against the tooth B, that is, instead of shoving the tool forward to produce the cutting, hold the tool still, and crowd the part of the case to be cut against it as described. By thus renewing the under cut of the catch edge, even a badly worn case may be made to shut and stay shut nicely.

For easing the cap or the back case of a watch when it opens too hard, rest the end *A*, of the tool, down on the inside of the dome, with the handle inclining backward at an angle of about 45°, and with one of the sharp edges extending from *A* to *C*, brought to bear against the snap edge that requires to be eased, in such a way that it will give a shaving (not a scraping) cut; carefully shave off the edge, thus, to the extent required. In this way even the most delicate case may be eased without the slightest marring or injury to it. In case of roughness of the snap edge, burnish it carefully with the back of the tool; or rubbing a bit of beeswax around the edge will often be found of service in cases of this kind.

WATCH HAND PLIERS. Fig. 196 shows Horton's combination watch hand pliers used for removing watch hands, second, hour and minute. It also takes the place of the 9-hole hand sliding tongs.

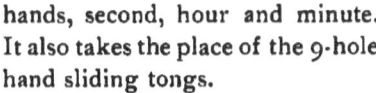

FIG. 196.

WATCHMAKERS. Sometimes the watchmaker and jeweler is desirous of telling how old a certain movement may be and the following alphabetical list of English watch and clock makers may aid him in fixing the age approximately. cc with date following indicates the year in which the person became a member of the Clockmakers' Company, of London. Watch, is watchmaker, and clock, is clockmaker.

Abbott, John, London, clock, cc 1703.
Abbott, Peter, London, clock, cc 1719.
Abbott, John, London, son of Peter, clock, cc 1740.
Ames, Richard, London, clock, cc 1653, died 1679.
Andrews, John, London, cc 1688.
Aspinwall, Samuel, London, watch, was in business in 1590.
Barrow, Samuel, London, cc 1696.
Bauge, Edward, cc 1695, an apprentice of Thomas Tompion; was in business in London in 1741.
Baylie, Jeffry, English, cc 1648.
Beauvais, Simon, London, clock, cc 1690.

Bell, Benj., London, watch, cc 1660, died 1694.
Bouchet, J., London, clock, cc 1728.
Bowley, Devereux, London, clock, cc 1718, Junior Warder of cc in 1756 and Master in 1759, born 1697, died 1773.
Boyear, William, London, clock, cc 1633.
Bradley, Langley, London, clock, was member of the court of assistants of cc and elected Junior Warder in 1724, Renter Warder in 1725, Senior Warder in 1724 and Master in 1726.
Brown, Henton, London, clock, cc 1726.
Cabrier, Charles, London, watch, cc 1697.
Cam, William, London, clock, cc 1686.
Chater, James, London, clock, carried on business at 14 Cornhill, London, from 1782 to 1790, when he was succeeded by Chater & Son, who were in business until 1800.
Clarke, George, London, clock, cc 1632.
Closson, Peter, London clock, cc 1633.
Cumming, Alexander, London, watch, commenced business in 1760. Died, 1813.
Decka, John, London, cc 1757.
East, Edward, London, watch and clock. One of the ten original assistants appointed by the Charter of Incorporation of the Clockmakers' Company in 1632. Was Warder in 1638-9, Master in 1645-52, Treasurer in 1637, being the only occupant of the latter office in the history of the company. He was watchmaker to Charles I.
East, Jeremy, London, clock, cc 1641.
Ebsworth, John, London, clock, cc 1665. Warder in 1695.
Ethrington, George, London, clock, cc 1684.
Everell, John, London, watch, in business in 1730.
Exelby, James, London, clock, cc 1718.
Goode, Charles, London, clock, cc 1686.
Green, James, London, clock, cc 1664.
Greene, James, London, clock, cc 1685.
Green, John, London, watch and clock, cc 1711.
Green, Joseph, London, clock, cc 1723.
Green, James, London, clock, Master of cc 1784.
Gregory, Jeremy, London, clock, cc 1652. Died 1685.

WATCHMAKERS.

Gregory, Thomas, London, clock, cc 1671.
Gregory, Robert, London, clock, cc 1678.
Gregory, Jeremiah, London, clock, cc 1694.
Grennel, Richard, London, clock, cc 1735.
Harper, Henry, London, clock, cc 1664.
Harris, Anthony, London, clock, cc 1683.
Hemmen, London, watch, in business in 1646.
Harris, Henry, London, watch, cc 1711.
Hodges, Nathaniel, London, clock, cc 1681.
Hohwii, Andreas, Amsterdam, Holland, chronometer maker to the Dutch Marine. Born 1803, died 1886.
Hunter, Thomas, Sr., London, clock, cc 1780.
Hunter, Thomas, Jr., London, clock, cc 1798.
Ireland, Henry, London, clock, cc 1668.
Irving, Alexander, London, clock, cc 1795.
Johnson, Thos., London, watch, in business at 9 Gray's Inn Passage, in eighteenth century. Was succeeded by his son John, who died in 1799, and was succeeded by Daniel Desbois, who died 1848.
Jones, Henry, London, clock, cc 1697.
Knibb, Joseph, London, clock, cc 1670.
Leconte, Daniel, London, clock, cc 1676.
LeCompte, James, London, clock, cc 1687.
Lecount, Peter, London, clock, cc 1787.
Lee, Cuthbert, London, clock, cc 1676.
Long, John, London, clock, cc 1677.
Long, John, London, clock, cc 1698.
Long, Henry, London, watch, in business at 200 High Holbon in 1780.
Markwick, James, London, watch, cc 1666.
Markwick, James, London, watch, cc 1692.
Mottram, John, Clerkenwell, clock, in business in 1790.
Nathan, Henry, clock, cc 1673.
Planner, Thomas, London, clock, cc 1701.
Planner, Thomas, London, clock, cc 1730.
Quare, Daniel, London, clock, in business from 1632 to 1724.
Reid, Thomas, Edinburg, watch and clock, born 1748, died 1834.

Rimbault, Paul, London, clock; born in Switzerland. In business in London in eighteenth century.

Rimbault, Stephen, son of Paul, succeeded him in business at 9 Denmark street, St. Giles, London, and was there in 1800.

Ringmader, ———, watch, Dublin, Ireland, in business in 1792.

Rivers, David, London, clock, cc 1773.

Rivers, William, London, clock, cc 1794.

Rooker, Richard, London, watch, cc 1728.

Swell, George, London, clock, cc 1688.

Sowery, Andrew, London, clock, cc 1676.

Storer, Robert, London, watch, cc 1760.

Taylor, Jasper, London, clock, cc 1694

Taylor, Thomas, London, clock, cc 1703.

Taylor, Jasper, London, clock, cc 1729.

Thomton, Henry, London, clock, cc 1699.

Townsend, Joseph, Helmdon, Eng., clock; in business in 1670.

Underwood, William, London, clock; was in business in Falcon street, Aldersgate, London, in 1790.

Vick, Richard, watch, cc 1702.

Vulliamy, Benj., Gray, Justin, London, clock, in business in 1790.

Webster, William, watch and clock, Master of cc 1765.

Wyse, John, London, clock, cc 1669.

Wyse, Richard, London, clock, cc 1679.

Wyse, John, London, clock, cc 1683.

Wyse, Thomas, London, clock, cc 1686.

Wyse, Joseph, London, clock, cc 1687.

Wyse, Peter, London, clock, cc 1693.

Wyse, Luke, London, clock, cc 1694.

Wyse, Robert, London, clock, cc 1695.

Wyse, John, London, clock, cc 1710.

Wyse, Mark, London, clock, cc 1719.

York, Thomas, London, clock, cc 1716.

WHEELS AND PINIONS. In the construction of watches and clocks it is necessary to transmit motion from one arbor to another, so that the arbor which is driven rotates more quickly than the one which drives it. If it were practicable to use rollers with smooth edges for transmitting such motion, the diameter of the rollers would be inversely proportionate to the number of rotations made by their arbors in a given time. For instance, the distance apart of two arbors from center to center measures 3.7 inches, and it is desired that for every time the arbor from which the power is taken rotates the other shall rotate eight times. The distance between the arbors is divided into nine equal parts of which eight are taken for the radius of the driver, which rotates only once, and one part for the radius of the follower as it is called, which rotates eight times. Although it is not practicable to drive with smooth rollers, which would slip unless pressed so tightly together as to cause excessive friction, the circles representing the rollers are the basis on which the wheel and pinion are constructed. They are called the pitch circles. The acting part of the teeth of the driver is beyond its pitch circle, and the acting part of the teeth of the follower within its pitch circle. In most of the toothed wheels with which watchmakers are concerned, the driver is the wheel and the follower the pinion. The shape for the acting part of the wheel is an epicycloid, a curve generated by rolling one circle on another.

FIG. 197.

In Fig. 197 is shown a portion of a circle representing the pitch diameter of the wheel, and on it a smaller circle rolling in the direction of the arrow. If these two are made of brass or any thin material, and laid on a sheet of paper, a pencil fixed to the circumference of the small roller will trace a curve as shown. This curve is the acting part of the wheel tooth.

The acting part of the pinion leaves must be produced by the same sized roller as was used for the points of the wheel teeth, but in a different manner. The pinion flanks should be hypocycloidal in form. A hypocycloid is obtained by rolling one circle within another instead of upon it. The most convenient size for the generating roller for both wheel and pinion is half the pitch diameter of the pinion. In Fig. 198 is a circle representing the pitch circle of the pinion, with another circle half its size rolling within it, and in this case the point described by the pencil would be a straight radial line, which is a suitable form for the pinion.

Fig. 198.

Teeth formed in this way will transmit the motion uniformly at the same speed as though the pitch circles rolled on each other without teeth, and will also meet another important requirement. The action between the teeth will take place almost wholly after the line of centers, that is if the pinion has not less than ten leaves. The difference between engaging and disengaging friction is great, especially if the surfaces in contact are not quite smooth. Wheels which have any considerable portion of their action between the teeth as they are engaging or before the line of centers, not only absorb considerable power thereby, but wear out rapidly.

Fig. 199.

With a larger generating circle more of the action between the teeth of the wheel and the leaves of the pinion would take place after the line of centers, which is a consideration with low numbered pinions, but then a larger generating circle traces a pinion leaf too weak at the root.

The pitch circle of the wheel is spaced out so that the teeth and the spaces are equal. To allow of necessary freedom the teeth or leaves of the pinion are less in width than the spaces. The distance between the center of one leaf and the center of the next may be divided into .6 for space and .4 for leaf.*

---

*The "pitch" of wheels and pinions is the portion of the circumference of the pitch circle between the center of one tooth and the center of the next.

WHEELS AND PINIONS.

The pinion leaves are finished with a semi-circular piece projecting beyond the pitch circle as seen in Fig. 199. They would work without if properly pitched, but would not be safe as the depth became shallow from the wearing of the holes. Some prefer a Gothic-shaped projection like Fig. 200, which is of epicycloidal form, the same as the wheel teeth. This is a very suitable form if the pinions are low numbered, for, although with it the action takes place more before the line of center, as afer depth is insured.

The teeth of the wheel are extended within the pitch line to allow of clearance for the addendum of the pinion. The root or part of the wheel tooth within the pitch line is generally radial.

The corners at the bottom of the tooth may be rounded strength, but these round corners must not be so full as to engage the points of the pinion leaves.

FIG. 200.

The action should be confined as nearly as possible to the epicycloid on the wheel, and the hypocycloid on the pinion. In watches, the roots of all the wheels and pinions are left square, except the roots of the barrel or great wheel teeth, and the roots of the center pinion leaves, which should always be rounded for strength. There is then less danger of the teeth stripping if the mainspring breaks.

If the pinion is to be used as the driver and the wheel as the follower, as is the case in the motion work of watches and clocks, the points of the pinion teeth must be epicycloidal, and the roots of the wheel teeth hypocycloidal struck with the same generating circle. For the convenience of using wheels and pinions indiscriminately as drivers and followers, engineers generally use a generating circle whose diameter = the pitch × 2.22 for the points and roots of all wheels and pinions of the same pitch. The tip of the addendum is removed in both wheels and pinions.

If more than two wheels gear together, the acting parts of all should be struck from the same sized generating circle.

The number of teeth in a wheel bears exactly the same proportion to the number of teeth in a pinion with which it gears, as the diameter of the pitch circles of the wheel and pinion bear to each other. If the pinion whose pitch circle is .8 of an inch in diameter has 10 teeth, then the wheel with a pitch circle of 6.4 inches in diameter will have 80 teeth, because .8 is contained 8 times in 6.4, and 10 × 8 = 80. But the out-

FIG. 201.

side or full diameter of a wheel or pinion is not proportional to the pitch diameter. The addendum or portion of the tooth beyond the acting part bears reference rather to the size of the generating circle and to the width of the teeth than to the diameter of the wheel or pinion.

Lantern pinions work very smoothly as followers, though they are unsuitable as drivers. The space occupied by the shrouds precludes their use in watches, but in the going parts of clocks they answer well.

For the convenience of ready calculation it may be assumed that the addendum of the wheel teeth increases the size of the wheel by three teeth. For instance, the pitch diameter of a wheel of 80 teeth is 2 inches. Then its pitch diameter would bear the same proportion to its full diameter as 80 does to 83; or 80 : 2 : : 83 : 2.07, which is the full diameter.

In the same way it may be taken that the circular addendum increases the size of the pinion by 1.25 teeth, and the epicycloidal addendum by 1.98, or nearly 2 teeth.

If the pinion is to be used as the driver, it must have the epicycloidal addenda to insure proper action. I believe an opinion prevails among some watchmakers that the circularly rounded pinions may be used as drivers if they are sectored large, and that they are so used for motion work, but such a practice is altogether wrong.

In the motion work of keyless watches the followers are used as drivers when the hands are being set, and a good form of tooth for motion work generally may be obtained by using for roots and points of both wheels and pinions a generating circle of a diameter equal to twice the pitch. This gives a short tooth which will run smoothly when at full width. The form of gearing suitable for the train permits of too much shake for motion work.—*Britten.*

FIG. 202.

WHEEL CUTTER. The wheel cutter is a valuable addition to the lathe. Several different styles of these tools are made, each possessing points of merit. They are designed for cutting all kinds of wheels and pinions used in key and stem-wind watches. When the cutter spindle is vertical the belt runs directly to it from the countershaft, but when horizontal the belt passes over idler pulleys held above the lathe. These idler pulleys are also used to run the pivot polisher. Fig. 201 illustrates the American Watch Tool Co.'s wheel cutter, while Fig. 202 is Moseley's pattern.

WHEEL VISE. Rose's patent wheel vise, shown in Fig. 203, is used for holding all kinds of watch wheels while undergoing repairs, such as putting in new teeth, removing rust from pinions, etc., and for holding balance wheels while putting in or removing the screws, taking the hair spring or collet from staff or for any work where the safety of the wheel is involved.

FIG. 203.

WIGWAG. The wigwag is used for polishing the shoulders of pinions, pinion leaves, staffs and pivots, and for numerous other operations. The formation of these tools differ according to the ideas of the various makers, but in principal they are alike. These tools are used extensively in all the American watch factories.

INDEX.

Abbey, 63
Acceleration, 9
Acid bottle, 11
Acids, and salts, 10
Adendum circle, 11
Adhesion, 11
Adjustable case springs, 62
Adjusting rod, 12
Adjustment, 12
Adjustment heater, 16
Adjustment to isochronism, 14
Ajustment to positions, 12
Alcohol cup, 16
Alcohol lamp, 16
Alloys, 18
Alum, 10
Aluminum, 22
    alloys, 18
    bronze, 18
    gold, 19
    silver, 19
    zinc, 19
Amalgam, 22
Anchor escapement, 23
Angular velocity, 26
Annealing, 26
    of steel, 262
Anode, 26
Aqua fortis, 10
    regia, 10
Arbor, 26
    barrel, 52
    saw, 244
Arc, 27
    balance, 44
Arcograph, 27
Arnold, John, 63

Assay, 27
    of silver, 251
Artificial gold, 16
Auxiliary, 30
Axle, 26
Balance, 27
    alloys, 18
    arc, 44
    auxiliaries, 30
    bridge, 44
    cock, 44
    compensation, 102
    expansion and contraction of, 28
    making, 28
    pivots, 234
    pivots, 49, 234
    Pool's, 30
    protector, 45
    size and weight of, 30
    staff, 46
    screw washers, 45
    spring, 46
    truing, 34
    to poise, 33
Banking pins, 51
Barrel, 52
    arbor, 52
    chiming, 78
    contractor, 52
    hook, 52
    ratchet, 52
    to true, 283
Batteries, 129
Beat, 52
    block, 53
    pins, 53

Beat, to put in, 176
Bell metal, 20
   metal, American, 21
   metal, Japanese, 21
Bench, 53
Bending gong wires, 240
Benzine, 55
   cup, 16
Berthond, Ferdinand, 63
   Louis, 63
Bevel gear, 55
Bezel, 55
   chuck, 89
Binding wire, 55
Bite, 55
Blow pipe, 55
   lamp, 17
Bluing, 55
   pan, 55
   shovel, 56
Bluestone, 55
Boiling out pan, 57
Borax, 10
Bouchon, 57
Bow, 57
Brass, 20
   to clean, 95
   polishing paste, 99
Breguet, Abraham, L., 63
Bridge, 58
   balance, 44
Britannia, 20
Broach, 58
Broaching second hands, 179
Bronze for medals, 21
   for ornaments, 21
   Japanese, 21
   manganese, 21
   Paris, 21
Bronzing, 129
   analine, 139
   antique, 140
   black, for brass, 140
   black, for gun barrels, 140
   blue, 140

Bronzing, blue, for iron or steel, 141
   brass, 141
   brown, 142
   brown, for copper, 142
   brown, for guns, 142
   Chinese, 143
   copper, 141
   gold, for brass, 143
   gold, for iron, 143
   gold, for silver, 143
   gray, for brass, 144
   green, for brass, 144
   liquid, 141,
   medal, 141
   steel, 267
   steel blue for brass, 147
Buff, 58
Bullseye, 58
Burnisher, 58
   wheel, 105
Burnishing tool, 59
Bush, 59
Bushing, 282
   pivot holes, 59
   punch, 59
   wire, 59
Butting, 59
Calipers, 59
   jeweled, 61
   jeweling, 184
Callet, F. 63
Cam, 61
Cannon pinion, 61
   pinion to repair, 285
Cap, 61
Capillary attraction, 61
Capped jewel, 61
Capsule balance making, 28
Carrier, 61
Cardinal points, 61
Case hardening, 61
   springs, 62
   spring vise, 62
   stake, 62
Cathode, 26

Celebrated watchmakers, 63
Centrifugal force, 77
Cement, 67
    acid proof, 67
    alabaster, 67
    amber, 67
    brasses, 69
    engravers, 68
    fire-proof, 68
    glass and brass, 68
    glass and metal, 68
    gold colored, 68
    jewelers, 69
    knife and fork, 68
    metal, 69
    silver colored, 68
    strong, 68,
    transparent, 68
    watchmakers, 68
Centering attachment, 71
    indicator, 73
Center of gravity, 73
    of gyration, 74
    of motion, 74
    of oscillation, 74
    pinions, to repair, 283
    punch, 73
    seconds, 77
    staff, 77
    wheel, 77
Centers, 70
Chain hook, 77
Chamois, 77
    to clean, 77
Chamfer, 77
Chamfering tool, 77
Chariot, 78
Chimes, 78
Chiming barrel, 78
Chloride of ammonium, 21
Chronograph, 78
Chronometer, 78
    escapement, 78
    marine, 78
    pocket, 78, 85

Chronoscope, 87
Chrysorine, 20
Chuck, 88
    adjustable, 88
    arbor, 88
    bezel, 89
    box, 93
    cement, 90
    dead-center, 90
    pivoting, 91
    screw, 88
    shoulder, 88
    split, 88
    step, 93
    wheel, 93
Circular error, 100
Clamps, 100
Cleaning of silver, 252
    of watches, 280
Cleansing, pickling and polishing 93
Clement's escapement, 23
Cleat, 100
Clepsydra, 100
Cliche, 100
Click, 100
    spring, 101
Clock bell alloys, 21
    wheel alloys, 21
Closing hole punch, 59
Club tooth, 101
Clutch, 102
Cock, 101,
    balance, 44
Collet, 102
    wrench, 102
Compass, 102
Compasses, 102
Compensation balances, 102
    curb, 103
    pendulum, 102
    files, 18
Concave, 102
Conical pendulum, 103
    pivot, 103
Conoidal, 103

Contractor, barrel, 52
Contrate wheel, 103
Conversion, 103
Convex, 103
Convexo-concave, 103
    convex, 103
Copper, 103
    durable luster on, 147
Corundum, 104
    wheels, 104
Counter balance, 104
Countermark, 104
Countersink, 104
Crank, 105
Crescent, 105
Crown-wheel, 105
Crucible, 105
Crystal, 105
Curb pins, 105
Cutter, screw head sink, 248
    rose, 243
Cycloid, 106
Cylinder escapement, 106
    plugs, 112
Damaskeen, 114
    imitation of, 133
Dead beat escapement, 114
Decant, 114
Demagnetization of watches, 213
Demagnetizer, 115
Dent, E. J., 63
Depth, 118
Depthing tool, 118
Detached escapement, 119
Detent, 119
De Vick, Henry, 63
Dial, 119
    cleaning metal, 121
    double sunk, 123
    drill, 119
    grinding backs of, 121
    pins, 281
    reduce diameter of, 120
    remove name from, 120
    remove stains from, 120

Dial, repairing, 120
Diamantine, 121
Diamond drills, 121
    gravers, 121
    laps and mills, 121
    files, 122
    powder, 122
Dipleidoscope, 122
Distributor, 122
Dividing plate, 122
Dog, 122
    screws, 122
Double roller escapement, 123
    sunk dial, 123
Douzieme, 123
Draw, 123
    plate, 123
Drifting tool, 123
Drill, 124
    rest, 124
    stock, 125
    lathe, 125
    diamond, 122
Drilling pinions, 286
Drop, 125, 194
Drum, 125
Duplex escapement, 126
    hook, 129
    roller, 129
Dust bands, 129
Electro-plating, 129
    aluminating baths for, 136
    brass baths for, 136
    copper baths for, 136
    dead luster in, 133
    doctoring in, 136
    gold baths for, 131
    grained surface in, 138
    green gold in, 133
    imitation damaskeening 133
    nickel baths for, 135
    recovery of metal when 137
    red gold in, 132
    silver baths for, 133
Emery, 147

Emery, buff, 58
    countersinks, 147
    files and pencils, 147
    sticks, 147
    wheels, 148
End stone, 148
Engine turning, 148
English watchmakers, 291
English hall mark, 177
Engraving block, 148
    on steel, 269
Epicycloid, 149, 295
Equation of time, 149
Equidistant lockings, 204
Escapement, 149
    anchor, 23
    chronometer, 78
    Clement's, 23
    cylinder, 106
    dead beat, 114
    detached, 119
    double roller, 123
    duplex, 126
    files, 151
    frictional, 154
    Graham, 168
    lever, 189
    pin pallet, 230
    pin wheel, 232
    recoil, 239
    resilient, 242
    right angle, 189
    straight line, 189
    two pin, 202, 277
    verge, 278
    vertical, 280
Escape pinion, 150
Escaping arc, 150
Eye glass, 150
Ferric oxide, 98
Ferrule, 150
Fetil, Pierre, 63
Fictitious silver, 20
Files, 151
    diamond, 122

Filigree to clean, 253
Filing block, 152
    fixture, 152
Flux, 153
Fly or fan, 153
Follower, 153
Foot wheel, 153
Friction, 153
    of train pivots, 235
Frictional escapements, 154
Frosting, 154
    of silver, 253
Full plate, 154
Fusee, 155
    advantage of, 33
Gas heater, 156
Guage, 157
    cylinder height, 164
    Dennison's, 157
    Douzieme, 158
    jewelers, 161
    micrometer, 159
    pinion and wire, 161
    registering, 162
    staff, 162
    staff length, 162
    twist drill, 165
    vernier caliper, 165
German silver pickle, 95
Gilding steel, 138
Gimbals, 167
Going barrel, 167
    fusee, 167
Gold alloys, 22
    blue, 22
    gray, 22
    green, 22
    Nurnberg, 21
    pickle, 95
    polishing powder, 99
    red, 22
    spring, 168
    yellow, 22
Gong and bell alloys, 21
Graham escapement, 168

Graham, Geo., 64
Graver, 172
　　diamond, 122
Gravimeter, 174
Gravity, 174
　　center of, 173
　　escapement, 174
　　specific, 174
Great wheel, 174
Grinder, traverse spindle, 276
Grinding and polishing pinions, 229
Grossman, Moritz, 64
Guard pin, 174
Gun barrels, stain for, 140, 142
Gyrate, 174
Gyration, center of 74
Hair spring, 175
　　stud index, 176
Half plate, 176
Hall mark, 177
Hand remover, 179
Hands, 179
Hardening of steel, 263
Harrison, John, 64
Hook, barrel, 52
　　chain, 77
Hooke, Robt., 64
Hopkins' jeweling tool, 182
　　lathe, 187
Horizontal escapement, 180
Houriet, F., 64
Hour glass, 180
　　wheel, 180
Huyghens, Christian, 65
Hydrochloric acid, 11
Hydrofluoric acid, 11
Idler, 180
Imitation silver, 21
Impulse pin, 180
Independent seconds, 180
Index, 180
Inertia, 180
Involute, 181
Isochronal, 181
Jocot pivot lathe, 181

Janvier, Antide, 65
Japanese bronze, 21
Jeweled calipers, 61
Jeweling, 181
　　caliper rest, 184
　　and staking tool, 182
Jewel, capped, 61
　　pin, 185
　　pin setter, 184
Jodin, Jean, 65
Joint pusher, 186
Jurgensen, Urban, 65
Kessels, M., 65
Knife and fork alloy, 21
Lacquer, 186
Lantern pinion, 187
Laps and mills, diamond, 121
Lap, 187
Lathe, 187
Lepaute, J. A., 65
LeRoy, Julien, 65
　　Pierre, 65
Lever escapement, 189
Lever, straight line, 269
Lime, Vienna, 280
Locking, 210
Logan jewel pin setter, 184
Lubricators, 223
Magnetism, 210
Magnets, to temper, 269
Mainspring, 214
　　cleaning of, 216
　　punch, 216
　　winder, 216
Maintaining power, 220
Malleable brass, 20
Maltese cross, 220
Mandril, 220
Manganese bronze, 21
Marine chronometer, 78
Mass, 221
Material cup, 221
Matt for steel, 264
Matting, 221
Meridian dial, 221

Medal bronze, 21
Metals, to clean, 94
Micrometer, 159, 221
    tables, 160
Millimeter, 221
Milling fixture, 221
Moinet, Louis, 65
Momentum, 221
Motel, H., 66
Motion work, 221
Movement, 222
    box, 222
    cover, 222
    holder, 222
    in beat, 176
    rest, 222
Mudge, Thos., 66
Nickel, cleaning, 94
    plating with battery, 135
    plating without battery, 138
    plating by boiling, 139
Nine-hole sliding tongs, 179
Nitric acid, 10
Non-magnetic alloy, 21
    watch, 223
Nurnberg gold, 21
Oil, 224
Oiler, 226
Oil sink, 226
Oiling a watch, 288
Oilstones, 227
Oilstone dust, 227
Opera glass alloy, 21
Oroide, 21
Oscillation, centre of, 74
Overbanking, 227
Overcoil, 227
Pallet, 227
    staff, 227
    stones, 228
    stone adjuster, 228
    to test, 194
Parallel bars, 34
Paris bronze, 21
Pendulum, 228

Pendulum, compensation, 102
    conical, 103
    to clean, 93
    spring, 228
Peg wood, 228
    cutter, 55
Pendant, 228
Perron, M., 66
Pickling of metals, 95
Pillar, 229
    plate, 229
Pinchbeck, 21
Pinion, 229
    cannon, 61
    grinding and polishing, 229
    lantern, 187
Pin vise, 231
    wheel escapement, 232
    pallet escapement, 230
Pivot, 234
    balance, 49
    conical, 103
    cylinder, 236
    friction, 32, 235
    guage, 48, 237
    hole bushing, 59
    lathe, 181
    length of balance, 234
    play of, 234
    polisher, 237
    polishing, 50
    shape of, 236
    to straighten, 235
    train, friction of, 235
Pivoting cylinders, 236
Plating, 129
Pocket chronometer, 78
Poising tool, 34, 238
Polisher, glass for steel, 269
Poising the balance, 33
Polishing agents, 98
    buff, 58
    metals, 94
Positive pole, 26
Potence, 101, 238

Prince's metal, 21
Pump center, 238
Punch, bushing, 59
    center, 73
    closing hole, 59
    mainspring, 216
Push piece, 238
Quare, Danl., 66
Quarter screws, 238
Rack lever, 239
Ratchet, 239
    barrel, 52
Recoil escapement, 239
Red stuff, 239
Regulator, 239
Reid, Thos., 66
Repair clamps, 239
Repairing of watches, 280
Repeater, 240
    gong wires, 240
Right angle escapement, 189
Ring guage, 242
Riveting stake, 242
Resilient escapement, 242
Robin, Robt., 66
Roller remover, 242
Romilly, M., 66
Roze, A. C., 66
Rose cutter, 243
Rounding-up tool, 243
Ruby pin, 244
    roller, 244
Rust, to remove from steel, 267
Safety pin, 244
Safety pinion, 244
Sal-ammoniac, 11
Sapphire file, 244
Saw arbor, 244
Scratch brushing, 99
Screws, 244
    to remove broken, 245
    to blue, 56
    left handed, 246
Screw driver, 247
Screw extractor, 247

Screw head sink cutter, 248
    holder, 262
    plate, 249
    tap, 249
Second hand holder, 179
Second hand remover, 250
Shellac, 250
Siderial clock, 250
    time, 272
Silver, 250
    assay by smelting, 252
    assay with tube, 251
    cleaning, 94, 252
    cleaning filigree, 253
    distinguishing, 251
    frosting, 253
    oxidizing, 144
    paste, 98
    soap, 98
    separating of, 250
Silvering for brass or copper, 145
    small iron articles, 145
    without battery, 146
Silver plating with battery, 133
    without battery, 146
Slide rest, 254
Sliding tongs, 179
Snail, 254
Snap, 254
Snarling iron, 254
Soldering, 255
    fluxes, 257
    forceps, 258
    tweezers, 277
Solders, 255
    hard, 255
    gold, 255
    silver, 255
    soft, 255
    to dissolve, 257
Solar time, 274
Specific gravity, 174, 259
Spectacle tool, 259
Split seconds, 261
Spoon alloys, 21

Spring, balance, 46
Sprung over, 261
Square, to repair, 284
Staff, 261
    balance, 46
    center, 77
Staining, 129
Stake, 261
    case, 62
Staking tool, 182, 261
Star wheel, 262
Steady pins, 262
Steel, 262
    annealing of, 263
    anti-rust varnish for, 267
    browning or bronzing of, 267
    colors of, under heat, 266
    engraving on, 269
    gilding on, 138
    glass polisher for, 269
    hardening of, 263, 268
    hardening liquids for, 268
    mat for, 264
    plunging of, 268
    rusting, to prevent, 267
    rust to remove from, 267
    tempering, 265
    tempering by electricity, 269
    working of, 266
Stem-wind wheels to fit, 285
Stop work, 269
Straightening pivots, 235
Straight line lever, 269
Stud, 270
    index, 176
Sully, Henry, 66
Sweep seconds, 270
Swiss universal lathe, 220
Table, 270
Tailstock, 270
    half open, 270
    screw, 271
    traverse spindle, 271
Tavan, Antoine, 66
Tea pot alloy, 21

Tempering steel, 265
Testing needles, 271
Third wheel, 272
Three-quarter plate, 272
Time, 272
    apparent, 272
    astronomical, 272
    civil, 272
    equation of, 149
    sideral, 272
    solar, 274
Timing, 274
    screws, 274
    to positions, 12
Tin putty, 98
Tompion, Thos., 66
Touchstone, 274
Train, 275
    examination of, 286
Transit instrument, 276
Traverse spindle grinder, 276
Tripoli, 98
Truing balance, 34
Turns, 276
Tweezers, 276
    balance, truing, 34
Twist drills, 123
Two pin escapement, 277
Universal face plate, 278
    head, 277
    lathe, 220
Vaughan mainspring winder, 217
Velocity, angular, 26
Verge escapement, 278
Vernier, caliper, 165, 280
Vertical escapement, 280
Vienna lime, 280
Vise, case spring, 62
Watch, 280
    bench, 53
    bow plyers, 289
    case tool, 290
    cleaning and repairing, 280
    hand plyers, 291
    hand remover, 179

Watch oil, 223
Watchmakers, list of, 291
Wathiers' stud index, 176
Wax, watchmakers, 69
Webster-Whitcomb lathe, 188
Wheel cutter, 299
    vise, 300

Wheels and pinions, 294
White metal, 21
Winder, mainspring, 216
Wire bushing, 59
Wigwag, 300
Wrench, collet, 102

Waltham Watch Tool Co.
SPRINGFIELD, MASS.

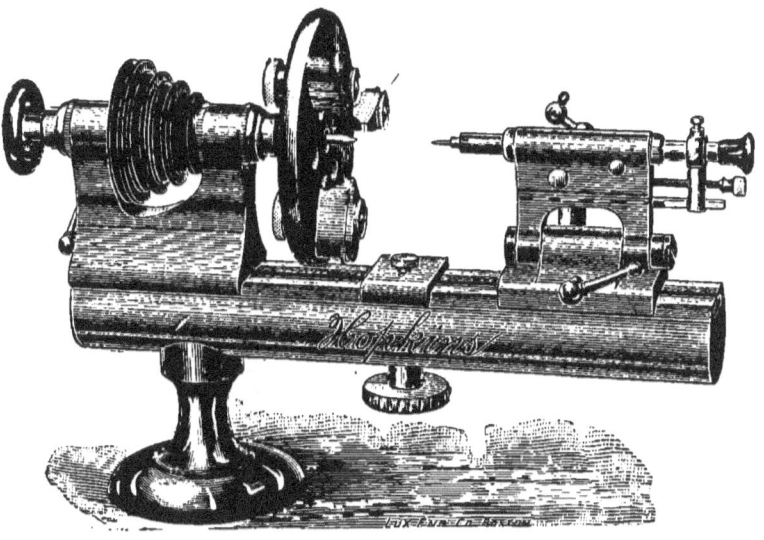

MANUFACTURERS OF THE

"HOPKINS" LATHES,
LATHE ATTACHMENTS, ETC.
THE BEST LINE OF LATHES ON THE MARKET.

PERFECT RUNNING
    ACCURATE IN ALL PARTS
        BEAUTIFULLY DESIGNED and FINISHED

The most Practical line of Attachments at low prices

The Best is the Cheapest, and the Hopkins 3x4 Lathe of to-day is the best on the American Market.

No Watchmaker can afford to buy a lathe without examining one of ours

SEND FOR ILLUSTRATED CATALOGUE.

Use the *CR* American Main Springs

L. H. KELLER & CO.

IMPORTERS OF
WATCHMAKERS' AND JEWELERS'

TOOLS and MATERIALS

OUR SPECIALTIES:

THE WELL KNOWN AND GUARANTEED

CR LEPINE MAIN SPRINGS
(OUR OWN)

SOLD BOTH IN SEPARATE FORCES
AND ASSORTED STRENGTHS,

AND THE . . . .

CR American Main Springs

THE BEST ARTICLE OF THE KIND IN THE MARKET
ELASTICITY AND BUT LITTLE BREAKAGE GUARANTEED

A Pleasure to use them.

THE JURGENSEN RECOILING MAIN SPRINGS
FOR HIGH GRADES OF WATCHES

MŒBIUS WATCH and CLOCK OILS	Ruby Balance Jewels with Olive-Shaped Holes
The Finest Lubricator for all Climates.	Sold both by number of hole and diameter of jewel.

We Solicit a share of your Patronage.

L. H. KELLER & CO.

NEAR MAIDEN LANE   64 NASSAU ST., NEW YORK.

American Watch Tool Co.,

STONY BATTER WORKS,

WALTHAM, MASS.

MAKE THE

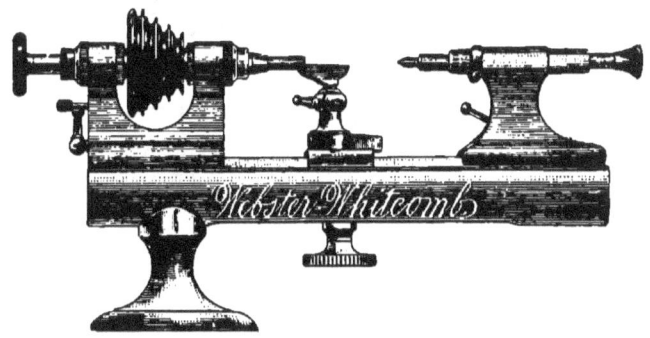

WEBSTER-WHITCOMB LATHE

Our Mr. Webster began designing lathes in 1860; This is his Latest and Best.

By the introduction of special and costly tools we have brought the price of lathes down from $80.00 in 1875, to $40 00 in 1890

WHO HAS DONE MORE FOR THE CRAFT THAN WE?

Remember our full address when you send for price lists

Greave's Demagnetizer

PATENTED, JUNE 5, 1888;
" **FEB'Y 5, 1889.**

Is the SIMPLEST, most DURABLE and EFFECTIVE machine ever made for DEMAGNETIZING WATCHES, and is indispensible to WATCHMAKERS having the responsibility and the care of FINE WATCHES, as it will REMOVE all traces of Magnetism without injuring the most delicate parts.

The size of the machine is only 4x8 inches, and can be attached to either a Battery or electric light wire.

PRICE COMPLETE, ONLY $20,
WITHOUT BATTERY.

In ordering please state system of electric light used.

If there is no electric light, and a Battery is to be used, it should be equal to two calls, type G, Edison-Lalande Battery which can be had from any electric supply store.

GREAVE'S DEMAGNNETIZER

can be had from L. H. KELLER & Co., 64 Nassau Street, NEW YORK; from any JOBBERS or directly from the manufacturers,

Jaccard Watch & Jewelry Co.

815 MAIN ST., KANSAS CITY, MO.

It is consistent with the future of this excellent work, in enlightening the craft with the latest methods of repairing the wheels of time, that we name our

Premier Brand
of Main Springs

as the safest and best to use. There are fewer breaks, they give a more uniform motion, and hundreds of the best workmen pronounce them the best.

Elgin Specialty M'fg. Co.
Elgin, Ill.

O. W. BULLOCK & CO.
SPRINGFIELD, MASS.

Manufacturers of the largest line of fine **BENCH TOOLS** for Watchmakers and Jewelers in the United States. Patented tools made in quantities to order, or on a Royalty.

The tools shown in Figs. 15, 16, 35, 36, 39, 40, 45 and 62 are a few samples of the great variety we make. They or anything else in our line can be procured directly from us if your jobber does not have them in stock.

For a full list send for our illustrated Catalogue, 100 pages, postage four cents.

We carry nothing but goods of our own manufacture. Our motto:

"AMERICAN TOOLS FOR AMERICANS."

Vaughan's Patent
CLOCK MAIN SPRING WINDER

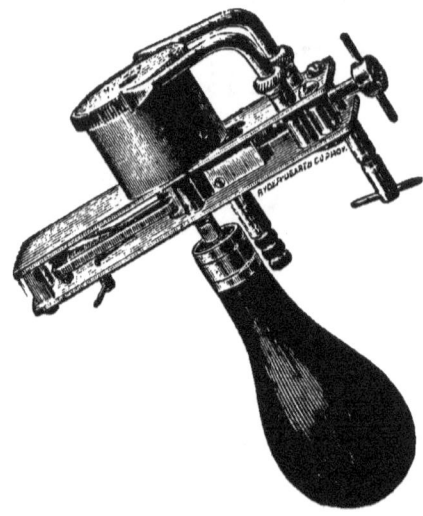

Takes the spring out of the barrel and replaces it, or winds a common clock spring for putting on a ring.

PRICE $3.50.

If your jobber does not have them, send to the manufacturers.

VAUGHAN & FIELD,

Pawtucket, - R. I.

JOHN BLISS & CO.,
MANUFACTURERS OF
MARINE CHRONOMETERS
128 FRONT STREET, NEW YORK.

To Watchmakers.—We have on hand a number of Chronometers by various good makers, not new, which have been in service for purposes of navigation, and are excellent instruments. They have been put in perfect repair, and will give satisfactory results as to performance. We will sell these chronometers at low prices, either for cash, or on accommodating terms to suit special cases, or will hire them at moderate rates, and allow the hire to apply on purchase. **Send for circular giving prices and terms.**

Do you need a New Lathe?

If so, get our prices before purchasing elsewhere. We carry all the leading varieties.

If you have trouble

in procuring Good Mainsprings, send to us for a sample dozen of our Celebrated G. & N. Gravier Mainsprings, and in the future you will use no others.

We carry a Complete Line of

Tools and Material of every description, for Watchmakers and Jewelers. You can order any tool mentioned in this book from us and you will receive it promptly.

Our Stock of

Watch Glasses, Watch and Clock Material, Lathes, Lathe Attachments, Bench Tools, Etc., Etc., is very complete.

Glickauf & Newhouse,

84 and 86 State Street,

CHICAGO.

Chicago Watch Tool Co.

MANUFACTURERS OF

FOOT WHEELS, ENGRAVING BLOCKS, WATCH RACKS,

POLISHING LATHES, AND ROLLING MILLS.

SCREW DRIVERS

COUNTER SHAFTS.

WATCH SIGNS.

STAKING TOOLS.

52 MADISON STREET,

SEND FOR CATALOGUE AND PRICE LIST.

CHICAGO, ILL.

Our Invariable Business Rules

PRACTICED SINCE MAY 10, 1882:

Positively No Goods Sold at Retail.
No Goods Sold to Peddlers, or to General Stores.
Price Lists Sent to Regular Jewelers Only.
Orders Filled Same Day as Received.

OUR LINES ARE THESE:

Watches, Chains, Spectacles,
TOOLS AND MATERIALS

We carry a very large stock and ship goods to every state and territory, and to all the Canadian provinces, and the universal verdict is in high approval of the quality, style and prices throughout our entire line. We send to all regular legitimate jewelers (and to no others) very complete Watch and Spectacle Price Lists, on application accompanied with a business card or satisfactory references.

We are large importers of Watch Glasses, Mainsprings, Jewels, etc., and have a superb stock of all the best Tools. One of our specialties is the "Guaranteed" Reversible Gravers, illustrtted on page 172 of this volume. These tools are far in advance of anything for the purpose ever offered to the trade, and they add a new delight to the fascinating art of engraving. Price with handle, 75 cents each; without handle, 50 cents each.

WE SOLICIT A SHARE OF YOUR FUTURE BUSINESS.

Bowman & Musser

IMPORTERS AND JOBBERS

Watches, Chains, Spectacles, Tools and Materials

Lancaster, Pa.

L. LELONG & BRO.

GOLD
AND
SILVER

REFINERS
AND
ASSAYERS

SWEEP SMELTERS

S. W. COR. HALSEY AND MARSHALL STS.,

NEWARK, N. J.

GOLD AND SILVER ASSAYING IN ALL ITS BRANCHES

Correspondence Solicited.   Letters Promptly Answered.

C. W. TERNAND & CO.

MANUFACTURERS OF FINE

Gold, Silver and Diamond Jewelry

ENGRAVING, COLORING AND
REPAIRING FOR THE TRADE

All work sent us from a distance will receive prompt attention.
Prices always reasonable.

155 State St., CHICAGO, Ill.

CHAS. KUEHNE & CO.

Wholesale Jewelers,

182 State Street, Chicago, Ill.

Watches, Diamonds and Jewelry.

MANUFACTURERS OF

WATCH CASES.

WATCH CASE AND JEWELRY REPAIRS.

WATCH WORK FOR THE TRADE A SPECIALTY

Write for Price List and give us a Trial.

The Manufacturing Jeweler

PUBLISHED EVERY TUESDAY.

Is devoted to the interests of not only Manufacturers, Jobbers and Importers, but also Retailers.

THE LEADING WEEKLY OF ITS CLASS IN AMERICA.

SUBSCRIPTION:
U. S. and Canada, $1.00 per Annum.
Foreign Countries, $3.00.

ADVERTISING RATES MADE KNOWN ON APPLICATION.

THE MANUFACTURING JEWELER,

42 Weybosset Street, - PROVIDENCE, R. I.

BENJ. ALLEN & CO.
Fine Watch Tools and Materials
141 & 143 STATE STREET,
CHICAGO, ILL.

We carry a complete line of Moseley Lathes and their attachments. Low prices furnished on application. We are also sole importers of the celebrated "*DIAMOND BRAND*" *of Main Springs*.

BENJ. ALLEN & CO.
Watches, Diamonds, Etc.   Chicago, Ill.

THE VERY BEST, BUT NONE TOO GOOD FOR OUR CUSTOMERS.

What Money and Perseverance Can Accomplish,

THIS GENUINE

WEBSTER-WHITCOMB HARD LATHE

TOGETHER WITH THIS COMPLETE OUTFIT,

All For $78.90 Net Cash.

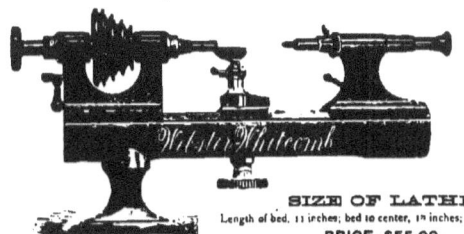

SIZE OF LATHE.
Length of bed, 11 inches; bed to center, 1⅞ inches; swing, 3¼ inches.
PRICE, $55.00.

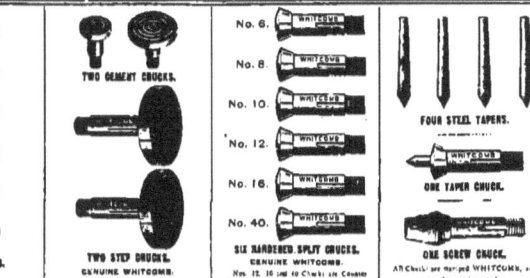

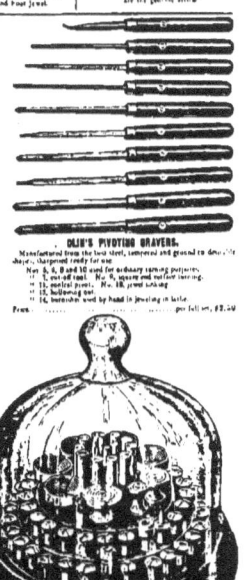

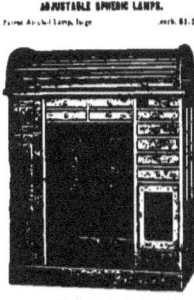

It has been our endeavor for years to get together such an ideal Lathe Outfit as would satisfy the most fastidious, and at a price that will be appreciated by our patrons. Remember we are selling the GENUINE Webster-Whitcomb HARD Lathe with GENUINE Whitcomb Chucks.

B. F. NORRIS, ALISTER & CO., 113-115 State Street, Chicago, Ill.

GOLDSMITH BROS.

OLD GOLD AND SILVER BOUGHT Refiners & Assayers **PLATED JEWELRY AND SWEEPINGS BOUGHT**

63 Washington St., Chicago.

OUR MOTTO:
"HONEST AND PROMPT RETURNS."

OUR PLAN:
"Immediately on receipt of shipment we will remit cash or draft, and if same is not satisfactory, we will return consignment in same condition as received and pay all charges.

Free on application, our book showing How to Test and Buy Gold.

A FEW EXTRACTS FROM LETTERS.

RICHMOND, VA., June 22, 1891.
GENTS:—Yours of 19th just received. Amount ($31.64) is perfectly satisfactory. E. A. SPOTT.

CLEVELAND, OHIO, May 8, 1891.
GENTS:—Check for $405.82 received; accept our compliments for satisfactory returns, together with your promptness.
THE PH. MILES JEWELRY CO.

ST. CLOUD, MINN., January 2, 1891.
GENTS:—Your check for $12.00 is very satisfactory. More than we expected to get. Many thanks.
Respectfully,
GEO. R. CLARK & CO.

MILWAUKEE, January 23, 1891.
GENTS:—Your favor of yesterday, enclosing check for $205.80 at hand, which is very satisfactory.
Yours truly,
C. PREUSSER JEWELRY CO.

FOOT POWER LATHES.

Are you looking for a foot-power, metal-turning, screw-cutting lathe? If so, you certainly want the best tool your money can buy, for however it may be in regard to other goods, it is indisputably true of machinery and tools, that the "best is none too good." We can give you the best foot-power lathe ever made, either in this country or in Europe. This is a strong statement and we are fully prepared to substantiate it.

Our lathes are superior to all others in elegance of design, workmanship and finish. More than this, they are COMPLETE tools. We can furnish you a lathe having back gear, reverse feed for right or left hand threads, hollow spindle and other indispensable features which you will not find in cheaper grade tools. Added to all this, our velocipede foot-power is incomparably the best ever applied to a foot lathe.

We make these lathes in different sizes, 9 to 13 inches swing, and taking between centers from 25 to 69 inches. In price they range from $70 to $200, and their high quality taken into consideration, are the cheapest lathes on the market.

We shall be pleased to mail to any address our complete catalogue and price list, which fully describes these lathes, as well as a large number of other machines which we manufacture.

W. F. & JOHN BARNES CO.
614 RUBY STREET, - - ROCKFORD, ILLINOIS.

HUTCHINSON'S
Practical School for Watchmakers,
LA PORTE, IND.

PUPILS RECEIVED IN WATCH MAKING, ENGRAVING,
OPTICS, SPECIAL TOOL WORK, ETC.

Students that desire to enter our Manufacturing Department while attending school are paid for their services.

Thorough Instruction and Competent Instructors in all Departments.

SPECIAL TOOLS FOR THE TRADE.   PARTICULARS ON APPLICATION.

J. L. HUTCHINSON,
LA PORTE, IND.

GENERAL
LETTER ✧ ENGRAVING.

For Watchmakers, Jewelers and Kindred Trades.

By G. F. WHELPLEY.

Price, Postpaid to any Address, $1.25.

GEO. K. HAZLITT & CO., PUBLISHERS,
CHICAGO.

PRACTICAL BOOKS FOR

WATCHMAKERS AND JEWELERS,

PUBLISHED BY

GEO. K. HAZLITT & CO.

351 Dearborn Street, Chicago.

*****The Watchmaker's and Jeweler's Practical Hand Book.** A workshop companion. Hundreds of valuable receipts and suggestions from private formulas and the best authorities, together with hints on making certain repairs. An invaluable book for the workman. The most valuable book for the money ever offered to the trade. 128 pp. Illustrated. Price........ 35c

*****General Letter Engraving.** By G. F. Whelpley, the acknowledged authority on engraving. His latest and best work. Contents; General Hints to Beginners; Lines and Curves; Originality; Practice Material; Position of Graver; Treatment of Gravers; Correct Spacing; Coffin Plate Engraving; Necessary Tools; Laying out the Work; Preparation of Plate; Use of Gravers; Methods of Cutting; Slope and Height of Letters; Inclination of Graver; Transferring; Letters Appropriate for Long and Short Names; Harmony in Laying Out; Touching Up; Difficult Materials and their Treatment; Tools and Materials; Sharpening Gravers; Proper Angles; Sizes and shapes of Gravers; Choice of Tools; Engraving in Rings; Gravers for Same; Engraving Blocks and Stands; Ciphers, their Formation and Ornamentation; Inscriptions; Best Manner of Cutting; Ciphers as Compared with Monograms; Monograms and their Treatment; Figure Monograms or Cipheroids; Intertwining; Complex Monograms; General Treatment. Copiously Illustrated. 116 pp. Cloth. Price.. $1 25

*****The Watch Factories of America, Past and Present.** By Henry G. Abbott. A complete history of watchmaking in America, from 1809 to 1888 inclusive. The only book on the subject in print. 140 pp. Illustrated with 50 engravings. Second edition. Half Morocco, Marbled edges, $2 25; English cloth.... .... $1 50

*****Watch Repairing.** By N. B. Sherwood. Contents: The Bench and its Accessories; The Vise and Oilstone; Lathe Appliances; The Jocot Lathe; Depthing Tool; Expanding the Web of a Wheel; The Spreading Tool and its Use; The Rounding-Up Tool; Stud Remover; Opening the Regulator; Roller Remover; Replacing Broken Teeth; Graining; Polishing Blocks; Polishing Steel Work; Polishing Pivots; Superiority of Conical Pivots; The Cutting Engine; To Cut 'Scape Wheels, Replacing Broken Arbors; Hardening and Tempering. 80 pp. Illustrated. Price................................... 35c

The American Jeweler. The leading horological journal of America. The only journal devoting its entire contents to practical articles on watchmaking, repairing and kindred subjects. 40 pp. monthly. Subscription per year, payable in advance.. $1 00

*****The Acme of Jewelry Repairs.** A simple and economical method of recording jewelry and miscellaneous repairs. Book of 1,000 entries, substantially bound.. $1 00

*Jewelers' Practical Receipt Book. Contains a mass of valuable receipts, formulas and information, gathered from the best and most reliable sources. 5th edition, revised and enlarged, 48 pp. Price..................$ 15

*Repairing Watch Cases. A practical treatise on the subject. By W. Schwanatus. Contents: Repairing the Pendant; Lining Pendant Holes; Work at the Joints; Soldering the Bezel; The Closing of the Case; Taking out the Dents. 40 pp. Price................................... 25

*Poising the Balance. An Essay of unusual merit. By J. L. Finn... 25

*Hairspringing. A complete treatise on the art of hairspringing. By A. Z. Price... 25

*Adjustments to Positions, Isochronism and Compensation. The only work on the subject in print. 50 pp. Illustrated. Price.............. 25

*Prize Essay on Watch Cleaning and Repairing. By F. C. Ries. This work took the first prize, (offered by The American Jeweler) in competition with thirty-six other writers. Contents: Examination of the Movement; Taking Down; Fitting the Dial; Fitting Center Pivot and Bridge; Bushing; Endshake; Worn Center Pinions; Truing the Barrel; Repairing the Ratchet; Putting on Square on a Fuzee; Examination of Mainspring; Stem-Wind Mechanism; Examination of Train; Imitation Gilding; Pivots; Making a Balance Staff; The Hairspring; Jeweling; Cleaning in General. 56 pp. Price 25

*Watch and Chronometer Jeweling. By N. B. Sherwood. A complete treatise on this subject, and the only one in print. Contents: Peculiarities of Gems used in Making Jewels; Requisite Tools and How to Use Them; Shaping and Polishing the Jewel; Opening the Jewel; Setting the Jewel; The End-Shake Tool; General Hints to the Repairer. 100 pp. Illustrated. Price.. 35

☞NOTICE.—We will not be responsible for books sent by mail. Send 10 cents extra if you wish package registered.
Any of the above books sent postage paid on receipt of price, to any part of the United States or Canada
Books not mentioned in this list can be procured promptly upon receipt of cash with order. Books will not be exchanged under any circumstances. Books will not be sent for examination with privilege of returning under any circumstances. They can be examined at our office. **Send for Complete Catalogue.**

The Jewelers' Weekly,

41 AND 43 MAIDEN LANE, NEW YORK.

A Wide Awake, Progressive Weekly, for the Watchmaking and Jewelry Trade.

Unsurpassed as an Advertising Medium. Advertising Rates Made Known on Application.

Subscription:	United States and Canada, $2.00.
Payable in Advance.	Foreign Countries, - 4.00.

If you want to buy or sell anything, try our Special Notice Column.

PARSONS' HOROLOGICAL INSTITUTE.

The First,

The Largest,

The Best.

Engraving,

Optics,

Jewelry Work.

LA PORTE, IND.

Established for the purpose of giving a

PRACTICAL & TECHNICAL EDUCATION

FOR WATCHMAKERS.

Write for Circulars and Terms.

Organized April 13, 1891.   C. D. Parsons, Principal.

CHICAGO WATCHMAKERS' INSTITUTE

...FOR...

Practical Instruction in every detail of Making, Repairing and Adjusting Watches, Chronometers and French Clocks; Jewelry Repairing, Engraving and Optics.

Gives you advantages that the combined capital of all other watchmaking schools in America could not afford, and at a moderate cost, and guarantees satisfaction.

Located in the elegant new building of the **Chicago Athenaeum, 18 to 26 E. Van Buren St.**, devoted solely to art and education, and especially adapted for the purpose.

• • • • •

VISITORS ALWAYS WELCOME.

www.ingramcontent.com/pod-product-compliance
Lightning Source LLC
Chambersburg PA
CBHW030742230426
43667CB00007B/810